MW00559729

The Guadagnini Family of Violin Makers

Ernest N. Doring

With a New Introduction by Stewart Pollens

Dover Publications, Inc.
Mineola, New York

DEDICATED TO
REUBEN A. OLSON
IN GRATEFUL RECOGNITION

Bibliographical Note

This Dover edition, first published in 2012, is an unabridged
republication of the work originally published by William Lewis &
Son, Chicago, in 1949. Stewart Pollens has prepared a new
Introduction specially for this Dover edition.

Library of Congress Cataloging-in-Publication Data

Doring, Ernest N. (Ernest Nicholas), 1877-1955.
    The Guadagnini family of violin makers / Ernest N. Doring;
    With a New Introduction by Stewart Pollens.
        pages ; cm
    An unabridged republication of the work originally published
by William Lewis & Son, Chicago, in 1949.
    Includes bibliographical references and index.
    ISBN-13: 978-0-486-49796-9
    ISBN-10: 0-486-49796-8
    1. Guadagnini, Giovanni Battista, d. 1786. 2. Violin makers—
Italy—Biography. I. Pollens, Stewart. II. Title.

ML421.G77D6 2012
787.2'19092—dc23
    [B]
                                                    2012027016

Manufactured in the United States by Courier Corporation
49796802   2014
www.doverpublications.com

Introduction to the Dover Edition

The violins of Giovanni Battista Guadagnini have long been favorites of professional musicians and are ranked closely behind those of Antonio Stradivari and Giuseppe Guarneri del Gesù with regard to responsiveness, tonal quality, and projection. Despite several recent publications about the Guadagnini family and an exhibition devoted to instruments made by G. B. Guadagnini, Ernest N. Doring's *The Guadagnini Family of Violin Makers*, published in Chicago in 1949, remains the most comprehensive study of this family's life and work and includes a *catalogue raisonné* of their instruments. Ernest N. Doring worked for the Rudolph Wurlitzer Company alongside noted violin experts Rembert Wurlitzer and J. C. Freeman and later for William Lewis & Son, which first published this book. In compiling information, he had access to the archives and Guadagnini instruments handled by these firms as well as by Hamma & Company, Emil Herrmann, and several notable collectors. Doring's book was originally published in a limited edition of 1500; today second-hand copies are extremely scarce and fetch a premium in the specialized violin book market. This modestly priced Dover reprint brings Doring's classic to the general public for the first time.

Though archival research tends to answer longstanding questions about the life and work of violin makers, it often raises new issues that confound the experts. For example, Stefano Pio's extensive investigation into violin-making in Venice and its environs (published in his *Liuteri Sonadori: Venezia 1750–1870*, Treviso, 2002, and *Violin and Lute Makers of Venice 1640–1760*, Treviso, 2004) failed to uncover any evidence of the purported violin maker Michele Deconet's supposed apprenticeship with Domenico Montagnana, his membership in the Arte dei Marzeri (the guild to which instrument makers and musicians had to belong in order to work legally in Venice), or that he maintained a commercial establishment for making or selling musical instruments in that city or in Padua, where he is also believed to have worked. However, Pio's research did reveal Deconet to be an itinerant musician and "singer of songs in the piazza" who probably could not even read music, which was a requirement for formal membership as a musician in the Arte dei Marzeri in Venice. Nevertheless, there is a sizable body of instruments fitted with printed labels bearing his name, as well as other instruments that have been attributed to him on the basis of their stylistic similarity to the labeled ones. Such instruments have been traded in good faith as authentic Deconets for over two hundred and fifty years, yet in the wake of Pio's findings, owners and dealers of these violins now find themselves in a predicament as to how to market them.

Similarly, Duane Rosengard's exhaustive research into the Guadagnini family, presented in his book *Giovanni Battista Guadagnini* (Haddonfield, 2000), failed to discover any record indicating that Lorenzo Guadagnini, the progenitor of this violin-making clan, ever made violins or apprenticed with Antonio Stradivari, despite violin labels that read "LAURENTIUS GUADAGNINI/fecit Placentie, alumnus Anto-/nius Straduarius anno 17__" (and other wordings). Instead, Rosengard uncovered evidence that he worked as an innkeeper, butcher, and baker. Giovanni Battista, Lorenzo's first son and the only one to go on to make violins, was born on June 23, 1711 in the small town of Bilegno, and not Piacenza as many biographers (including Doring) have speculated. He was to become the premier violin maker of a family that would include his two violin making sons, Giuseppe and Gaetano, as well as several grandsons, great-grandsons, and their progeny who plied the craft into the twentieth century.

In eighteenth-century Italy, apprenticeships traditionally began at the age of twelve or thirteen, but there is no evidence that Giovanni Battista ever formally learned the craft of violin making in his native Bilegno, a town that is not known to have had a resident violin maker during Giovanni Battista's formative years there. In 1738, at the age of twenty-six, he left home and settled in Piacenza, where he married, became a member of the wood-workers' guild, and evidently began making violins there by 1740. This is the earliest date found on a label in an extant G. B. Guadagnini violin and represents a rather a late start to begin a career in those days. In 1749 he and his family began an itinerant existence, leaving Piacenza for Milan, then resettling in Parma in 1758, and finally departing in 1771 for Turin, where he continued making violins until his death on September 18, 1786. These details regarding Lorenzo Guadagnini and G. B. Guadagnini's birthplace, guild membership, and the precise dates of his relocations correct lacunae and a few minor inaccuracies in Doring's book.

Some historians suggest that G. B. Guadagnini spent several months in Cremona in 1758 prior to his arrival in Parma, and several of his instruments bear labels indicating that they were made in Cremona in that year. Labels subsequently printed in Parma state that he was Cremonese, which strictly speaking was untrue. Labels printed in his Turin period go so far as to state that he was also an "alumnus," or former apprentice, of Anto-nio Stradivari; however, Stradivari died in 1737, so if Guadagnini passed through Cre-mona in 1758, he could not have worked with him, or with the two sons who assisted him, Omobono and Francesco, who died in 1742 and 1743. Nor is there any evidence that he apprenticed in his youth with Stradivari; if he had done so, why wait so many years to proclaim this on his labels? Clearly, Guadagnini misrepresented the facts to bolster his reputation as well as the desirability and price of his violins. In attempting to explain his relocations (which was not at all common with violin makers at that time), Doring sug-gests that he was so productive that he flooded each of these markets with instruments and then had to move on to greener pastures; however, he does consider Guadagnini's appoint-ment as court instrument maker in Parma and the subsequent political intrigue that led to the loss of his stipend as plausible reasons for his arrival and departure from that duchy.

6

One of the pivotal figures in Giovanni Guadagnini's life was Count Ignazio Alessandro Cozio di Salabue, an amateur violinist and violin historian who became his principal patron during the Turin period. Between 1773 and 1776, Count Cozio acquired some fifty instruments from Guadagnini, and attempted to serve as the maker's mentor by offering to lend him Antonio Stradivari's forms, patterns, and tools, which he had purchased in 1776 from Paolo Stradivari (Antonio's youngest son and a merchant by profession). Writing in 1804, Count Cozio stated that Guadagnini made instruments under his supervision using Stradivari's violin forms and patterns, though Guadagnini's instruments, in fact, bear little resemblance to those of Stradivari, and thus it is unlikely that he actually made use of these materials. The Count did collaborate in the finishing of some of Guadagnini's instruments, for we know that he obtained instruments "in the white" and sent them to the Mantegazza brothers (active 1747–1801) in Milan for varnishing. Among the Count's letters and papers that are preserved in the Biblioteca Statale in Cremona are sheets of Guadagnini's printed violin labels with a few of them cut out, further evidence of his involvement in the fabrication of Guadagnini's violins. When offering violins to a fellow collector, Count Cozio priced Amati violins at 300 *zecchini*, the biggest and best Stradivari violins at 150 *zecchini*, other Strads at 80–100 *zecchini*, Bergonzi's at 30–50 *zecchini*, and Guarneri and Guadagnini violins at 15–18 *zecchini*, which gives some indication of their relative worth at that time, as well as the reevaluations that have occurred since.

Included in Doring's book are translations of twenty-eight letters exchanged between Count Cozio, G. B. Guadagnini, and Paolo Stradivari that shed light on their business dealings. Several of these letters first appeared in translation scattered throughout George Hart's *The Violin: Its Famous Makers and Their Imitators*, published in London in 1875. A year after the appearance of Doring's book, Renzo Bacchetta published transcriptions of all of Count Cozio's correspondence and notes in a book entitled *Cozio di Salabue: Carteggio* (Milan, 1950); an English translation of these writings was recently published by Brandon Frazier in his *Memoirs of a Violin Collector: Count Ignazio Alessandro Cozio di Salabue* (Baltimore, 2007). These days, Cozio's name is invoked in virtually every book, article, lecture, and informal discussion on the violin. Doring's selection of letters provides an excellent introduction to this fascinating and historically important material.

Each of the cities in which G. B. Guadagnini lived is associated with a stylistic period in his development as a violin maker. Doring's catalog of extant Guadagnini violins, violas, and cellos is organized by city and provides a detailed provenance for each instrument. From his vivid descriptions of these instruments, we get a sense of the stylistic characteristics of each period, such as the yellowish-brown varnish used on the Parma-period instruments, which stands in contrast to the brilliant red varnish that is typical of those made in Milan. Of Guadagnini's Turin period, Doring characterizes it as exhibiting "broader patterns of sturdier form, flattened arching with an almost complete absence of channeling in the plates, wider rims, and notably, varnish of a different texture, sometimes almost colorless, mark the first Turin works of the maker, comprising a type quite different from that of the daintier, more effeminate creations of the late Parma period." He notes other general earmarks, such as the distinctive pin pricks around the volutes of the scrolls that resulted when Guadagnini marked the outline of the spiral from a pattern, as well as the pear-shaped lower eyes of the f-holes, a stylistic flourish that is generally associated with Guadagnini's later work but which Doring astutely identifies in an early cello dated 1743. Still, despite Doring's efforts and more recent investigations, questions remain regarding the geometric design of Guadagnini's instruments, which exhibit a wide range of shapes, dimensions, "stops" (the distance between the top of the body and the bridge), and f-hole positions.

Doring provides a chapter on Guadagnini's labels, with photographs showing the various wordings and typefaces used in different periods and locales. He points out that a great many of Guadagnini's violins still have their original labels intact, which enabled him to trace with a fair degree of precision the maker's movement from city to city. There is also a table of measurements of twenty-one violins, violas, and cellos as well as a tally of the number of instruments he was able to locate, city by city, totaling 248 in all. Finally, he lists instruments made by G. B. Guadagnini's sons Giuseppe and Gaetano, and presents details about the life and work of their sons and grandsons. Throughout *The Guadagnini Family of Violin Makers*, Doring reviews and evaluates the facts, speculations, and conclusions presented by virtually every violin historian and biographer of Guadagnini who preceded him. He bemoans that fact that "serious historians of the violin may be regarded as a modern institution, younger by perhaps two centuries than the evolution of the instrument itself. It is regrettable that a deeper interest did not exist in years when the living still retained memories of the pioneer violin makers and their careers were still fresh in the minds of their generation, and thus possible to investigate and record." While secondary sources provided much of the biographical and historical information presented by Doring, he was relatively objective and refrained from aggrandizement, a pitfall of many of the Guadagninis' earlier and subsequent biographers.

STEWART POLLENS

8

INTRODUCTORY NOTE

An inalienable prerogative of romancers is to indulge their imagination, and thus, in the weaving of tales there is afforded an unlimited freedom to invent suitable characters, heroic or otherwise, with every degree of descriptive fantasy admissible in the telling of their mythical deeds. A certain latitude is also permitted writers of more serious works, allowing them to propound theories and present arguments on debatable subjects. When such theorizing has to do with the lives and accomplishments of living characters, whether of the present or past, a historian falls short of his obligation to posterity when through his pronouncements error and misinformation become recorded on the printed page.

Unfortunately, in many cases—of which our present interest lies with the violin makers Lorenzo and Joannes Baptista Guadagnini—dearth of real information did not deter early violin historians from proclaiming beliefs which may, to give due respect, have been held by some to be correct, but with others were mere hazard or reiteration. Hypothetical matter of such nature became source-material for subsequent writers, and in that manner a background since found to be inconclusive, often contradictory, has been so firmly established on the records that truth does not easily penetrate.

Able minds of later eras have applied themselves to the subject in order to bring enlightenment on controversial points. With the evidence afforded by study and comparison of authentic works of the makers under consideration, about whom suppositious rumors have so long revolved, it has been possible to establish their working periods as well as to clarify some of the doubtful conceptions previously existing.

In offering this review it is not without certain misgivings, such as must prevail when an involved subject forms the major topic of a discourse. Patently not intended as a criticism of those early writers who gave us the groundwork on which to build, it is in true humility, lest error be found, that I submit this work for the consideration of the reader as a tribute to the patient craftsmen of the Guadagnini Family who worked without thought of reward other than fair recompense for their labor, certainly not with dreams that future generations of scribes would labor to perpetuate their fame!

Evanston, Illinois   Faithfully,
1949   ERNEST N. DORING

9

ACKNOWLEDGMENTS

As the names of authors are mentioned in connection with herein quoted matter no further acknowledgment of my indebtedness to such sources seems needful here. I do, however, deem it fitting to express a deep sense of gratitude to Doris Commander for unselfish devotion in collaborating in the preparation of the manuscript of this work. To my former associates at the Rudolph Wurlitzer Company, Jay C. Freeman and Rembert Wurlitzer, to Fridolin Hamma of Hamma & Company, Emil Herrmann, Erich Lachmann, Nathan E. Posner, other colleagues and private owners of Guadagnini instruments, for coöperation in providing photographs and data, as well as to my friend Attilio Ortolani, who was reared near Cremona, for translations from the Italian—my humble thanks.

ERNEST N. DORING

FOREWORD

Intensive research, pursued over scores of years, has been directed to ascertain facts concerning the historical background of the old violin makers. Mainly devoted to the Stradivari and the Guarneri families, they have been memorialized in impressive manner by scholarly works which form an important part of the literature pertaining to the art of the *liutaro*.

There need be no brief to explain why similar notice of the lives and works of other eminent makers has been more or less neglected. Until comparatively recent times public interest was apathetic toward learning about those who were not included within the small circle of the great classic figures in the craft. Owing to the gradual rise of Guadagnini instruments in the estimation of the public, and their consequent enhancement in value, the need for a treatise concerning their creators has prompted the writer to prepare this essay to provide a better medium of information, more complete and specialized, than notices available in existing biographical works.

Later generations of the Guadagnini family who were interrogated on the subject apparently retained small recollection of their forebears, and were possessed of still less information concerning their lives and habitat. Without statistical or other documentary confirmation, the little they offered is neither important nor reliable. Consequently, some of the more or less haphazard statements which appeared in early recordings remained uncontested, to be enlarged upon and further distorted by subsequent writers.

In order to present a broad view of what has been said before, I have incorporated in this review a progressive series of extracts from published works on the topic, leading up to the most recent opinions. A theory that there were two makers of the name Joannes Baptista Guadagnini has long been held—it will be seen in what manner this originated and how, finally, it was adjudged fallacious by eminent authorities in the branch. It must be remarked, however, that a minority still persists in the belief that there were two, contending that one was Cremonese, the other of Piacenza. J. B. Guadagnini employed a variety of labels with which he marked his works, altering their form as he removed from one city to another and also, during each period of residence, using different methods of wording. Labels used in his early career bear the inscription Placentinus which, according to the common practice of the time, indicated his origin to have been Placentina (Piacenza) at birth; of a later period, at Milan, he reaffirms this by naming himself as of Placentina fecit Milan; lastly there are labels imprinted Cremonensis, which according to the same usage would suggest his birthplace to have been at Cremona. However, there are good reasons to doubt that the maker actually intended that to have been the meaning. Such an interpretation is found incompatible with the evidence of his earlier forms of labels which reflect a complete absence of any mention of Cremona. This does not occur until his stay in that city for a few months during 1758, subsequent to which and while working in Parma, he first employed the term "Cremonensis" on his labels and continued to do so thereafter until his death in 1786.

We have nothing to indicate that either Lorenzo or J. B. Guadagnini produced instruments at Piacenza previous to the year 1740; it is evident, however, that they were highly accomplished in their art at that time, and in order to have attained that skill must have been trained by some master of uncommon ability. It is believed that this was at Cremona and a few works of Lorenzo Guadagnini will be mentioned for which the claim of Cremonese origin is made dated prior to 1740. None can be forwarded as actually the work of J. B. Guadagnini dated from Cremona previous to 1758.

The output of J. B. Guadagnini must have been of very large number; many of his works of which there is no record available to this writer unquestionably survive. Regarding the works of later generations of the family, descendants of the famous maker, no trustworthy information can be offered. Lacking characteristics such as those which indelibly mark the works of their illustrious predecessor, their products have largely passed without notice. It should be observed that many obscure though deserving makers, no kin of the family, whose style of work approached in any manner more or less closely that of the Guadagninii, have been deprived of the credit due them as makers through the removal of their labels and insertion of others bearing the more famous name.

These various subjects will be more fully investigated and discussed in chapters to follow.

IMPORTANT

The fact that instruments are entered in various tabulations throughout this work must not be misconstrued as assurance of their authenticity. All possible care has been devoted to the end that only genuine works are enumerated, so known to the author or reported by reliable informants.

CONTENTS

❈ ❈ ❈

CONTENTS—*Continued*

GUADAGNINI INSTRUMENTS HEREIN PICTURED

19

PART I

LORENZO GUADAGNINI

Circa 1695-1745

We who know the attraction of old violins can readily understand the urge which possessed others of a bygone day, similarly enthused, to own, to cherish and to write about them. We stand indebted to those of the quill and pen for laying a groundwork upon which succeeding generations pieced out the framework of many stories from which emerged a yet uncompleted narration of the achievements of workers in the violin-making craft. Although a vast accumulation of biographical data is available today, it is not, nor can it ever be, completely correct in the presentation of a subject so broad and varied, and so shrouded in mystery and doubts. Some writers followed blindly on paths prepared, others probed more or less deeply in research, and revised and corrected.

With a few exceptions, Italy, the cradle of violin making, has produced little in the way of printed records to memorialize the deeds of her violin makers, and that directed only to the more prominent of her sons.

For many years the violin maker Lorenzo (Laurentius) Guadagnini, like others who probably enjoyed only local recognition, was not to be regarded as sufficiently important to warrant close scrutiny, either as to his nativity or antecedents. The fame which is now accorded him is due largely to the eminent position attained by his illustrious son, Giovanni Battista (Joannes Baptista). But recognition goes to Lorenzo not undeservedly, as it is merited by the evidence of the excellence of his lamentably small number of surviving works.

21

Labels used by Lorenzo Guadagnini might be variously interpreted to suggest Cremonese schooling in his use of the words "alumnus Stradivari," but cannot be mistaken as to their meaning in naming himself as hailing from Placentina. Descendants living in the late nineteenth century are known to have averred that Lorenzo, and also his son, Giovanni Battista, were natives of the last named city.

Contemporary thought is inclined to agree with that premise, quite unreservedly as concerns Lorenzo Guadagnini, but somewhat less so concerning his son who in his late epoch introduced reference to Cremona on his printed labels. The indisputable evidence remains, however, that at the outset of his career and for some twenty years following, he consistently referred to himself on his labels as of Placentina (Piacenza).

Lorenzo Guadagnini is said to have worked at Cremona prior to his short era as an active producer at Piacenza. His output could not have been large, at least of instruments turned out under his own name and so labelled, whether at Cremona or at Piacenza, and as the demands of the wealthy class had been largely satisfied by the time of his advent as a producer, such works that he completed were probably created for an occasional rather than a steady call.

Whatever may have been their destination, it is evident, from what we know today, that their maker, Lorenzo Guadagnini, was long to remain an obscure, little known personality, mentioned by historians, it is true, but vaguely as to his qualifications and unintelligibly as to the merit of his instruments. This may in part be accounted for if Lorenzo, like others of the old makers, neglected to identify all of his works by supplying them with labels bearing his name.

His status among the Italian violin makers was eventually

to be established, yet for a long period recognized only as a name, remarks thereto supplemented largely pure invention.

Whether his works were absorbed by plebian or aristocratic clientele will never be known, but with his qualifications as a craftsman of unquestioned ability meriting fair compensation for his labor, his patronage would appear to have been in the higher stratas of society.

The world today owes much to the privileged classes of early times for their encouragement to craftsmen in the arts. It is due to their lavish outpouring of wealth that great talents applied their supreme efforts to the creation of masterpieces, of which our heritage is rich in violins and their kindred instruments. With regard to the latter, it is safe to say that their aristocratic possessors of those times acquired them less in the sense of art lovers or collectors than they did for the practical purpose of equipping privately supported groups of musicians. Readers familiar with the history of the violin are acquainted with great names, many of noble lineage—kings and princes of church and state—who are recorded as one time possessors of the works of Stradivari and others and whose names have thereby been immortalized in musical history.

Probably the first of the titled Italians to become so deeply enamoured of the violin that he accumulated fine works to satisfy his hobby as a collector and thus became a leading figure in the archives of violin lore was the wealthy Count Ignazio Alessandro Cozio di Salabue of Casale-Monferrato in Piedmont, born 1755. The story of this nobleman has been variously told and is well known. He has been regarded as a generous patron of J. B. Guadagnini at a time in the career of that maker when he was in need of succor, a belief, as to the humanitarian nature of his interest, latterly subject to attack.

A memorial to Count Cozio exists in a monograph written by the Italian biographer Federico Sacchi, published at London in 1898, edited by Towry Piper. In this, certain notes concerning Cremonese violin makers which Cozio prepared in 1823, incorporating data concerning Guadagnini, were presented in the original Italian.

Before proceeding, it is in order to remark that the notes of which Cozio was the author provide one of two sources to which are attributable much that has been written concerning Lorenzo Guadagnini and his son Giovanni Battista. As the first biographer of violin makers to record these makers, Count Cozio was best fitted to provide reliable data as he was intimately acquainted with Giovanni Battista during years of his last period at Turin and must, therefore, have been in position to speak of him with authority. It is realized today that his notes concerning Guadagnini, though not of great length, correctly record the major circumstances of the maker's career.

It will be read that he not only named the various cities in which Giovanni Battista Guadagnini lived and worked, but also placed his epochs in their proper sequence.

Thus, chronologers of violin history owe the Italian nobleman recognition for having provided a well grounded thesis on which to elaborate.

Noteworthy in a far different sense as exerting a contrary effect, the second work requiring mention here is that of another wealthy amateur, the Russian Prince Nicolai Borisovich Yusupov (Youssoupow), to which is traceable a tragic consequence subsequently to create opposing factions among writers on our subject, one of which was to follow blindly along in support of a false premise. It is the hope of this writer that its fallacy will become evident to readers of this book.

COUNT COZIO'S NOTES

Although not bearing directly on Lorenzo Guadagnini, to whom this opening chapter is dedicated, Count Cozio's biographical mention of the family will follow at this place. Submitted to a Cremonese biographer, Vincenzo Lancetti, with the purpose that he should incorporate mention of the Guadagnini violin makers in his proposed work on Cremonese Worthies, Cozio's notes were dated at Milan in 1823. In broad translation we read:

"Meriting enumeration in this biography is the deceased Gio. Battista Guadagnini, son of the deceased Lorenzo, who often referred to himself on his tickets as Cremonese. . . . Though we do not know certainly that he worked in Cremona . . . it is established that he did first at Piacenza, afterwards for a length of time in Milan, then in Parma where he worked for the duke, and when all grants were withdrawn from the artists, he went to Turin in 1772, ultimately to die in that city. We mention his work as in reality copied after the celebrated Stradivari in the interior construction, in the arching, and particularly in the neatness of his instruments. He used the most beautiful woods and his instruments are of similar class or type as Stradivari's. But due to circumstances, either of the times or persecution of makers who were his inferiors and ill-informed, or because, by his self-conceit, he did not seek to imitate the master in the volute (scroll), the ff, the edges, and the varnish, and possibly because of his fiery nature and outbursts, he incurred the disgust and dislike of many professors of his time, and his work received little consideration in Italy. None the less, his work was appreciated by some professors, but at low prices, and these were players who demanded the power and evenness of tone required in the orchestra. It is to be noted that many of his instruments found favor with speculators in Holland and Germany and there brought prices comparable to good Cremonese works. . . . Any intelligent, impartial person can judge for himself of the quality of instruments made expressly of chosen woods in Turin from 1773 to 1776 at the behest of Count Cozio, commissioned of the maker for his collection in order to sustain him and his large family. While yet new, but well seasoned, some, like two violoncellos and two violas already adapted by the brothers Mantegazza for their present use, all still have their original finish; they do not show wear as easily as good Cremonese violins on the outside, and when seasoned with use the varnish will last as long as the best, and give as good service."

The note continues, mentioning as among children surviving: ". . . two of which, Gaetano and Giuseppe, followed their father's vocation, the first named in adjusting and finishing violins. He left a son of the same name who made violins and guitars. And Giuseppe made various violins and violas, but in Pavia, where he had removed his household and where he died without offspring; his works do not merit being mentioned in this biography."

The original Italian phraseology of the Count's notes is susceptible of differing interpretation, but it is due to them as the nuclei, that later scribes painted the maker as a man of violent temper, built fanciful stories about certain dukes of Parma long dead before Guadagnini's arrival there in 1759, and otherwise through embellishment enlarged upon the only recorded data originating from first hand acquaintance with the maker.

In the same month of January, 1823, that his notes were forwarded to Lancetti—on the 31st to be exact—Count Cozio despatched a letter, in his own handwriting, to Lancetti, a facsimile of which appears in Sacchi's memorial. The communication insofar as it concerns the Guadagninii is here presented in translation and indicates that Count Cozio had decided that they were to be definitely regarded as Cremonese:

"The latest news which reached me from Turin after our last meeting, makes it appear that Gio. Batt. Guadagnini, deceased, and also his father Lorenzo, were belonging to a family that originated in Cremona; also that both of them were born in Cremona. . . ."

It is to be gathered from the above that, other than the brief mention by Count Cozio of the name, the better part of a century passed subsequent to Lorenzo Guadagnini's demise before his existence received more than cursory attention from biographers, and, lacking definite basic information, the subject has been variously approached since that time.

YUSUPOV'S ESSAY

The year 1856 witnessed publication of the first edition of the essay written by a Russian musical enthusiast, Prince Nicolai Borisovitch Yusupov.* He was born at St. Petersburg, in 1827, and died at Baden-Baden 1891. An accomplished violinist, he maintained a private orchestra in his palace, was the composer of a number of works including a concerto for violin, and the author of several essays. Published anonymously under the *nom de plume* "un Amateur," his *Luthomonographie historique et raisonnée* went into five editions.

In it the author divulged his identity, as he mentioned himself in connection with "a grand collection of violins conserved in the palace of Prince Nicholas Youssoupow (French version) at

---

*Variously spelled Youssoupow, Jusupof, Yousoupoff, etc.

St. Petersburg." Not dreaming that he was perpetrating the offense of a hoax against posterity in the train of consequences to follow, he caused to be printed, among his notes on *Imitateurs et élèves de Stradivarius:*

ORIGINAL	TRANSLATION
"*Milani (Francesco)* 1742 imitateur scrupuleux de Stradivarius, travailla long-temps à Milan, d'après les données qui lui avaient été transmises par: *Guadanini (Laurenzius)* 1710, de Milan, élève de Stradivarius. Le frère de ce dernier *Jean Baptiste,* de 1709-1754 quitta Crémone pour se fixer a Placentia où il travailla jusqu' à sa mort à titre d'élève distingué de Stradivarius. . . ."	Francesco Milani,* 1742, worked a long time at Milan; scrupulous imitator of Stradivarius after the art was transmitted by Lorenzo Guadagnini, 1710, of Milan, pupil of Stradivarius. The brother of the last (Lorenzo) Jean Baptiste, 1709-1754, left Cremona to settle at Piacenza where he worked until death a distinguished pupil of Stradivarius.

And again, under *Differentes Ecoles d'Italie:*

". . . Dans l'école de Milan sans parler de Testator, qui en est pour ainsi dire le fondateur, nous remarquons les deux frères, *Guadanini,* dont nous avons parlé dejà dans l'article concernante les élèves de Stradivarius, *Lacasso (Antonio Maria) Sanza Santino* (1634) et puis enfin *Testore (Carlo Giuseppe)* (1750) ce dernier ainsi que *Guadanini (Laurenzius),* peut être placé au rang des bons luthiers."	In the school of Milan, of which Testator† may be said to have been the founder, we remark the two brothers Guadagnini, of whom I spoke in connection with my remarks concerning pupils of Stradivarius; Lacasso . . . and finally Testore . . . lastly Lorenzo Guadagnini, as deserved to be ranked the good luthiers.

* The name Francesco Milani does not occur in the work of Vidal; it is mentioned by Valdrighi; and Lütgendorff repeats it with the same date, 1712, given by Yusupov, with the statement that Milani was a pupil of Lorenzo Guadagnini, "one of the best copyists of Stradivari among the Milanese." Vannes (1932) repeats, in essentially the same words, adding "living in Milan about 1742."

† The name Testator was probably a fiction, a corruption of Testore.

We have here the root of an innocuous growth which fastened itself upon the records. Prince Yusupov committed the double error of terming Lorenzo Guadagnini a Milanese and naming J. B. Guadagnini as his brother. No mitigating factor can be suggested to reduce the enormity of the offence, which though unwittingly committed, has worked harmfully ever since. His statement, brief in itself, has been enlarged upon and distorted, and although its fallacy is realized today, it is entirely to the thoughtless utterance of Yusupov that we must attribute the repetition of fantastic references to one Giambattista Guadagnini, called brother of Lorenzo, as apart from Giovanni Battista Guadagnini,* the son of Lorenzo.

As this review proceeds it will be seen how the seed planted by Prince Yusupov fell upon fertile ground, causing the emergence of a myth that spread and gained credence widely, and how, eventually, its fallacy became apparent and truth prevailed.

GEORGE DUBOURG

The writings of British enthusiasts figure prominently in the literature of the violin. One of the earliest, the scholarly work of George Dubourg entitled "The Violin," commands attention. Its theme is principally biographical narrative concerned with famous players of the instrument, but includes an intriguingly told story of the early history and development of the violin family, as well as remarks about famous makers and sundry recounting of anecdotes and experiences relevant to the subject. The book received wide acclamation and required a number of reprintings, yet is now rare and counted as a collector item. The first edition appeared in 1836, and in the

---

* The two forms, as well as the Latin Joannes Baptista and the French Jean Baptiste, have the same significance the modern J. B. being the abbreviated derivative.

chapter devoted to violin makers there is no mention what-
soever of members of the Guadagnini family. The book went
into five editions, and in the fourth, published 1852, the author
extended his remarks to more fully list makers. In this appears:

"Lorenzio Guadagnini, of Placentia, a pupil or apprentice of
Straduarius, copied the small-pattern fiddles of his master. His
instruments give a round and clear tone from the first and
second strings—but are dull on the third. . . ."

As the first English mention of the Guadagnini violin makers,
to the writer's knowledge, this entry, though obviously fantastic in the matter presented and particularly so in the description of tonal characteristics, is significant in naming Lorenzo's
locale "of Placentia."

The French musical historian François Joseph Fétis produced
his famous work, "Antoine Stradivari, Luthier Cèlébre" (etc.),
in 1856. An English translation by John Bishop of Cheltenham
appeared in 1864, in which same year Sandys and Forster published their "History of the Violin." Then, in 1875, the first
edition of George Hart's classic, "The Violin: Famous Makers
and Their Imitators" was produced.

The French work of Jules Gallay, "Les Luthiers Italiens,"
published in 1869, contained nothing of interest pertaining to
our topic; a compilation of the names of owners of Italian
instruments therein included, does not mention the name Guadagnini. The same author's "Les Instruments des Écoles Italiennes," published by Gand and Bernardel in 1872 at Paris
contains a more extensive list of owners. This provides, under
the simple title "Guadagnini," four violins, three violas, five
violoncellos, with one other violin mentioned in the appendix.
Antoine Vidal's great work "Les Instruments à Archet" (etc.),

was published in three volumes; the second appearing in 1877, deals with the subject of violin makers. His "La Lutherie et le luthiers" was published in 1889 in response to a demand for a reprinting of that section of the earlier work.

As coming subsequent to the notes of Count Cozio and regarded as the most important biographical works on the subject of violin makers of their epoch, those which I have mentioned may be accepted as providing the source material which directed later writers, to be by them reconstructed as suited their whim. There can be no question as to the sincerity of purpose of the various authors, and as pioneers in a largely unexplored field, errors and discrepancies were no more possible to avoid than it is today given us to warrant the absolute accuracy of our own utterances.

F. J. FETIS

Reverting to the above mentioned works, and to examine them more in detail, if we consider that of Fétis, it should be approached with the regard due an eminent scholar, a learned man who ventured his treatise with the devotion of a true votary. With very little previously recorded data on which to rely, it must be assumed that he drew upon the knowledge and experience of the contemporary French connoisseurs and dealers of his time to furnish material for his book. It is generally accepted that J. B. Vuillaume was his principal informant, some indeed going so far as to virtually characterize Fétis as his mouthpiece. Whatever the source, the work was of its time the most erudite on our subject of early violin makers, directed principally, as indicated by the title, to a notice of Antonio Stradivari. His remarks referring to other makers are more or less vague and incidental, making it a matter open to question whether Vuillaume himself, shrewd tradesman and eminent connoisseur though he was, had more than cursory knowledge of the background of many of those mentioned by Fétis, makers who had not achieved the status of a place among the very great in then popular estimation.

It is a safe assumption that to Fétis, rather than due to the brief note in Dubourg's book or Yusupov's essay, the premise of a connection of Lorenzo Guadagnini with the shop of Stradivari, either as workman or apprentice, found its origin. As presented in Bishop's translation, the words of Fétis are made to read that among the "immediate pupils of Anthony Stradivarius" there was "Lorenzo Guadagnini, Cremonæ, 1695 to 1740."

SANDYS AND FORSTER

Next in the order of works referred to, we find in the Sandys and Forster book:

"Lorenzo Guadagnini was born at Placentia towards the end of the seventeenth century, and was living in 1742. He was a pupil of Antonius Stradiuarius, whose models he followed, generally of the small pattern. He finished with care, using good oil varnish, his S S holes are elegant, and his purfling neat; the first and second strings brilliant, but the third occasionally dull. After working for some time at Placentia he removed to Milan. . . ."

Here we find repeated the inanity of tone characterization which Dubourg committed in 1852. It is worth noting that these English writers name Lorenzo a native of Piacenza in direct contradiction of Fétis' statement, thus in agreement with what is said to have been asserted by descendants of the maker.

JOSEPH PEARCE

To further illustrate how blindly one writer copied the words of another, I mention the work of Joseph Pearce, of Sheffield, who was the author in 1866 of "Violins and Violin Makers —Biographical Dictionary of the Great Italian Artistes" (etc.). Evidently much of his material was drawn from the words of Fétis (whom he quotes) and Sandys and Forster, but some display of his imagination appears in his notes of Guadagnini. Certainly with no knowledge that a second maker by name Lorenzo Guadagnini was to be forwarded at a later day, Pearce did just that in giving us two of the name, one as of Cremona, 1690 to 1720 . . . "Pupil of Straduarius and highly esteemed as a maker. . . . Followed the style of his celebrated teacher," supplemented by the naive statements: "Guadagnini is one of the makers especially recommended by Spohr when one of the three great masters cannot be procured. A good specimen of his work will always command a good price." Then follows the second note concerning a Lorenzo Guadagnini, "Placentia and Milan, 1742. Made instruments generally of the smaller model. Was a careful workman and finished his instruments well, and used a good varnish." This reference, obviously, was a corrupted version drawn from notices to (as he has it) "Guadagnini, Baptista. Same places and about same dates, and made similar instruments." These various writers essayed to outline features displayed by Lorenzo's instruments, which, in their vague generalities, are equally applicable to any other of a large variety of types. The works of various Italian makers, such as those of the Amati, Stradivari and Guarneri families, possess characteristics which to the trained eye betray not only the makers but also the approximate life-periods in which they were constructed. This cannot be said of Lorenzo Guadagnini's instruments. The great scarcity of his works of itself prohibited familiarity with his technique, but that fact obviously did not deter conjecture and theory to enter into discussion of his style.

GEORGE HART

Over the same period during which the aforementioned British works appeared, George Hart was collecting data in preparation for his renowned book. When the first version appeared (London 1875), it carried an extended notice to Lorenzo Guadagnini, as follows:

GUADAGNINI, Lorenzo, Cremona, 1695-1735. The name of Guadagnini carries with it considerable weight, and their instruments are rapidly increasing in value. No matter to which of the Guadagnini the instrument may owe its origin, if it bears the name of these makers, importance is attached to it, often without due regard to the merits of the particular specimen. . . . The great makers of the Guadagnini family were Lorenzo and Johannes Baptista. The former has been considered the chief maker, but if the merits of each be duly weighed, they will be found to be nearly equal. It is probable that Lorenzo has been looked upon as the principal maker from the association of his name with that of Stradiuarius, a fact which it must be granted lends to his name a degree of importance.

"The instruments of Lorenzo are exceedingly bold in design. . . . Lorenzo frequently changed the style of his sound-hole, giving it the pointed character of Joseph Guarnerius in some instances, and sometimes retaining the type of sound-hole perfected by his master. The model is inclined to flatness, the declivity being of the gentlest kind; the breadth of the design commands admiration. . . . The scroll is certainly not an imitation of that of Stradavari; it has considerable originality, and is more attractive on that account than for its beauty. . . ."

*   *   *

In Hart's subsequently revised editions the notes concerning Lorenzo have similar introduction. Cremona is mentioned, the period, however, changed to read 1695 to about 1740. An additional paragraph is introduced which reads:

"Lorenzo Guadagnini was born at Piacenza, and upon leaving the workshop of his master returned to his native town, where he remained until about the year 1695, at which period he is said to have removed to Milan. In the last named city he continued to work until about the year 1740." An explanatory footnote follows: "This and other information relative to the Guadagnini family I have recently obtained from its descendants at Turin." In view of the fact that no mention of any other habitat than Cremona occurs in the original and the subsequent paragraph headings, the new matter is distinctly contradictory in nature, an oversight on the eminent author's part which is hard to explain. Having pointed out the discrepancy existing in Hart's note as regards location of the maker, if its context calls for discussion the newly added paragraph would suggest the question: at what period of his life did Lorenzo work in the shop "of his master" if he returned to his native town and remained there "until about the year 1695?"

Judging from examples of Lorenzo Guadagnini's work, there seems no justifiable reason to believe him to have acquired training or experience in the shop of Stradivari. It is well to consider that the consensus of modern opinion discredits all theories linking members of other families than Stradivari's own with the Cremonese master. Particularly misforming is the inference that Lorenzo Guadagnini worked at Milan from 1695 until about 1740. It is extremely doubtful that he worked in that city at all; no record exists, to my knowledge, of instruments produced or dated from that city, and it is probably chargeable to Yusupov's blundering that Lorenzo's name became associated with Milan. The eminent German chronicler Lütgendorff remarks in this connection (translated):—"That he also worked in Milan has been stated, but seems to have been founded on mistaken identity."

SIR GEORGE GROVE

Following Hart's work, Grove's *Dictionary of Music and Musicians* appeared in 1879. E. J. Payne wrote the notes concerning many of the old violin makers; of the first generations of the Guadagnini family the entry reads: "Lorenzo and John-Baptist . . . their exact kinship is uncertain . . . both claimed to be pupils of Stradivarius."

Later editions of the Grove work indicate matured opinion. Prepared by the Reverend E. H. Fellowes, Mus. D., after consultation with Alfred Ebsworth Hill, the notice reads: "The first . . . was Lorenzo, who worked at Piacenza and died there about 1740. He is one of those who styled himself a pupil of Stradivari, but no proof of this claim has ever been forthcoming. (2) Giovanni Battista (c. 1745-90) was the son of Lorenzo . . . both . . . did their best to copy the Stradivari model for the reason that they recognized it to be the best, and not because they had been his pupils . . . Lorenzo left but few violins, and his violoncellos are very scarce; some of the violins are meritorious . . ."

The notice as it concerns J. B. Guadagnini will be given further mention at another place. The words "did their best to copy the Stradivari model" are not without significance; in my experience, little is to be found in any of the instruments produced by the Guadagninii which would suggest teaching of Stradivari. The outline in some, perhaps, but in their archings, purfling, the size and method of insertion of dowel pins, sound holes, heads, and other refinements typical of the older master, the trained eye immediately recognizes a technique incompatible with that which might be expected of a hand trained by Stradivari.

JAMES FLEMING

In 1883 James M. Fleming published his "Old Violins and Their Makers." In this he reiterates that Lorenzo was a pupil of Stradivari who "established himself at Piacenza from 1700 to 1743." But in his "Fiddle Fancier's Guide," published 1892, he modified the statement, attributing Piacenza as Lorenzo's native city and the reference to his teacher to read ". . . worked for a number of years with Stradivari—so it is said—and returned to Piacenza about 1700. The words "so it is said" express obvious doubt, as well as his final words of the notice commenting on the wording of "alumnus", on Lorenzo's labels: "This ticket is probably the foundation for the notion that he worked with Stradivari." His notice also includes ". . . curiously enough, a goodly number of them bear Nicolas Amati labels." It is regrettable that Fleming commited the error of naming the chimerical "brother" of Lorenzo in his revised work, a blemish which the original was spared.

HORACE PETHERICK

As an example of how far imagination can stretch theory, we find not only error but gross exaggeration and build up of faulty premises in what was furnished by the English writer Horace Petherick, unquestionably a sincere enthusiast, one who collaborated with George Hart, and who was never deterred by a sense of modesty to put his ideas, fantastic or otherwise, in print.

In his work on Stradivari (1900), he ventures to tell us much about Lorenzo Guadagnini, and as at once branding his utterances devoid of the background of fact, he speaks of the maker as a Milanese, probably an echo from Yusupov. Writing about Stradivari, he goes on to say: "Among the earliest of his pupils (the precise number or even the names of all will never be known), may be placed Alexander Gagliano of Naples, working with him about the period of 1680* and some years later . . ." and, further, "Lorenzo Guadagnini, Joannes Battista, his son, and Josef of Pavia all claim to have lent a helping hand and there is nothing in their art that is in contradiction. The first became a great master of the Milanese school [!] and was afterwards rivalled by his son, who was more cosmopolitan and was not identified with one place in particular."

To further emphasize the inconsistency of his remarks, pertaining to tone qualities of instruments produced in various localities, of itself always a moot subject, Petherick ventures to say:

"Taking for instance the Milanese maker, Lorenzo Guadagnini, who tells us himself that he learnt his art under Antonio Stradivari, we find distant traces of it in his tone, the general calibre is the same and most of the fine, distinguishing features noticed in the tone produced by his master; the difference, however, is that which is peculiar to the master makers of

---

* Or at the time Stradivari was still working for Amati!

Milan, that of a slightly less reedy emission of sound. Some have called it harder, which is not a correct description. Chords are produced with it as easily and roundly as with any other, the individual notes blend beautifully and give an impression of homogeneousness in no wise inferior to anything produced in Italy. There was no apparent difficulty in the way of Milan acquiring and cultivating the variety of Italian tone known as the Cremonese had they been so disposed; we are therefore led to infer that each place with its musical worlds held its own opinions as to the most satisfactory quality of tone for its purpose and considered it the best. Milan is situated in Lombardy, northwest of Cremona, and distant from it between forty and fifty miles; not a very long distance at any time, but quite sufficient for each place to cultivate or indulge in any artistic or musical fancies or whims independently of each other. We find maker after maker in Milan keeping within certain limits as regards the quality of tone produced there; I do not know of one whose instruments emitted other than the Milanese quality.

"We may, I think, safely assume that so far from loosely and superficially instructing his pupils, Stradivari's tuition was of a deeper, far-reaching kind than has ever been suspected. If the tone of Lorenzo Guadagnini is compared with that of the makers who were working in Milan when he arrived*, it will not be difficult to perceive that the Milanese type is still retained, although much enlarged and matured, in fact becomes freshly developed, throwing out the additional qualities for the obtaining of which the great master of Cremona had carefully trained his gifted pupil. All this is not in the least interfered with by the fact of Joannes Battista

------

* Which, it is safe to say, he never did!

Guadagnini's tone differing in some respects—and more at times—with that of his father, but rather helped by it; both assert on their tickets that they were instructed by Stradivari, and both show the results of their training in that largeness and impressiveness which is so much beloved of violinists and which without doubt came from their great teacher. Josef, the son of Joannes Battista Guadagnini, appears also to have been instructed by Stradivari or to have assisted under his personal supervision—which would amount to much of the same thing. We may perceive in the tone of this maker also the influence of the great master in the same directions as are manifested in the works of his father and grandfather, they are all of the Stradivarian school."

The reader can readily sense the innocuous prattle indulged in as utterly pointless, aside from its blundering in classing Lorenzo Guadagnini among the Milanese makers. Not content to ascribe the teaching of Lorenzo and Joannes Baptista Guadagnini to Stradivari, Petherick also associates the latter's son Josef as a pupil of the master.

CONTEMPORARY WORKS

Turning to the recordings of more modern writers, two French violin-historians of this century add to the variety of misinformation concerning Lorenzo Guadagnini. Henri Poidras' "Critical and Documentary Dictionary of Violin Makers," published at Rouen in 1923, names him of Cremona, circa 1695-1755, and commits the blunder of confusing Lorenzo with J. B., in stating that he worked at Parma, Milan and Plaisance. The characterization of Lorenzo's violins, i.e., "small pattern," repeated from other writings, is rendered the more meaningless by the additional remark that they were "of medium height with a personal touch." The work of René Vannes, "Essai d'un Dictionnaire Universel des Luthiers," published at Paris in 1932, exhibits still greater lapse in reiterating "Lorenzo (I) was the brother of Giambattista (I), born Plaisance about 1695, died at Milan after 1760."

The excellent work of Hamma & Company, "Meisterwerke Italienischer Geigenbaukunst," published at Stuttgart about 1930, names Lorenzo's period as of Cremona-Piacenza 1695-1760. Departing from the long prevailing custom of describing Lorenzo's patterns as small, Hamma characterized his violins as generally built on large and broad form. Cremona is mentioned by Hamma as the source from which certain works of Lorenzo emanated. Examples shown in picture in the book present views of tops and backs of violins: (1) Cremona, 1740 (doubtful); (2) Piacenza, 1743; (3) Piacenza, 1745. The specimen of 1743 will be mentioned later, as it is one which was in possession of Efrem Zimbalist at one time and figured in an unusual episode.

RECAPITULATION

It is obvious why little has been learned from sources quoted concerning Lorenzo Guadagnini's origin, either as to locality or period. However, relative to the location, the cities of Cremona and Piacenza were but a short distance removed from each other as measured today—a mere half-hundred miles, which even in those days of slow travel would have made Cremona the logical and convenient place for a native of Piacenza who was planning to follow the craft of the violin maker to choose. Cremona was the Mecca for many; that few who went to gain admission to the sanctum of Stradivari were successful is known to us now. Yet, we may believe that opportunity was afforded the tyro wishful of learning to observe methods and imbibe knowledge to carry home with him. On such grounds it is quite reasonable to assume that self-chosen titles, such as "alumnus," were adopted by some makers, notably Lorenzo Guadagnini.

Our dictionaries define the word alumnus to mean *loosely any pupil of a college or school,* and the word school as the *disciples or followers of a teacher.* Considering these interpretations, the quoted words from Grove's Dictionary should be recalled.

The period of Lorenzo Guadagnini's birth has been generally placed as about 1695. Granting the fecundity of the Italian people, it is, nevertheless, difficult to accept the generally recorded date of 1711 as that of the birth of Joannes Baptista, thus making Lorenzo a father at the boyish age of sixteen. Count Cozio's concern that his protégé should be included among the "Cremonese Worthies" may account for his writing, as has been read, that both father and son were natives of Cremona. Otherwise, judging by the labels used by them in 1740 and later, on which they proclaimed themselves as of Piacenza, there is nothing known to us to justify Cozio's belated report, which so soon followed his first statement that there was no information in his possession other than that J. B. Guadagnini had used the term Cremonese on some of his tickets.

*   *   *

There is positive proof that both Lorenzo and Joannes Baptista Guadagnini began their Piacenza epoch in the year 1740, and, also, that they worked independently of each other; this exists in labels, those used by the father including the word "Pater," and those employed by the son the words "filius Laurentius." The small number of existing works attributed to Lorenzo dated from Piacenza is readily explained by the fact that his death took place within a few years subsequent to the beginning of the Piacenza period, about 1745 it is believed. This being so, readers will recognize the fallacies contained in the writings of historians who connect him with Milan and of the period 1760 onwards! The truth, as said, seems to be that Lorenzo never worked in that city. There can be no doubt that he was industrious and that he must have completed the making of more than a few instruments before his advent at Piacenza in 1740. The question therefore arises, what has become of them? If such existed, and reason prompts the belief that a number did, they cannot all have disappeared and, as mentioned by some writers, they probably pass as the works of other hands.

HILL ON LORENZO'S LABELS

An excerpt from Hill's work on Stradivari (1902), page 84, presents the following:

"Lorenzo Guadagnini may have been a pupil of Stradivari, though this matter . . . is shrouded in some doubt. Was he a Cremonese, or are we to believe, as stated by Hart, on the authority of the present members of the Guadagnini family, whose knowledge of their ancestors we have found by personal intercourse to be most hazy, that he was born at Piacenza? In certain of his works there are traces of Stradivari's influence, and we possess an original label, one of the only three ever seen by us, on which he states, 'Laurentius Guadagnini, fecit Placentiæ, alumnus Antonius Straduarius, 1740.' We obtained this label, with several others, from the executors of the late Charles Reade, and on the paper to which it is attached we read the following significant remark. 'N.B.—At Piacenza it was easy to call himself a pupil of Stradivari—he dare not have said so at Cremona.' With which characteristically terse statement by Reade we are inclined to agree."

At the time of that writing only three genuine Lorenzo Guadagnini labels were known to the authors.

LORENZO'S LABELS

Through the courtesy of our contemporaries of the Hill firm, it is possible to illustrate two types, reproductions of originals.

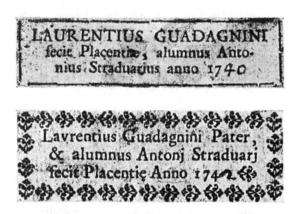

Lütgendorff illustrates the line bordered type shown above. It is identical with the label of the elsewhere illustrated violin of 1740.

Reproductions of these labels are to be found in various books. The original edition of Vidal contains a pen drawn illustration picturing the ornately bordered type, the date 1743. This was evidently sketched from the same label which is reproduced in photogravure in the 1889 edition of Vidal, on which the date reads 1745. It is of interest to note that J. B. Guadagnini employed the use of one small floral ornament, identical to those which form the border of the pictured label, on his own earliest type.

It has been said that Lorenzo Guadagnini's employment of the spelling Straduarius or Straduarj, as found on the illustrated labels, indicates an illiteracy quite incompatible with a maker who asserted service under the master, it being assumed that an Italian who claimed such association, whether for short or long period of time, or even ordinary acquaintance with the old Cremonese name of Stradivari (or with the cursive form U as in Stradiuari, followed by the maker himself until about 1730 when he adopted the Roman V) could not possibly have been guilty of the omission of the letter "i" after the "d". Various books, such as Hart's, show supposed types of labels set in type including the term Cremona, the discrepancies evident in their spelling makes it obvious that such types were not copied from genuine tickets used by the maker.

* * *

With little factual material at hand upon which to draw in an effort to construct a logical thesis on Lorenzo Guadagnini's career, the writer must indulge in recourse to theory. The story, then, would read:

A native of Piacenza, born there about 1695, having elected to become a maker of violins and there being no opportunity to learn or work in the craft at home, Lorenzo Guadagnini proceeded to Cremona and there worked and became proficient. Under whose training, or with whom he shared his labors during the years prior to his return to Piacenza about 1740, is left open to surmise. According to labels used by him at Piacenza, his adaption of the words "alumnus Antoni Straduari" has been interpreted to mean that he was a disciple of the master. But, so were other makers of the time who felt and obeyed the influence of their great contemporary. Joseph, son of Andreas Guarnerius, fell under that influence, as did his pupils, among whom his own son, Joseph del Gesù, Carlo Bergonzi, and, not beyond the bounds of reason, one other who might have been fellow worker in the same shop—Lorenzo Guadagnini—as well as later, the son of the last named, Joannes Baptista, all disciples of or carrying on in the tradition of Stradivari, if we can stretch the interpretation of the word to mean adherence to the principles of *a* master than, strictly, to *one's* master! As modern belief holds that Stradivari neither trained nor employed outside helpers, a reasonably logical conclusion points to the Guarneri establishment as offering, in Lorenzo Guadagnini's youth, opening for aspiring applicants for work, learning and employment.

Hart remarked that the sound holes of Lorenzo's violins sometimes have the "pointed character of Giuseppe Guarneri," perhaps too broadly interpreted if taken to suggest a connection with that master, nevertheless worthy of consideration. That the style of Lorenzo's violins varies cannot be denied; the strong personality exhibited in the works of J. B. Guadagnini which makes them easily recognizable, fails to stamp the instruments produced by the father. Working concurrently with his son at Piacenza for a mere five years, and allowing for a few instruments presumed to have been previously made in Cremona, Lorenzo's career as an individual maker was short-lived and, consequently, unproductive of many instruments.

*   *   *

This record of existing works attributed to Lorenzo Guadagnini embraces a period terminating 1745. The small number of instruments here named, presumed to be authentic works of the maker, testifies to their great rarity. An asterisk indicates specimens actually handled by this writer.

TABULATION

VIOLINS

17....* An outstanding work. The label it bears is a reproduction of the bordered type used by the maker at Piacenza, dated 1739. Described as a work at Cremona, this violin was loaned by Mrs. James W. Husted of New York for exhibition at the Stradivari Bicentenary Observance at Cremona, Italy, in 1937. It was again one of a number of rare instruments exhibited in the Brooklyn (New York) Museum in 1945, commemorating the 300th anniversary of Stradivari's birth (1644) and the 200th of the death of Joseph Guarnerius del Gesù (1744). The violin was illustrated and commented upon in a souvenir volume published subsequent to the Cremona affair, and a brochure distributed at the Brooklyn exhibition referred to it as the *ex* Kemeny, after a former European owner. Another owner was Professor Wünsch of Magdeburg, Germany. In 1928 the violin was acquired by Emil Herrmann and later passed to the possession of Mrs. Husted. The violin has a back of handsomely figured maple, added wings at the lower flanks being original with the maker. The varnish is of a rich orange-red color.

1738   A catalog issued by Hamma & Company of Stuttgart, Germany, about 1910-12, listed a violin described as a work at Piacenza, seemingly an error as to the date as the maker is not known to have produced instruments in that city prior to 1740. The back of the violin was pictured in the catalog, showing it to be in two pieces of small flamed maple cut slab. The varnish is of a yellow color.

1740   Catalogues issued by Lyon & Healy in 1917 and 1918 showed in color a violin described to be of large proportions. The varnish of red-orange color and the back in one piece of maple of handsome figure.

1740   Hamma's book "Meisterwerke Italienischer Geigenbaukunst" illustrates a violin showing strong characteristics of J. B. Guadagnini's style. It is described as a work of Lorenzo Guadagnini and has a two piece back of handsome strongly figured maple.

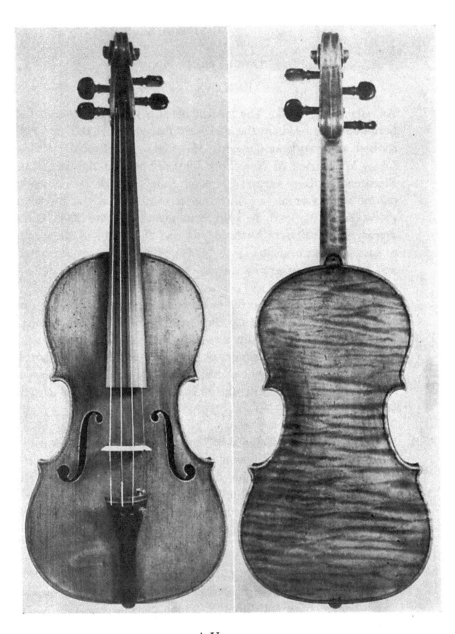

A VIOLIN BY
LORENZO GUADAGNINI
PIACENZA, 1740
ex Andreæ

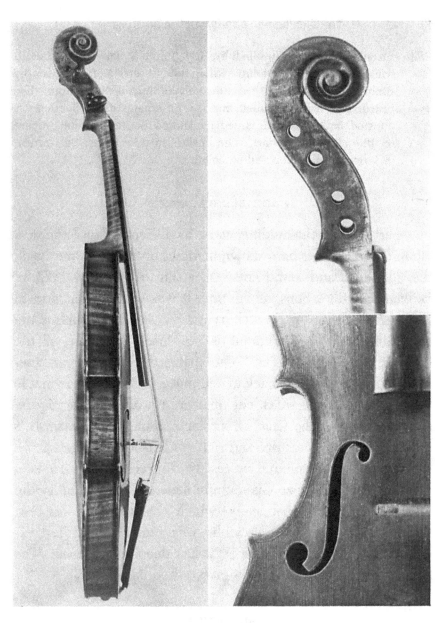

SIDE, HEAD, SOUND-HOLE
LORENZO GUADAGNINI
PIACENZA, 1740
ex Andreæ

49

1740   From information supplied by Mr. Ralph P. Powell, of Smethwick, England, this violin was in the possession of Mr. George
Blain, prominent English violinist, at the time of this writing. The
instrument bears no label, but (as informed) its authenticity is
attested in a certificate issued by Hart & Son of London, signed
by the late George Hart. The back is in two pieces; the varnish
of a beautiful golden yellow color.

A NOTABLE EXAMPLE

A particularly outstanding work by Lorenzo Guadagnini, a
violin dated 1740, is here shown in views of the front and back,
the side, head and sound hole. A certificate issued in 1922 by
William E. Hill & Sons, at the time it was sold by that firm to
Leslie B. Andreae of Christchurch, New Zealand, contains the
statement:— "The instrument is the finest specimen of the
maker's work known to us." Our plates depict the even, fine-
grained spruce top; the back in one piece is of handsome maple
cut on the slab; the sides, cut quarter, are of matching figure,
and the wood of the head of similar marking. The varnish is
very lovely, of soft texture and rich golden-brown in color.

It would be of definite interest to the record to know how
many works of Lorenzo Guadagnini have been recorded by the
House of Hill. Whether many—which seems unlikely—or few,
the fact that this particular violin was named as the best example known to the firm in 1922 has deep significance. The
type of label it bears has been pictured on page 44.

TABULATION

1740* *ex*-Andreæ. Above remarked, a violin characterized by W. E. Hill
& Sons as one of the finest works of Lorenzo Guadagnini. It was
acquired in London by William Lewis & Son of Chicago, subsequently to be purchased by William M. Douglas. (*Illustrated*)

1743   This is the second of two violins attributed to Lorenzo Guadagnini exhibited at the Stradivari-Guarneri commemorative observance at Brooklyn, New York, in 1945. The instrument was
titled *ex* Hammig and authenticity is established in certificates
issued by W. H. Hammig and W. E. Hill & Sons. It is in fine
condition, has a one piece back of curly maple and varnish of
yellow-orange color. Owned by Mrs. Barbara Kempner, who
acquired it from Emil Herrmann.

THE ZIMBALIST LORENZO

An unusual chain of events attracted world-wide notice to
a fine violin by Lorenzo Guadagnini, which, with a famous
Stradivari, was part of the equipment carried by Efrem Zimbalist when he left New York on a world tour late in 1926.
During a concert in Los Angeles early in the following year,
it was taken from his dressing room while the artist was an-
swering one of a number of curtain calls during his performance
of the program. Recovery of the instrument took place in May,
1927, when it was offered for sale to dealers at Chicago. Like
other famous masterpieces, the Guadagnini was known, and
recognized as the property of Zimbalist. The culprit was a
musician and his story to the Chicago police was that as an
employee at the Los Angeles theater and having access back-
stage, he made off with the valuable instrument while it was
left momentarily unguarded. With recovery of the instrument
the story might have ended had return to its owner been immediately possible. Mr. Zimbalist had by then arrived in Australia, where his wife (the late Alma Gluck) was to join him.
Apprised by cable of the developments, he instructed Mrs.
Zimbalist to regain possession of the violin and bring it with
her. This plan was not carried out, and it was subsequently
dispatched to Sydney, Australia. But when it arrived, Zim-

balist had gone. Exchange of cables then brought about its shipment to Tokyo where again it arrived too late. The sequence of disappointments continued; the instrument followed the trail of the artist—always a little too late—to Shanghai, Hong Kong, Manila, Calcutta, Bombay, Madras. A final effort brought about its return to Sidney where Zimbalist expected to make a return engagement, which, however, was canceled. As time did not permit a special trip to Sydney, the violin was then returned to New York, in care of the Wurlitzer Company. It was expected that violin and violinist would be reunited when Zimbalist arrived in New York from his European engagements, but the instrument did not reach New York until after the Zimbalist family had left to spend the summer months at their country place at West Hartford, Connecticut. The incidents were widely publicized by the press at the time as rare material for a human interest story. Delivery of the violin was effected in the company of a bodyguard of newspaper men and photographers, and assumed the nature of a ceremony. A succession of flashes recorded the action and photographs taken were shown in newspapers throughout the country. Among other photos taken, particular interest connects with a group which portrays Ruvin Heifetz, father and first teacher of Jascha Heifetz, Efrem Zimbalist, Jr., the late Alma Gluck Zimbalist, and Mr. Zimbalist wearing the rural garb he preferred for country wear. Mr. Heifetz was a guest at the Zimbalist cottage, and at the time was teaching Efrem, Jr., to play the violin.

TABULATION

1743* The Zimbalist Lorenzo. This violin is one of those mentioned as illustrated in the Hamma book. The instrument was brought to this country by Erich Lachmann, and through the Wurlitzer Col-

A VIOLIN BY
LORENZO GUADAGNINI
PIACENZA, 1743
ex Zimbalist

lection was acquired by Zimbalist. It subsequently passed to other ownership. A finely preserved specimen with orange red varnish. *(Illustrated)*

1743   Hug Collection of Zurich. This violin is illustrated in Franz Farga's book. One piece back; apparently of medium arching.

1744   A violin, in the possession of Mr. Roland Sirrell of Birmingham, England, as advised by Mr. Powell in 1947. It bears Hill certification as an authentic work of the master, with exception of the head. The label is said to be an original. The violin has a two-piece back; the varnish of deep golden yellow color.

1745   Pictured in the Hamma book, this violin bears a marked resemblance in the wood of its one-piece back to the Zimbalist specimen, as well as to the one of 1740 previously mentioned as having been in the Lyon & Healy Collection. The wood of which these backs were formed apparently came from the same log.

1745   One of the artistic brochures distributed by Hamma & Company, about 1912, shows a violin listed as a work of Laurentius Guadagnini at Cremona. The plates depict a fine violin showing Guadagnini characteristics, but incorrectly dated if a work at Cremona. It has a two piece back with broad curls descending downward from the left in each part; the varnish is described as Bordeaux-red in color.

?   Hug Collection of Zurich. Illustrated in Franz Farga's book. Although recorded as a work at Cremona, the portrait suggests the hand of some other maker.

A VIOLA

1745   A viola. Illustrated in a catalogue issued by Emil Herrmann in 1926. The plates show it to have a one piece back of maple of which the figure slants downward from the left to right.

PART II

J. B. GUADAGNINI AT PIACENZA

Over two centuries have passed since Lorenzo Guadagnini founded the dynasty of violin makers bearing the family name, yet no genealogical background has emerged which, as in the case of Antonio Stradivari, provides details of family or other intimate personal nature. Beyond that which was contained in Count Cozio's notes, we have nothing to cite from church or census records, and notwithstanding statements credited to descendants that the family was of Piacenza, an element of speculation on the subject of the birth and early careers of both Lorenzo Guadagnini and his son, Joannes Baptista, has remained. Two theories have been held, which may be argued as follows:

(1) J. B. Guadagnini born at Cremona: Some present day connoisseurs adhere to the belief that Cremona was the locality of the maker's birth. Other than Count Cozio's amendments to his original notes there seems nothing to substantiate the theory. Lorenzo Guadagnini must have been either fifteen or sixteen years of age at the time he betook him a spouse if, as is generally conceded, Giovanni Battista was born in 1711, the month and day not recorded. The name of the mother, nor the locality of her origin, is likewise not recorded on any available material. Lorenzo must have removed to Cremona at an earlier year if a son was born to him there in 1711.

(2) J. B. Guadagnini born at Piacenza: The earliest recordings mentioning J. B. Guadagnini name him as of Piacenza. Count Cozio's first mention of the maker is plainly doubtful of Cremonese connection and only in a subsequent letter to Lan-

cetti suggests it, quite obviously with a purpose that both father and son should be entitled to rank with other "Cremonese Worthies." The very first labels known to have been used by Giovanni Battista Guadagnini record him as of Piacenza (Placentina); those used by him thereafter at Piacenza and later during his Milan period continue to assert Placentina nativity, not only in naming the city, but also in designating it by the letter "P" beneath his monogram, which he continued to use at Cremona in 1758 as well as at Parma later.

Considering these unalterable facts, logic prompts and strongly supports the assumption that Piacenza should be regarded as the locality in which Giovanni Battista Guadagnini was born.

Had his origin been Cremonese, he could not have been unaware of the prestige attached to connection with that school during the twenty year period at Piacenza and Milan and would so have announced on his labels from the beginning of his career. Theorists contend that both Lorenzo and Giovanni Battista Guadagnini lived and worked in the city of Cremona prior to 1740.

Cremonese records have been most thoroughly searched in quest for records pertaining to the old violin makers; nothing seems to have been found there to connect the family Guadagnini with the locality and notwithstanding a claim made by Count Cozio that investigations *at Turin* had established the city of Cremona as that of their origin, the subject may be considered closed to further discussion at this time.

As will be mentioned, information concerning J. B. Guadagnini as presented by Count Cozio in his notes to Lancetti was not made public for many years subsequent to their writing in 1823. Nor did their significance penetrate widely outside of

Italy for another term of years. We know that George Hart had some knowledge of their purport at the time he brought out the revised edition of his work in 1884. Obviously, such was not the case at the time he prepared his first manuscript and was misled into following the lead of Prince Yusupov and Sandys and Forster. That the false trail blazed by these pioneer biographers of the Guadagninii was one blindly followed has led to the errors that spoil otherwise excellent works.

As the earliest biographer of violin makers to direct more than casual attention to Guadagnini, Count Cozio was apparently a loyal and ardent champion, wishful that his protégé receive such honor and glory that was his due, and of which he had been largely denied throughout his life. It is to be assumed that Cozio was better informed of the intimate facts of the maker's career than was given us to know by him through his notes to Vincenzo Lancetti. Thirty-five years had elapsed since the death of J. B. Guadagnini at the time his earliest biographer prepared the material forwarded in 1823 to Lancetti at Cremona—a tribute directed to memorialize the great earlier Cremonese masters in the main, but also evidencing a particular concern that he, Guadagnini, who had been his collaborator and advisor during the years devoted to a fancy for fine violins, should be immortalized in the Cremonese biographer's contemplated work. It cannot have been a lapse of memory entirely that carried no recollection of Guadagnini's origin, and it is conceivable that he subsequently found it essential, in order that Lancetti's record of Cremonese worthies should include the violin maker, to name not only Giovanni Battista, but also his father, Lorenzo, as Cremonese by birth. Whether made to fit that purpose or not, Count Cozio might well have been in position to divulge other facts relating to Guadagnini's background had there been reason or occasion to do so. That many details only now to appear in a new publication soon to be released* were unknown to this and other historians is regrettable, but a far greater misfortune was theirs who, in ignorance of that small measure of information for which we are indebted to the Count's notes to Lancetti, indulged in fantasy and brought confusion to the thought of many subsequent biographers.

For, as we know today, Count Cozio gave an entirely correct recital of J. B. Guadagnini's active career in so lucid a manner that there remained no sensible reason to invent a second person of the same name. Verification has come about through the evidence of the maker's own labels, examples of which survive in goodly number to this day, untampered with and clearly designating the place and time of their insertion in violins, violas and violoncellos.

There are those who defend the theory of J. B. Guadagnini's Cremonese origin on the ground of his employment of the term on labels dated from Parma, subsequent to a short visit to Cremona in 1758, a practice he continued throughout his Parma and Turin epochs. As now regarded, this has no significance other than business expediency, adopted to enhance his reputation by asserting a connection with the violin-making school of Cremona, a claim not entirely immune to contradiction, as it could then be based on an actual working period in the famous cradle of the art. Surely, had he the right to so term himself in his earlier career, he would not consistently have proclaimed himself of Piacenza even during his stay at Cremona in 1758.

Neither to insinuate agreement with, or deny the premise

---

* A work of Renzo Bacchetta, in process of printing at Milan, Italy, will divulge the contents of Count Cozio's private diaries, correspondence and records.

that J. B. Guadagnini had been employed at Cremona in his youthful years, there are certain characteristics not incompatible with the theory to be found in his works—as also in those of his father—that suggest experience gained under the guidance of master hands, and, there being none such at Piacenza, and Cremona not far away as distance is measured, that would have been their logical choice to learn and practice. Any direct connection with the shop of Antonius Stradivarius, hazarded as possible by many early historians, is no longer credited, notwithstanding interpretation given J. B. Guadagnini's Turin labels on which he employed the term *alumnus Stradivari*, which is believed to owe its origin to the suggestion of Count Cozio. If at Cremona, a likely source of employment would have been in such an establishment as that maintained by Giuseppe, son of Andrea Guarneri.

* * *

Turning from discourse on such debatable matter to indisputable facts, we find corroboration of Count Cozio's words telling of Guadagnini's movements in the following table designating the various periods of his working career:

1740-1749, at Piacenza;
1750-1758, at Milan;
1758, a few months at Cremona;
1759-1771, at Parma;
1771-1786, at Turin.

* * *

In striking contrast to the exceeding rarity of works by his father, a rich heritage was left by J. B. Guadagnini. Admittedly far from providing a complete tabulation, the record of his productions as hereinafter presented will show that he must have worked with unflagging energy and diligence year after year producing violins, violas and violoncellos in a style uniquely his own and in number amazing to contemplate. Many sources have been drawn upon to gather information about existing examples believed to be his authentic work yet a vast augmentation would accrue if the whereabouts of still other privately held specimens in this and other countries could be known. Whereas a universal interest in the works of Stradivari and Guarneri de Gesù has caused their movements to be made public for recording in the majority of cases, very little effort has ever heretofore been directed towards keeping track of Guadagnini instruments.

J. B. Guadagnini built substantially; he employed excellent materials, due to which and a seeming immunity to vicissitudes that have brought ruin to many fine works of the older masters, his survive plenteously, many in immaculate state.

A subtle difference in the style of work and finish marks each change of the maker's habitat without, however, any loss of a distinctive individuality that characterizes his style. Largely due to those periodic removals from one city to another, and the noticeable variations which mark each epoch, it can be readily understood that early writers fell into the error of attributing his instruments to the labor of more than one pair of hands, and, for reasons to be presented, accepted a premise that two makers of the same name, working in different cities, lived and worked concurrently. This belief came to be so firmly rooted that it persisted without challenge until fairly recent years.

*   *   *

The world outside Italy was slow to accord recognition to J. B. Guadagnini during his lifetime, nor, judging by his migrations from one community to another, was his presence honored by fellow-townsmen. It cannot be gainsaid, however, that notwithstanding his changes of habitat, an innate assiduity compelled unremitting application to his art and aside from an actual demand for his products, his industry was such that in each of the cities that claimed him as a resident, with the single exception of Cremona, he created a far greater number of finished works than did any of his violin-making contemporaries.

Discounting Cozio's insinuation remarking Guadagnini's hasty temper, a more logical premise might be offered to account for the periodic removal of J. B. Guadagnini from one city to another in taking into consideration that the man himself was of a roving nature and further, that through his very prodigal, unceasing productivity he glutted each local market in turn, and thus was impelled to seek new fields. There was no interruption of his steady labor—and it is correct to use the singular, "his," as his and only his impress is delineated in the great number of his works until the last years of his life. It seems reasonable to believe that a major part of his output was absorbed close to the point of origin as, although dealers outside of Italy, in northern European and British centers, were actively engaged in violin traffic as far back as during Guadagnini's time, early historians paid him scant notice and evidenced disregard of the merits of his work by classifying it as second rate.

Before the dawn of the nineteenth century, Italian musicians had been carrying instruments with them to the northern cities, and among others, certainly works of Guadagnini. However, study of published lists of instruments contained in famous collections of the past century indicate that Guadagnini's violins had not attracted that class of buyers who, as collectors, sought only the works of the then recognized "great" masters. Nevertheless, a steady northward movement of violins produced in Italy had begun to draw heavily on the existing supply of that country, even before the now famous Luigi Tarisio rose from obscurity to prominence as a connoisseur of and trafficker in fine fiddles. His story is well known; his name connects with many masterpieces and he is mentioned here not for the fame accorded him as the one-time owner of Stradivari, Guarneri or other great Cremonese works, but because even in his day the name of Guadagnini seems to have had little significance. That he did bring numbers of them with him on his pilgrimages to his northern patrons, particularly in the French cities, can be taken for granted. However, in a list of important works exhibited at Paris in 1865, compiled by Jules Gallay, not a single owner of Guadagnini instruments is mentioned. The work contains reference to Lorenzo and J. B. Guadagnini without alluding to family connection. Vidal (1872) mentions J. B. as the son of Lorenzo. I remark these French works here for more than one reason—not only to stress the point that popularity had as yet seemingly failed to have been achieved by Guadagnini instruments in Paris at the time of their writing, but also because only *one* J. B. Guadagnini was mentioned.

Reverting to previously listed works on the subject, George Dubourg, author of *The Violin, Some Account of That Leading Instrument, etc.*, wrote in the fourth (1852) edition of his book, in the mention of Lorenzo Guadagnini: "He had a son, who worked at Milan, till about 1770, after his father's mode." Small comment, yet significant as it bears on our story, in mentioning only *a son* as successor to Lorenzo.

Following the appearance of Yusupov's treatise, first at fault in publicizing and thus lending support to the illusory theory concerning the Guadagninii we find the British collaborators, Sandys and Forster. William Sandys, F.S.A., was a member of the bar and writer on musical subjects, and Simon Andrew

Forster, was one of a prominent English violin making family. Unknowingly fathering the growth of a misconception, they referred to Yusupov's words in their notice to the Guadagnini family of makers in their *History of the Violin,* published (first of many editions) in 1864. As it concerns J. B. Guadagnini, the notice reads:

"Giovanni Baptista Guadagnini is generally called his [Lorenzo's] son, but if a ticket we have seen with this name and the date 1731 is genuine, it would appear probable that he was his brother, as stated in 'Luthomongraphie'; he worked at the same places, and made instruments very similar to those of Lorenzo, and of about the same value; he calls himself in some of his tickets a pupil of Antonius Stradiuarius."

Unconscious of encouraging a fiction, the author of those words was assuring permanence to Yusupov's ill-conceived premise. It was to follow that the work of Sandys & Forster attained a tremendous distribution, carrying its word far more widely and weightily than the limited printings of "Luthomonographie," and thus to offend generations of students of violin history, as the book has been reprinted time and again without revision or change in its text.

The French work of Fétis on Stradivari, published 1856 (English translation 1864), gives us the names of Lorenzo and Giovanni Battista without further detail as to family relationship, yet even at this day, notwithstanding the pronouncement of learned authorities to the contrary, there are those who still argue the belief that there were two makers of the name Giovanni Battista Guadagnini.

*   *   *

Since serious historians of the violin may be regarded as a modern institution, younger by perhaps two centuries than the evolution of the instrument itself, there is little cause to wonder why those who first elected to discourse on the topic were prone to err in forwarding their conclusions. It is regrettable that a deeper interest did not exist in years when the living still retained memories of the pioneer violin makers and their careers were still fresh in the minds of their generation, and thus possible to investigate and record. Attention which eventually focused itself on the subject as far back as a century ago, was principally directed to the great trio of Cremonese makers—the families of the Amati, Stradivari and Guarneri—as also the great Tyrolese master Jacobus Stainer, who long held a deservedly prominent place among the artists of first magnitude, with a lesser interest in the early Brescians. The works of many gifted makers who had not achieved the distinction of importance were disregarded and held of minor attraction by collectors. This becomes obvious when we note how insignificant is the number of instruments contained in some of the famous British collections, their comparative scarcity made further noticeable if we consider the modest sums derived at public sales during the '70s of the last century. Of these, I offer extracts from several important auctions:

The Gillott Collection, dispersed in 1872:

Lots 14, 18 —a tenor by J. B. Guadagnini, 1733 *(sic)*, and a small violin, with case, £40 0.

Lots 41, 45 —A violin by J. B. Guadagnini, and another by Carlo Bergonzi, in double case, £70 0.

Lots 47, 48 —A tenor by J. B. Guadagnini with case; and a Double-bass, by Gaspard di Salo, formerly Signor Dragonetti's, with case, £56 15.

Lots 130, 131—A violoncello by J. B. Guadagnini, with case, and another violoncello by Guadagnini, £76 0.

The Corsby Collection, dispersed in 1874:

A violin by J. B. Guadagnini 1730 *(sic)*, £16 0.

The Thornley Collection apparently contained no works by J. B. Guadagnini, but, at its dispersal in 1876, there was sold:

A violin by Joseph Guadagnini, 1802, £13 0.

Similarly, the Parera Collection, dispersed in 1877, contained only one work of the Guadagninii:

A violin by Joseph Guadagnini, 1755, £22 0.

From these extracts we find that Guadagnini's works were available to purchasers of comparatively modest means in those days, indicating that his instruments were not then sufficiently appreciated to make them desired or to command high prices.

HART ON J. B. GUADAGNINI

George Hart's popular work *The Violin, Famous Makers and Their Imitators* has been, and will long remain, a standard item of violin literature. In its first edition—the original manuscript of which must have been in work before date of publication in 1875—it is apparent that he had read the aforementioned item in Sandys & Forster's work, as we find:

"Guadagnini, Johannes Baptista, Placentia, 1710-1750. His relationship to Lorenzo has never been stated, but it is probable that they were brothers. Lorenzo has always been regarded as the only pupil of Stradiuarius in the Guadagnini family, but if their respective works be closely examined, it will be found that those of Johannes Baptista more closely resemble the instruments of Stradiuarius than even those of Lorenzo, and one is thus led to the conclusion that Johannes Baptista was also a pupil of Stradiuarius. It is quite evident that he considered the model of Stradiuarius as that to be followed, and he does not appear to have changed his views on this point at any time, all his work being in accordance with the teachings of the great master." No doubt subsequently to cause Hart some rueful thought, his separate mention of "Giovanni Battista" Guadagnini, Piacenza, 1754-1785, in this first edition, stated simply: "The instruments of this maker are frequently equal to those of Johannes Baptista. His wood is also excellent." Equally regrettable is the next entry: this names Giuseppe Guadagnini, Parma, "1760-1800. Brother of G. B. Guadagnini. Very good wood; model a trifle more raised than in the instruments of his brother; sound-hole well cut, in imitation of Stradiuarius."

We do find, in Hart's writing, a genuine appreciation of the early works of J. B. Guadagnini; however, if his Piacenza and Milan works, as can be said, bear a slight similarity to the style of Stradivari, his later works show still less, unless it be allowed that the general pattern of the Violin provides a basic design, followed with variations unique with each maker.

It is to his credit that Hart corrected some portions of his original manuscript before publication of later editions of his work; it is significant that reference to the "brother" theory was thus deleted, as in the edition of 1884 of his book, in which he quotes Count Cozio, we read:

"Guadagnini, Giovanni Battista, Piacenza, 1711-1789. Son of Lorenzo. He was born, according to Count Cozio de Salabue, at Cremona, and Lancetti states that he worked with his father in Milan. Later he worked at Piacenza, then at Parma, where he became instrument maker to the Duke. Upon the pensions to the artists of the Duke's court being discontinued in 1772, he went to Turin, where he died." A footnote states: "The present representatives of the family mention Piacenza as the city of his birth"—a direct contradiction of the statement attributed to Count Cozio di Salabue that it was at Cremona. The Hart item continued:

"Count Cozio communicated to Lancetti the following particulars relative to Giovanni Battista Guadagnini. He says, 'He imitated Stradivari, but avoided close imitation of all detail, and prided himself on not being a mere copyist.' He is said to have excited the jealousy of other makers, which caused him to remove so frequently, but most likely he offended chiefly with his hasty temper. Many of his instruments made in Turin between 1773 and 1776 have wood of the handsomest kind. Count Cozio ordered from him several instruments which he added to his collection, among them two Tenors and two Violoncellos. The interest Count Cozio manifested with regards to this maker is shown in his having obtained from the parish registers the dates of his birth and death. He states that he was born in Cremona in 1711, and died in Turin, September 18, 1786. The last-named date is in conformity with that of 1785, recently given to me by the representatives of the family at Turin, as the last year in which he made instruments. . . ." Some of the material incorporated in the original notice to the maker (1875 edition of Hart's book) then follows, to be amended with: "In the correspondence which passed between Count Cozio di Salabue and Vincenzo Lancetti, in the year 1823, the Count says, 'The instruments of G. B. Guadagnini are highly esteemed by connoisseurs and professional men in Holland and Germany.' . . ." Preceding statements should be compared with the original words of Count Cozio as presented earlier in this work.

The excerpts from George Hart's writings have a deeper significance than that which is found in their mere reader interest. They emphasize the power of the printed word to sway the opinion of the multitude and thus fasten upon the records erroneous matters which may easily survive long after their faults have been exposed. Further, they point out that although "first editions" of great works often become rarities of considerable worth in the collector sense, it does not follow that their contents can be depended upon to provide reliable guides or information when the discourse is on controversial topics. It is important to note, in this connection, that whereas George Hart reversed himself in the later editions of his book, the first edition retains its position as an authoritative treatise and, there can be little doubt, was the agent consulted by many subsequent historians of the violin, who, without scruple, continued to refer to J. B. Guadagnini in the dual personalities of uncle and nephew.

ED. HERON-ALLEN

An example of such gross negligence is chargeable to the English writer Ed. Heron-Allen, erudite student of matters pertaining to the violin and its making though he is regarded to have been. He permitted his most famous work, published in book form in 1884, thus contemporaneously with George Hart's revised work, to reiterate the false premise referred to, an inexcusable blunder as it evidences his failure to avail himself of knowledge then possessed by others in his particular field of study. The work to which I refer is that entitled "Violin Making, as It Was and Is," and has had probably the largest sale of any treatise devoted to the subject. The matter of which it consists had been in large part published in serial form subsequent to 1882. The completed work acknowledges the author's

indebtedness to others for data presented therein and conveys
thanks to contemporaries for aid and advice. In view of this,
his reiterance of the uncle and nephew myth (one of other inaccuracies) weakens the position assumed by him in the Preface
of the book, charging the onus of faulty recording to "amateurs"
and others. This is particularly in bad taste as he directs the
attention of his readers to those two very works to which the
fallacious theory of brotherly relation of Lorenzo and J. B.
Guadagnini and the dual personality of the latter as uncle and
nephew is traceable. In this, he committed an offense against
posterity which might have been spared him (and all those who
suffered reprinting of the book without corrections) had Heron-
Allen availed himself of information known to have been in
the possession of his contemporary George Hart and in print
in the latter's revised work. Thus, all who have acquired and
studied Heron-Allen's work in any of its many editions, continue to read that "the anonymous 'Luthomonographie,' written
by the Russian prince Youssoupow (or Jousoupof), is so full of
strange mistakes as to be of little value apart from its bibliography rarity; and there is no doubt that Sandys & Forster's
'History of the Violin' owes its popularity and value entirely to
the fact that to the charming style and cultivated research of
Mr. Sandys, F.S.A., was added the practical knowledge of the
great Simon Andrew Forster."

Heron-Allen paid scant notice to Guadagnini, and the many
thousands of readers to whom his works are precious will continue to remain misinformed concerning the maker unless they
turn elsewhere in pursuit of knowledge on the subject. Generally speaking, this was of course possible only in a limited
field in Heron-Allen's day, yet it was in his time that the Lancetti papers (to which Hart refers) were made available, and

their translation in Hart's revised work had become publicized.

Obviously, Heron-Allen, at the time his book was printed, was unacquainted with the newly published facts, nor could he have had actual experience with instruments made by J. B. Guadagnini. His notice states that ". . . pupil of Stradivarius, whom he copied persistently, particularly in the form of his scroll. . . ." Anyone who has seen a Guadagnini scroll will know that this is definitely misinforming. Similarly lacking of significance is another reference contained in his book:—"It was towards the decline of the Cremona violin manufacture that gum-lac was introduced, and with it J. B. Guadagnini spoilt the tone of many of his instruments." How far wide of meaning this statement was has its answer in the great popularity of J. B. Guadagnini instruments among professional artists!

GROVE'S AND THE STAINER DICTIONARY

That the manner of George Hart's wording as found in the first edition of his book impressed the writers of the day becomes apparent in notices which appear in various other important reference works, wherein the legendary brother of Lorenzo continued to be recorded.

Following shortly after George Hart's first edition, Grove's *Dictionary of Music and Musicians* was published, the introduction dated 1879. Edward John Payne, eminent British attorney and a true votary of the violin, contributed a number of items. Mr Payne's remarks concerning Guadagnini were permitted to stand unaltered in later editions of the Grove work (to the writer's knowledge at least as late as the edition of 1899), notwithstanding George Hart's publication in 1885 of the correct facts eliminating all reference to the mythical brother of Lorenzo. It is of interest to mention that the early edition of Grove's Dictionary states, in reference to violins by

J. B. Guadagnini: ". . . good specimens command prices varying from £40 to £80."

What was, I believe, the first specialized "Dictionary of
Violin Makers" in the English language, under which title it
was published, was compiled by Miss Cecilia Stainer. She and
her brother, J. F. R. Stainer, collaborated with Sir John Stainer,
their father, in research on musical subjects, and all were
contributors to the Grove Dictionary. Books with the violin
as the general topic, which included as part of their text more
or less extended listings of violin makers' names, had been in
circulation in various languages for many years, but that from
the pen of Miss Stainer, dated from Oxford in 1896, true to its
title contained only names of violin makers in alphabetical
order, accompanied by the general type of complementary data.
The "Dictionary" has had several editions and is widely consulted as an accredited biographical English language dictionary of the workers in the violin-making craft.

The information provided therein relative to J. B. Guadagnini
follows that of Grove's Dictionary, and Miss Stainer acknowledges indebtedness to it and the works of many others, two
pages being devoted to a bibliography naming their authors.
Oddly, Miss Stainer's notice to J. B. Guadagnini is strangely
at variance with that written by her contemporary, Mr. Payne,
who, as she also, had been a contributor to the Grove work.
This will be noted in extracts from the writings of Mr. Payne
and Miss Stainer, as will be shown in juxtaposition.

It is readily understandable that, depending upon which of
these reference works was available for consultation, remarks
therein contained became a base upon which subsequent writers
prepared their notes; exercise of imagination provided embellishment to contribute further to the confusion!

GROVE'S DICTIONARY

"The first generation of the Guadagnini family consists of Lorenzo and John-Baptist; the latter seems always to have been a family name. Their kinship is uncertain. They worked from about 1690 to 1740. Both claimed to be pupils of Stradivarius. The violins of John-Baptist fully justify this claim. They are finely designed and covered with a rich dark red varnish, easily distinguished from the glaring scarlet varnish used by the second John-Baptist, and are in all respects worthy of the Stradivarian school. John-Baptist dated from Milan, Piacenza and Turin; he sometimes describes himself as 'Cremonensis,' sometimes as 'Placentinus.' . . . The second John-Baptist (probably a son of Lorenzo) made a large number of useful violins of the commoner sort. They are mostly of the Stradivarian pattern. The second John-Baptist introduced that unpleasantly high-coloured varnish which is often supposed to be the special characteristic of a 'Guadagnini.' "

STAINER'S DICTIONARY

"Giovanni Battista Guadagnini, brother of Lorenzo. Worked in Milan, Piacenza and Turin about 1695 to 1775. He made a great number of instruments, of ordinary workmanship, but some violins are well finished and the tone is good; they are made on a small pattern, slightly arched, the sound holes long and well put, the varnish a rich dark red colour, very different from that used by his nephew Giambattista. . . ."

"Giambattista Guadagnini, son of Lorenzo. . . . A pupil of his father, his violins and basses show the same form, the same qualities and the same defects. He followed the Stradivari pattern, and his instruments stand high in public opinion. He often suffers in reputation from having the same Christian name as his uncle. Giovanni Battista, Lorenzo's brother, whose work was much inferior. He used wood of the finest quality, and the varnish, which shows unmistakable signs of inferiority to that of the great makers, was that brilliant golden-red colour which is often considered a characteristic of a 'Guadagnini.' "

❋   ❋   ❋

At the dawn of this century there were those who still relied on the information contained in George Hart's first recording. I mention Hart alone, for his was the first definite statement supporting the theory of a brotherly relationship between Lorenzo and "Johannes Baptista"* Guadagnini. The few lines devoted to Giovanni Battista Guadagnini in his first book, as separate from those regarding Joannes Baptista Guadagnini, served further to create misunderstanding. Hart probably did not realize that his regrettable reiteration and recording of an error would be reflected in an aftermath of argument and controversy! We must assume, had that been foreseen, he would have remarked more pointedly upon the matter to explain his error of opinion at the earlier time when he so soon afterwards more accurately presented the revised editions of his work.

Laurent Grillet, a French writer, was the author of the first twentieth century biographical work concerning violin makers to correctly record the facts regarding the identity of J. B. Guadagnini. The work includes a historical survey and dictionary of violin makers and is titled *Les Ancêtres du violon et du violoncelle.* It was published in two volumes in Paris in 1901. Profusely illustrated, it relates the story of the ancestry of the violin family and contains well over a thousand biographical notes of makers, many replicas of their labels, etc. A scholarly review, its author was a noted conductor, composer and violoncellist. He was born 1861, and died at Paris in 1901, the year which witnessed the publication of his work. It is much to his credit that Grillet did not fall into the error of mentioning the fiction of a J. B. Guadagnini as a brother of Lorenzo.

---

* I have frequently been asked whether the latter "h" was used by the maker on his tickets; his labels show the spelling Joannes, which in the Hart book is found in an example mentioned. Hart's introduction of the "'h" may be attributed to an author's privilege to use that form, one of several of the Italian "Giovanni."

As properly a part of this record, Andreas Moser, eminent German violinist and associate of Joseph Joachim, mentions in his *Geschichte des Violinspiels* (1923), dedicated to Joachim: "Also belonging to the school of Stradivari, Lorenzo Guadagnini and his son Giambattista. . . ."

*   *   *

Although we have no documentary record of J. B. Guadagnini's whereabouts prior to 1740, a few words may be devoted to his appearance at Piacenza in 1740.

Recollection of the scenes of childhood, of early home and environment remain strongly impressed on the mind of man. In the European custom, apprentices in various crafts served their terms in different localities, rarely forgetful of the memories that sentimentally bound them to the place of their youth. Presuming Piacenza to have been where Lorenzo, and Joannes Baptista Guadagnini were born, such considerations may have been a compelling factor in their choice of that city in which to begin an actual career as individual makers of violins.

Capital of the province of the same name, Piacenza is situated on the River Po, about a score of miles southwest of Cremona and forty-three miles southeast of Milan, which is one of Italy's largest and richest cities and where for many years prior to the time of which we treat violin making had flourished, a craft then practically unknown at Piacenza. Whatever impelled the Guadagninis, father and son, to locate at Piacenza, it was obviously not a locality where finished artists of the attainments shown by the earliest dated works of the Guadagninii could have received their training.

Piacenza was possessed of considerable wealth, particularly rich in art. It was there that Raphael did the celebrated Sistine Madonna; the famous painting was sold by the monks of San

Sisto to Frederick Augustus of Saxony in 1754—during J. B. Guadagnini's period at Milan. A number of fine churches at Piacenza required instruments for their music; with no resident makers to serve players of the string family, there was an incentive, in addition to civic love, to attract the Guadagninis, father and son, to begin a career in the city as holding out promise of establishing a remunerative following. Although the elder maker left small evidence of industry or even success, judged by the few surviving works possible to enumerate, the existing productions of J. B. Guadagnini, as will be shown in the tabulation to follow, attest his productivity during his epoch there.

During his period at Piacenza J. B. Guadagnini employed several types of labels; on one he designates himself simply Joannes Guadagnini; another form, which establishes his relation to Lorenzo, bears the inscription Joannes Baptista filius Laurentius Guadagnini fecit Placentiæ 174... Also, as previously remarked, apparently establishing Piacenza as the city of his birth in accordance with Italian practice, we find labels later employed at Milan which read: Joannes Baptista Guadagnini Placentinus fecit Mediolani 175.....

TABULATION

The recording of works of J. B. Guadagnini at Piacenza which are believed beyond question authentic and correct as to their period of production, begins with instruments dated 1740. Although different writers have mentioned earlier dates in connection with works attributed to the maker, none such are known to the author. From all that can be gathered, father and son were working at Piacenza in 1740, each signing his own name to his product. That they found reason to direct attention to their identity, Lorenzo by including the word "pater" on his labels, and Joannes Baptista, "filius Laurentius," clearly indicates at least friendly rivalry, but, nonetheless, establishing that they maintained independent shops.

———————

Location of Guadagnini instruments as herein indicated is from my most recent information.

PIACENZA PERIOD VIOLINS

1740* This violin bears the original label, a rare type elsewhere illustrated, on which the maker designated himself simply as Joannes Guadagnini. The authenticity of the instrument is attested by the Messrs. Hill of London, and the late Alfred E. Hill is authority for the statement that Guadagnini did not at first incorporate his middle name, Baptista, in the setting of his labels. This violin was for some time the solo instrument of the late Evelyn Davis, of Chicago, before it passed to the present owner, Alfred Lustgarten, Chicago violinist.

1740 This violin, certified by Hill as original and a typical work of the period, bears an original label of the type with the maker's name Joannes Guadagnini. It was sold by Ralph P. Powell of Smethwick, England, to a client named Pawson, about 1941.

1740* A fine example which, from W. E. Hill & Sons, passed to the Wurlitzer Collection. Nicolas Garagusi purchased it; in an exchange the violin reverted to Wurlitzer, later to be acquired by Miss Clara Reisenberg.

1740* A characteristic work of the period, flat patterned, with two piece back of broad figured curly maple, bearing a label of the "filius Laurentii" type. The varnish is of an orange-brown color. William Lewis & Son collection.

1740 Plates which illustrate this violin in Max Möller's book, *Italiaansche Vioolbouw*, indicate a very fine example, clearly exhibiting the characteristic form of sound holes typical of the maker.

1741 *ex* Rich. Bearing a label of Milan dated 1751, this very fine violin is a typical work of the Piacenza early period. The circumstances of its passing from the possession of Albert Caressa to Dr. Thaddeus Rich were of unusual nature; he was closely connected with John and Rodman Wanamaker and was an important factor in forming the famous Wanamaker collection of stringed instruments. While at Caressa's place of business in company of Rodman Wanamaker, Rich expressed admiration for this particular Guadagnini violin, among others which Wanamaker acquired at the time. Upon reaching agreement with Caressa for their purchase, Wanamaker presented this violin to Rich. He retained possession until 1944 when it was purchased by Wurlitzer. An outstanding work of the maker, it has a two piece back of handsome maple and varnish of a brilliant wine-red color. The dimensions are slightly under normal. Now owned by a Californian.

1741* From the collection of August Herrmann of Berlin, this violin passed to concertmaster Alfred Hess, of Frankfort-on-the-Main, Germany. In more recent times, it was brought to this country and has been in the possession of Ludwig Schmidt, of Rockford, Illinois, for some years.

1741* The "Venus." The violin was so named because of its great beauty of wood and richness of varnish. It is illustrated in a catalogue of the 1927-28 collection of Emil Herrmann, and since that time has been in the possession of various owners—Mischa Mischakoff, Wurlitzer, Nathan E. Posner, and lastly, Max Polikoff.

1742 *ex* Bazzini. This violin was once in the possession of the famous Italian violinist Antonio Bazzini, who also owned another Guadagnini, a work at Cremona dated 1758, to be mentioned later in this review. Bazzini traded both of the Guadagnini violins with Giuseppe Scarampella for a Joseph Guarneri del Gesù which he retained until his death. The Guadagnini of 1742 subsequently was owned by Professor Mattolini of the Conservatory at Florence. In that city it was purchased, as well as the Cremona work mentioned, by Mario Frosali, who later brought them to this country. The 1742 specimen bears a label of the type inscribed "filius Lau-

A VIOLIN BY
J. B. GUADAGNINI
PIACENZA, 1742
ex Bazzini

rentii fecit Placentiæ." The violin has a body 13-27-32 inches long, with widths across the bouts 6-9/16, 4-1/2, and 8-1/16 inches. It is in a fine state of preservation and has varnish of a golden-orange color. *(Illustrated)*

1742 *ex* James. This violin bears a label of the first type, on which the maker announced himself as Joannes Guadagnini. It was purchased at Hill's in 1903 by Henry James, later passing to the possession of Mrs. Wershaw, from whom it was acquired by Wurlitzer in 1940. The present owner is a prominent ensemble player residing in the middle west.

1743* *ex* Szanto. This violin was in the Hill collection when Robert A. Bower effected its sale to Hamma & Company. Jani Szanto purchased it and brought it with him when he came to this country where he attained eminence as player and teacher of the instrument at Philadelphia. Julius Hegyi acquired possession recently. *(Illustrated)*

1744 From the collection of Emil Herrmann. Owned by Leon Goldwasser of Los Angeles, California. Mr. Goldwasser was a pupil of Leopold Auer at the Petrograd Conservatory; he was a member of the Los Angeles Symphony from 1913 to 1940 and since then connected with the motion picture studios. The Guadagnini violin has a two piece back and orange-red varnish.

1744* Formerly owned by Richard Burgin, concertmaster of the Boston Symphony Orchestra, this violin passed through Emil Herrmann to the possession of Mrs. M. Margulis of Portland, Oregon.

1744 Owned by Camillo Foltzer in 1937, and loaned by him for exhibition at the Stradivari Bicentenary observance at Cremona in that year. Plates illustrate the violin in the commemorative brochure published at Cremona.

1744* Contained in the Friedrich collection in 1921, and illustrated in a catalogue issued at that time.

A Violin by
J. B. GUADAGNINI
Piacenza, 1743
ex Szanto

1744 Illustrated in Franz Farga's book, and therein indicated to have been at the time in possession of Hug & Co., of Zurich. A characteristic work is shown, the back in one piece, and the label recorded as of the filius Laurentius type.

1745 *ex* Roentgen. Ernest Roentgen acquired this violin in London, at Hill's, and their certificate issued April 7, 1921, attests its authenticity and states it to be an exceptionally fine state of preservation. The varnish is of a red-brown color, the wood of the two piece back and sides marked by a broad curl, and that of the head plainer. Through Joseph Settin, of New York, the violin was recently acquired by Mr. Herbert L. Cohen. A letter addressed to him, written by W. E. Hill & Sons under date of April 18, 1948, informs that prior to selling it to Mr. Roentgen, the violin had been owned by the well known violin fancier, Gustavo Herten, of Buenos Aires, Argentina, and before him, by a Mr. Symes (deceased) who lived in Bognor, England. *(Illustrated)*

1745 *ex* de Cuvillion. An indication of prices paid for Guadagnini violins in earlier times, Monsieur de Cuvillion became the owner of this fine violin in 1875 at the price of a thousand francs, paid to the Paris house of Chanot & Chardon. The instrument remained a French possession until 1916 when it was acquired by Wurlitzer from Caressa & Français. Now privately owned.

1745 Plates in one of the early catalogues issued by Hamma & Company, of Stuttgart, illustrate this violin. It is described as of high excellence, with varnish of golden yellow color; the plate shows a two piece back of broad figure.

1745* *ex* Friedrich. The catalogue of the Friedrich collection of 1924 lists this violin; it is described as having a two piece back of lightly figured maple, the varnish of red-brown color.

1745 A fine example owned by John Pennington of the London String Quartet. The violin is said to have long been in a Russian collection. It was acquired from Albert Caressa by Miss Vera Barstow, for her pupil Miss Ruth Wilson, subsequently passing

A Violin by

J. B. GUADAGNINI

Piacenza, 1745

ex Roentgen

to the possession of Mr. Pennington in 1945. It has a two piece back and varnish of a golden-yellow color.

1745   *ex* Petre. Thomas Petre, formerly of the famous London String Quartet, acquired this violin at Hill's in 1927. It has a two piece back and varnish of a golden-orange color. Now in the possession of Louis Feiler.

1746* *ex* D'Ambrosio. This violin is one of several said to have been owned by the Italian violinist-composer, Alfredo D'Ambrosio (1871-1914). Erich Lachmann acquired possession, from the Paris dealers, Maucotel & Deschamp, bringing it to New York, where it eventually passed to Wurlitzer. *(Illustrated)*

1746   *ex* D'Ambrosio. The second of two Guadagnini violins said to have been owned by Alfredo D'Ambrosio. If correctly informed, it is a coincidence that this violin also passed through the hands of the Parisian house of Maucotel & Deschamp, by which it was recorded as once D'Ambrosio's, when it was sold to Fritz Hirt of Basel, Switzerland, in 1923. The instrument was recently in the collection of Emil Herrmann.

1746   A fine work of 1746, certified as authentic by Wurlitzer, was owned by Miss Arlie Furman in 1931.

1747* *ex* Countess of Kingston. When Harry Blech, of the Blech String Quartet (London, England), was in Chicago with the Royal Air Force Band in 1945, he had this violin with him. The history of the instrument as supplied by W. E. Hill & Sons is that it was originally sold by their house to the Countess of Kingston in 1888. It later passed to Josef Bláha, a Bohemian violinist, who was for some years attached to the teaching staff of the Royal Conservatory of Music, and a member of the Crystal Palace Orchestra. Later the violin was in the possession of Robert A. Bower (Bauer), a Chicagoan who became a resident of England, and during the world war adopted the Anglicized spelling. His name connects with a number of fine masterpieces. Hill's certificate naming this Guadagnini violin was issued to Bower in 1936; Mr. Blech obtained possession more recently. The back is rather plain, but

A Violin by
J. B. GUADAGNINI
Piacenza, 1746
ex D'Ambrosio

the sides are of handsome wood; the varnish is of a rich orange-red color. The head is by the maker, but of a later period.

1747* A striking work is this violin, certified as original including the label by Hill September 4th, 1946, while in the possession of Maurice Clare of Ludlow House, Hampton Wick, England. The back is in two pieces of handsome medium broad flamed maple, small added wings at the lower flanks original with the maker. The head is of wood showing very small strongly marked curls, similar to that found in the back of the *ex* Wirth violin of 1757. The varnish is of a rich deep orange-red color. Acquired by Reginald Kell, noted clarinetist, the violin was brought to the U.S.A. and was in the possession of Leonard Sorkin at the time of this recording.

1747 Many fine Italian instruments are in the possession of South American owners. An excellent violin by Guadagnini, dated 1747, is owned by Señor Antonio Antoncich, of Santiago, Chile. His collection includes several other fine instruments purchased from Hill & Sons.

1748 This violin was formerly in the Lyon & Healy Collection and is mentioned in their catalogue of 1909.

1749* *ex* Max Lawrence. Formerly in the Wurlitzer Collection, this violin was purchased by a member of the Toronto Symphony Orchestra.

174? A Guadagnini violin of this period, acquired from Hills, was long in the possession of Willy Hess, famous German violinist, born at Mannheim, 1859; at the age of nine he came to the U.S.A. and was later engaged to play with the Theodore Thomas Orchestra. He returned to Germany, where he received the distinction of the title "Royal Prussian Professor" in 1900. He was professor at the Royal Academy of Music in London (1903), then, returning to America, he became concertmaster of our Boston Symphony Orchestra (1904-1910), succeeding Franz Kneisel. Until his retirement, Hess was famous as a quartet player and highly esteemed as a teacher.

A Violoncello by
J. B. GUADAGNINI
Piacenza, 1743
von Zweygberg

A VIOLONCELLO BY
J. B. GUADAGNINI
PIACENZA, 1743
von Zweygberg

VIOLONCELLOS

1743* First of two cellos of the year here illustrated, each of which is a superb masterwork in every detail of workmanship and finish. Professor Lennart von Zweygberg, a native of Finland, and for many years on the faculty of the School of Music of Indiana University, brought the instrument with him when he came to this country. It remains in his possession at the time of this recording. Comparison with the illustrations of the Lorenzo Guadagnini violin of 1740, shown on pages 48/49, reflects the influence of his father. The sound holes indicate an early development of the pear-shaped lower openings. The label is of the "filius Laurentii" type. *(Illustrated)*

1743* The second violoncello of 1743 illustrated was brought to this country by Nathan E. Posner. It was characterized by W. E. Hill & Sons as one of the finest examples of the maker's work. It was sold through William Lewis & Son to Nicolai Graudan. Mr. Graudan and his wife Joanna, a concert pianist, are well known to concert goers, having toured widely through this and other countries as a duo. *(Illustrated)*

1743* *ex* von Kohner. The Baron von Kohner of Budapest owned a quartet of Guadagnini instruments, this cello acquired about 1906 from Caressa. Von Kohner was an enthusiastic amateur music lover. The cello was again part of a quartet of Guadagnini instruments when it passed to the possession of the well known violinist, Professor Popoff. About 1927 Emil Herrmann sold the instrument in Berlin. It then passed through Hamma & Company to the dealers Schreiber & Lugert of Hamburg, eventually again acquired by Emil Herrmann from whom it was purchased by Mrs. Elizabeth Gerson. A certificate attesting the authenticity of the cello was issued by Hill in 1938. (One of the violins of the von Kohner quartet is recorded among the Milan works of 1752.)

1744 This cello passed from the collection of Emil Herrmann to the possession of the Lewisohn family, of New York.

1746 A fine and well preserved example was recently contained in the Herrmann Collection.

A VIOLONCELLO BY
J. B. GUADAGNINI
PIACENZA, 1743
Graudan

1748   *ex* Wanamaker. A fine example which was acquired by Wanamaker from Maucotel & Deschamp in Paris. Subsequent to the passing of the Wanamaker collection to Wurlitzer, the cello was purchased by Constantine Bakaleinikoff. It has a two piece back and golden-orange varnish.

1749   *ex* Hill. The cello was purchased from W. E. Hill & Sons in 1937 by Jean Werro (now deceased) of Berne, Switzerland. The late Jean Werro was well known to an American clientele; his son Henry succeeded to the ownership of the business.

Part III

J. B. GUADAGNINI AT MILAN

Before discussion of the Milan epoch of Guadagnini remarks will be directed to, among others, an important contribution to violin literature. Prior to its coming there had been progress in classification of violin makers, but all that had gone before in that branch of biographical recording was to be eclipsed by a stupendous work, the like of which will perhaps never be duplicated nor surpassed in the breadth of its scope and the detail encompassed. This work, though not infallible, has become a standard reference work whenever information concerning violin makers is sought.

LÜTGENDORFF

The author, Professor Willibald Leo Freiherr (Baron) von Lütgendorff is known by name to all within the fraternity of violin lovers. International fame attaches to his *Die Geigen-und Lautenmacher von Mittelalter bis zur Gegenwart*. Errors exist in the work, but are of minor significance weighed against its undeniable worth as a whole. It evinces a glorious enthusiasm in his subject, a tremendous energy applied in the accumulation and compilation of data, and the fullness of matter concerning the lute, viol and violin making craft compels admiration. Unfortunately, through the very fact of its high prestige as a reference work, it is demanded that a thorough exposure of its fallacies and contradictions should be pointed out, particularly in its reiterations of the concept that there were two makers by name Joannes Baptista Guadagnini.

For the information of readers who may not know the background of the compiler, it is proper that something should be said of the personality of the man who conceived and brought it to completion. He was born at Augsburg, Bavaria, July 8th, 1856, and died at Weimar, December 31st, 1937, after an illness of but a few days, during a visit to his daughter. His early education was at Pressburg, and he completed his studies at Munich, his chief interest then being in literary work and painting. In pursuing his artistic bent he completed a number of paintings which have been hung in public buildings and art galleries. At Lübeck, where he established a school of art, he was appointed Director of the Dom Museum, where he lectured on art and history. One of his great works in the latter field was a history of the city of Lübeck, comprising several volumes. Such were some of the accomplishments of Lütgendorff, and it was with an equal enthusiasm that he approached the task of writing a treatise on our subject of violin makers. During the progress of his research he not only investigated every available source of information, and studied every specimen of the violin maker's art possible for him to see, but also concerned himself to learn at first hand the practical making of the instrument and is said to have been successful in completing finished works.

The culmination of such earnest and well directed effort is found in his notable writings and had he rested content with the first edition which appeared in one volume, that in itself would have provided a lasting monument to his fame. Hailed as a remarkable contribution at the time, the author proceeded to enlarge its scope, eventually to publish a two volume set, one devoted to historical survey of the craft from earliest times, the second listing makers with biographical data. Written in German, the various editions were speedily absorbed;

were they available in the English language, many more than the published number would have been required to meet demands.

The first edition appeared in 1904, a single volume comprising over 800 pages. As pertinent to our subject, we find therein the belief that there had been two makers of the name Joannes Baptista Guadagnini, an opinion that was strongly held at that time, and Lütgendorff, swayed by that theory, unfortunately gave notice to such as Giambattista I and Giambattista II. His remarks were potent in their effect on the recordings put forth by subsequent writers, and as presented they read (translated):

"Guadagnini, Giambattista I.

Mailand. Parma. Born in Piacenza 1685, died after 1768.

"Regarded as brother of Lorenzo. It is said that he was working in Milan until 1740, then going to Parma where he remained for a long time in the service of the Grand Duke. He was very industrious but his violins are often considered mediocre when compared with those of Lorenzo and those of the latter's son Giambattista. He is often confused with the latter. He followed the pattern of Amati as well as Stradivari, and possessed a fine golden varnish. In tone his violins are generally good. His labels make reference to his birth-place in that he either names 'Placentinus' or, under his initials, the letter P in a circle, also when he, probably for business reasons,

"Guadagnini, Giambattista II.

Piacenza, Turin. Born in Cremona 1711, died September 1786, in Turin.

"Son of Lorenzo and like his father probably a pupil of Stradivari. He was the equal of his father in every particular, building, as he did, quite correctly on Stradivari's models, less so in cutting the scrolls, also his f holes are slightly changed. He favored the flat model, used excellent wood—backs mostly two piece— and golden-yellow, brilliant and transparent varnish. His works are highly prized and fetch prices up to 14,000 marks. After the death of his father, he succeeded to his workshop and later went to Turin, where he died."

termed himself 'Cremonensis.'
Through these he may be easily
distinguished from Giambatt. II,
who was born in Cremona."

Information thus presented is manifestly a mixture of the
real and fantastic. As previously noted, the evidence provided by the maker's labels indicates that J. B. Guadagnini's first
signed works emanated from Piacenza in 1740 onwards until
1750, when we find him working at Milan, the Parma period
following from 1759. It is obvious that Yusupov's influence
dictated Lütgendorff's entry concerning "Giambattista I", in
locating him at Milan "until" 1740, and Cozio's notes are reflected in the long service at Parma in the "service of the Grand
Duke." That "Giambattista I died after 1768," in reality indicates the closing period of the maker at Parma, from whence
he, as noted in Lütgendorff's reference to Giambattista II, "later
went to Turin."

The new form of Lütgendorff, in two volumes, appeared
about 1921. The first of these is devoted to a comprehensive
survey of the lute and violin making craft. All countries, their
various divisions and cities, are individually mentioned, and an
entire section pictures works of famous makers. The plates used
for the latter purpose had in many instances been previously
utilized in the catalogues of prominent collectors and dealers
of Germany and Austria, including Hamma & Company, Eugen Gärtner of Stuttgart, Theodore Hämmerle of Vienna, the
Musical Museum of Wilhelm Heyer at Cologne, etc. A number
of examples of the works of the Guadagninii are portrayed, of
which some will be commented upon in this review.

As the author's final contribution to our subject, this vastly
augmented edition offers silent tribute to Lütgendorff's untiring
zeal and calls for further remark. The opening paragraphs

evince the sincerity of the author; freely translated, they convey his purpose:—

"As a keystone of the Story of the Violin, I permitted my work concerning Violin and Lute Makers, the fruit of an over ten-year-long period of labor, to be published in 1904. I entertained the hope to provide, with it, perhaps, a source of enjoyment for all those who, like myself, are intrigued and—let us say—enamoured with love for the Violin. My hope was not a delusion; far sooner than I could have wished or anticipated, a second, and now a third edition has been required, and these I present to lovers of the art and connoisseurs with the same sentiments as the first.

"I have proceeded without intermittance in gathering data and am thus able to considerably enlarge my book, as well as to introduce corrections and amendments where necessary, so that now, in many respects, a new work has emerged. The sequence previously followed is retained but I have added a general survey which presents in concise form matter which appears in the comment on individual makers. I have endeavored to do this as best it could be done. I am thankful to many advisers to whom I gratefully acknowledge my indebtedness, but realize that I have undertaken a task which is almost beyond the capability of one person to properly discharge. I pray the friendly reader, therefore, for future co-operation and for notice of omissions and errors. . . ."

The survey opens with a review of the *Lauten und Geigenmacher* of Füssen in the Tyrol. A short historical sketch tells of the antiquity of the town and names as one of the earliest lute makers working there, Jörg Wolf, in 1493. In such manner, the story progresses, covering in sequence, Brescia, Cremona, then Milan, second only to Venice as the richest city of Italy in former times. A well presented picture of Milan, telling of its greatness in art and music, as well as its early lute and violin makers, first brings us to our subject of the Guadagninii. Milan having been the second city in which Giovanni Battista (J. B.) Guadagnini tarried for a considerable period, the data presented in Lütgendorff's narrative will be entered in its place as it appears in the progress of the maker's wanderings.

In the order of presentation, Mantua comes next in the book, then to be followed under one heading, by Parma, Piacenza, and Pavia, three cities in which the Guadagninii produced. As our present interest lies with "Giambattista" (J. B.), and as his story begins at Piacenza, a review of the Lütgendorff paragraph follows (translated):—

"Piacenza was founded by the Romans during the same years as was Cremona and in the middle of the XVI century feder-ated with Parma. The influence of Cremona and the attraction of Parma were felt by the resident Piacenza violin and lute makers. The very first makers had their apprenticeships at Cremona and also worked at Parma. These were the brothers Giambattista and Lorenzo Guadagnini (Illustrations 15c, d, 75). The younger, Lorenzo, of course was the better; he records him-self as a pupil of Stradivari, and his work is no dishonor to him. Giambattista, as already remarked, also learned at Cremona and later from his brother, so that he lacked but little as his equal. While, however, Lorenzo tarried at Piacenza, Giambat-tista went to Parma and later to Milan, but never, in the text of his labels, named the city of his birth. Both were makers of the first rank, and Lorenzo's son, Giambattista II, already showed such indisputable talent that his father took him to his old teacher, Stradivari, in his early youth, to become one of his last pupils, it is said. The younger Giambattista became a worthy successor to his father and if he failed to equal him in some small particulars he was nevertheless a master of whom Piacenza might be proud. It seems, however, that he also learned that the prophet is not recognized in his own land, as he, when over fifty years of age, changed his place of residence to Turin, where he died September 18th, 1786. If he was influenced to make the change by his older brother, Giovanni Antonio, as one may believe, this cannot be stated definitely, as nothing further is known of this Giovanni Antonio. The survivors of this young Giambattista to this day have become the main representatives of the Turin school."

We do not have to seek afar to discover that the writer of the quoted lines sought to make his story fit with the conflicting statements of his predecessors. Providing, as he attempts to do, a background for the fictitious "brother" of Lorenzo, we are given the date of 1685 as that of his birth, yet he is called the younger brother in spite of the fact that Lorenzo's birth is recorded as having occurred in 1695. As to him whom Lütgendorff names Giambattista II, there is no reference to his whereabouts between the years of his residence at Piacenza and removal "when over fifty years of age" to Turin—the inference remaining that they had been passed at Piacenza. Introduction of the mythical "older brother," Giovanni Antonio, is obviously meaningless and uncalled for as the author's own remark explains that nothing is known of him. It must be regretfully noted that the quoted paragraph should be regarded as pure invention.

In our study of Lütgendorff's revised biographical notes concerning J. B. Guadagnini, we find a strange divergence from what he had entered in the original version. In order to emphasize the point, it is again of interest to present the original and so to show both, with the most glaring inconsistencies stressed in the employment of bold-face type:—

EARLY EDITION

"Guadagnini, Giambattista I. Mailand. Parma. Born in Piacenza 1685, died after 1768.

"Regarded as brother of Lorenzo. It is said that he worked **in Milan** until 1740, then going to Parma where he remained for a long time in the service of the Grand Duke. He was very industrious but his violins are often **considered mediocre when compared with those of Lorenzo and those of the latter's son Giambattista.** He is often confused with the latter. He followed the pattern of Amati as well as Stradivari and possessed a fine, golden varnish. In tone his violins are generally good. His labels make reference to his birth-place in that he either names 'Placentinus' or, under his initials, the letter P in a circle, also when he, probably for business reasons, termed himself 'Cremonensis.' Through these he may be easily distinguished from Giambatt. II who was born in Cremona."

REVISED EDITION

"Guadagnini, Giambattista I. Mailand. Parma. Born in Piacenza 1685, died after 1770. Presumed to be the brother of Lorenzo G. **with whom he is said to have worked at Piacenza in the beginning.** Then for a longer time he went to Parma where he entered the service of the Grand-duke. After 1750 he worked at Milan. He was very diligent and his **violins bear comparison with those by Lorenzo quite well and are better than those of his son Giambattista."** Matter which follows is identical with the original but there is, in addition, mention of certain examples, viz., "a violin of 1750 owned by Prof. Gustav Holländer of Berlin; a cello of 1755 in the Hämmerle (Vienna) collection; a small violin owned by J. H. Zimmerman Leipzig; a violin of 1753, Dr. Thommen, Vienna; a violin, A. S. Bauer of Rein; and a glorious concert violin belonging to Stefi Geyer:"

Column I, it will be noted, states that Guadagnini indicated his natal city as Piacenza; the preceding extract contained the statement, ". . . never, in the text of his labels, named the city of his birth." In the light of present day knowledge, there is a certain humor in remarking on efforts to make comparisons intended to characterize differing qualities attributed to the works of two individuals who, in fact, were one and the same. Thus, we have read in the first notice that the work was mediocre as compared with that of the "son," whereas the revised opinion avers that it was better! It is also to be noted that Lütgendorff eliminated the words "working in Milan until 1740" in the biographical note as here translated, but it will be read that the statement was allowed to remain in remarks contained in his historical survey.

Again to allow comparison with what Lütgendorff had to say about "Giambattista II," the first version is presented in juxtaposition with the revision:

EARLY EDITION

"Guadagnini, Giambattista II. Piacenza, Turin. Born in Cremona, 1711, died Sept. 1786 in Turin. Son of Lorenzo and like his father probably a pupil of Stradivari. He was the equal of his father in every particular, building, as he did, quite correctly on Stradivari's models, less so in cutting his scrolls, also his f holes are slightly changed. He favored the flat model, used excellent wood—backs mostly two-piece—and golden-yellow, brilliant, and transparent varnish. His works are highly prized and fetch prices up to 14,000 marks. After the death of his father, he succeeded to his workshop and later went to Turin, where he died."

REVISED EDITION

"Guadagnini, Giambattista II. Piacenza, Turin. Born 1711 in Cremona, died Sept. 18, 1786, in Turin. (Matter contained in the revised version is otherwise identical with that of the original except that, with regard to the scrolls, there is inserted) . . . "which he liked massive" (and after the reference to the varnish, the following): "in all its excellence it does not, however, equal in quality that of Lorenzo, as it is generally somewhat hard and lacks elasticity. In tone, also Giamb. II rates below Lorenzo, as Violins which possess really outstandingly fine tone are rare, whereas it is commonly the case that Violins which are outwardly

wonderful in appearance fall short
of their promise in tone quality.
His best works are those produced
during the final third of his life
and indicate Turin as their origin.
His Violins are highly prized and
already, before the war [that was
another war!] brought prices up
to 14,000 Marks, a sum which
now [1922] has been quadrupled.
That he should have also worked
at Brescia, as has been claimed,
cannot be substantiated."

In his first version, Lütgendorff rated Giambattista II "the equal of his father in every particular," yet the revised edition places his work below that of Lorenzo both as to quality of the varnish and the tone.

The Lütgendorff narrative of the violin making craft, as it relates to Milan and J. B. Guadagnini reads (translated):

"From Piacenza came Giambattista Guadagnini who remained at Milan until 1740, to return again after extended absence (illustrations 4a, 33, 57, 77, 78). Even if he did not equal his brother Lorenzo, he must be correctly designated as one of Milan's best violin makers, as his works can only have suffered in opinion because he endeavored to produce too many."

How far astray from the facts! Though correct in saying that J. B. Guadagnini came to Milan from Piacenza, the period is incorrectly named; Lorenzo, here called the brother of J. B., can quite definitely be said never to have worked in Milan at all. Failure to check with the matter contained in the biographical section—where the correct statement that J. B. Guadagnini worked in Milan *after* 1750 is found—can only account for the error apparent in "Giambattista Guadagnini who remained at Milan until 1740."

Due to such erroneous and conflicting entries, figures on Guadagnini labels have been altered to conform in dating. Concerning the instruments illustrated, it is noted that the violin remarked as No. 4a (from the Hamma Collection), apparently a work of the maker of the Milan period, is recorded made in 1740. No. 33, a violoncello from the Hämmerle Collection, is impossible to classify from the illustration, but is at least correctly dated as a Milan work of 1755. No. 57 shows a violin from the Eugene Gärtner Collection, named of Milan with the date given as 1747; not only incorrect as to period, but not a work of Guadagnini at all, as according to the well known authority Erich Lachmann, it was made by Vincent Panormo and was in the possession of Max Menge, a violinist of Hamburg, prior to the last war. No. 77 shows a violin from the Hamma Collection, date not mentioned, and No. 78 another violin from the Hamma Collection, dated 1750 and probably one of the examples to be mentioned under the listings of that date, the same illustration being one of the number shown in the excellent work on Italian masterpieces published by the brothers Hamma—as Plate 82—and which will be remarked later.

*　　*　　*

Lütgendorff correctly stated that J. B. Guadagnini must be considered as "one of Milan's best violin makers." Before his time that city had been the center of a flourishing industry which produced large numbers of violins and kindred instruments. Among the Milanese makers, those of the Grancino and Testore families are prominent; they were industrious and during the late seventeenth and early eighteenth centuries were prolific in the production of less costly instruments than those of their contemporaries of Cremona. Hill, in the Stradivari book, twice characterized the makers then working in Milan as the "Milanese cheap-jacks," first when remarking their free use of the finest description of pine even for their cheapest productions, and again when alluding to the outline of their instruments, in which was notable "in a marked degree that refreshing originality . . . never entirely absent from the work of the many other Italian makers who flourished . . . even among the Milanese cheap-jacks. . . ." A footnote explains the reference to apply "to such makers as Grancino, the several members of the Testore family, and their followers."

Thus, J. B. Guadagnini entered upon ground well prepared to appreciate a higher product than had been the average before his coming.

With reference to the gradual disappearance of the Cremona varnish, I quote Hill:

"With Stradivari's death, the decay of the higher standard of instrument-making rapidly set in. Very probably the waning prosperity of the Church in Italy, coupled with the large number of fine instruments then existing, was the principal cause. . . . Elsewhere than at Cremona the craft was still actively carried on, notably at Milan and Naples; but works cheaply produced, rather than those of fine workmanship and fine varnish, seem to have been what the age required throughout Italy. The demand, therefore, for slower-drying varnish no longer existed; to use it meant extra cost, and its supreme importance passed either unnoticed or unheeded. . . . From time to time generous patrons caused the old traditions to be revived, and we thus catch glimpses of the true recipe for Cremona varnish still now and then in use; but as the years rolled on these instances became rarer and rarer. They occurred at Milan until about 1760. We meet the true recipe again, and for the last time, at Turin, used occasionally by J. B. Guadagnini, no doubt under the auspices of Count Cozio, up till 1780-84. . . ."

Here, we see, that with Guadagnini at Milan between 1750 up until "about 1760" (the master left there, judging by dates found in his works, in 1758, although the date 1760 and Milan has been recorded), it was he who raised not only the standard of violin making above that which Milanese craftsmen had previously achieved, but, also, revived the art of varnishing at that place, rivalling the Cremona quality.

As to Lütgendorff's remark that the master's work suffered in opinion because he endeavored to produce too many, there is but little justice in that criticism, because the instruments produced at Milan by Guadagnini are generally of a very high excellence. Their model is on the flat order, slightly channeled towards the edges, with the rims carefully worked, and the varnish of fine texture and rich color. An occasional specimen indicates a departure from that care which would be lavished on well-remunerated effort, but on the whole, fine instruments mark the Milan period of the master's work and it is possible to record a large number.

FRITZ MEYER'S BOOK

Fritz Meyer, a German violin enthusiast, was the author of a narrative which, under the title "Berühmte Geigen und ihre Schicksale" (*Famous Violins and Their Fate*), was published by P. J. Tonger at Cologne in 1920. Those who have had occasion to read the work may have noted various discrepancies in his romancing. For the benefit of those who have no knowl-

edge of the book, a translated version of the section that
touches on our subject is presented here:—

"Highly regarded are the works of the elder Giovanni Battista Guadagnini, who, about 1685, saw the light of this world
at Piacenza, where he died about 1768. Even Joachim recommended Guadagnini's violins to those to whom possession of a
Stradivari or Guarneri del Gesù was denied. A fine violin by
the master which originated at Milan in 1721 *(sic)* is owned
and played up by Professor Carl Wendling of Stuttgart; despite
a patch in its back it is an outstanding concert violin which
had already charmed auditors while in the prior possession of
Professor Abel of Munich. Also, Joseph Joachim's one-time
solo violin, during the entire period of his activity at Hannover,
was one which was produced in the period 1750-1755 in Milan.
Until recent years the violin remained in Germany but is at
this time (1920) in Switzerland. A rather high-modeled, entirely perfect concert-violin of 1755, with very beautiful, thick
orange-red varnish which is surprisingly fresh and unworn, and
with a two piece back the flames of which extend upwards from
the center joint, was acquired by Albert Hamma not far from
Milan, the city of its origin. This long-unused instrument now
belongs to Concertmaster Nagel in Düsseldorf.

"Before Carl Flesch acquired the famous Brancaccio Stradivari, he also used a violin by the elder Guadagnini. The label in
this violin indicates Milan as its origin, where the highly-gifted
Giambattista worked until 1740; the violin therefore, was not
produced later.* Its back shows broad flames and it is covered
with soft varnish of finest texture. The top has a breast patch.

---

* The absurdity of the phrase is obvious as Herr Meyer previously mentioned
Joachim's Milan violin of 1750-55, and his book pictures another violin of Milan
the date 1755, as the one which Albert Hamma acquired and Nagel of Düsseldorf
subsequently owned.

Notwithstanding, the violin sounds—especially on the G string —wonderful, for which reason it was long a favorite with Henri Vieuxtemps. The Belgian virtuoso relinquished it however towards the end of the '70s in favor of his pupil Madame d'Exarque, whose husband was the then Bulgarian Representative in Bucharest. It was acquired from her by Carl Flesch, who, ten years later, passed it to his pupil Professor Robert Pollack in Moscow.*

"The great Polish virtuoso Stanislaus Barcewicz of Warsaw played a Giovanni Battista Guadagnini II, the wonderfully round and far-carrying tone of which reminds one of a Joseph Guarneri del Gesù. Also, the solo violin of the 1916 deceased pedagogue Gustave Hollaender [his death occurred at Berlin, December 6, 1915] was by the same master and made in 1750.† Another violin produced at Turin in 1773, which is free of any blemish, belonged to the late chamber-music player Eduard Rappoldi of Dresden; it was bequeathed to his son, Adrian. Two other works of Turin must be mentioned because of their remarkable tone qualities. The one, the life of which began 1776, is known by the name Pearson; the beautiful violin was brought from England by Hamma and after a period of some years in North Germany was bought by a Frenchman. The other, light brown, with two piece plain back dated 1779, is in England. The grand, outstanding in its handsome and bold contour redbrown Guadagnini instrument of the highly gifted Hungarian Palma von Pàszthory has often, because of the sweetness of its golden-clear tone, been compared with Sarasate's violin. It is to be hoped, however, that the noble violin may not suffer the lot of the Sarasate Stradivari and be doomed to everlasting

---

* This violin is still owned by Mr. Pollak, now resident of Los Angeles.

† Erich Lachmann is authority for the statement that the violin is a work of Camillus Camilli.

silence immured in a Museum, to experience a death of lone-
someness. This [Guadagnini] instrument was produced in Cremona in 1784 *(sic)*.

"Such violins have today attained a value of 12,000 to 20,000
Marks, but their tone is as fine as that of renowned Cremonese
instruments of highest value."

Meyer's book provides interesting though extravagantly ver-
bose reading. In his remarks concerning J. B. Guadagnini he
followed the common error of speaking of two makers of the
name, regrettable particularly as the false premise had been
definitely laid to rest by eminent authorities before his time.
Its reiterance by German writers may perhaps have been due
to unswerving faith in the recording of native historians, but
more likely, because enlightenment had not penetrated their
realm. The source material of Meyer's work is to be found in
his references, much of it from the old firm of Hamma & Company, to which attention follows.

THE HAMMA GALLERY

An important work which demands high regard is that of
the brothers Fridolin and Emil Hamma, who comprise the
Stuttgart firm of Hamma & Company. They contributed largely
of their knowledge to the work of von Lütgendorff. Fridolin
Hamma was the author of the text of their "Meisterwerke
Italienischer Geigenbaukunst" (*Masterworks of Italian Violin-
making*), published 1930, an impressive volume comprising in-
formative text but mainly devoted in its many hundred pages
to numerous plates illustrating the works of famous Italian
makers.

It is pertinent to refer to the comment concerning J. B.
Guadagnini, not so much to quote the notations which accom-

pany a number of fine illustrations, but to particularly emphasize the statement contained therein, setting forth the opinion
of the authors in unqualified terms that specimens portrayed
were the product of two different makers of the same name.
It is but natural that readers of the work would be prone to
accept its dictum and for such that are not already correctly
advised, it is to the credit of the brothers Hamma that Fridolin
Hamma (as will be presently read) eventually reversed his
position on that long debated point, acknowledging the existence of only one J. B. Guadagnini as the maker of all those
instruments so long divided into two classes.

Although to a certain extent reiterating the views of others,
the Hamma book contains remarks of interest not elsewhere
found. Translated they read:

"GUADAGNINI, JOANNES BATTISTA.—MAILAND, PARMA 1685-1770.
(Brother of Lorenzo Guadagnini.) Stradivari pattern of
faultless execution. Often somewhat arched. Nice purfling.
Very characteristic workmanship, particularly the sound holes
provide a typical mark of identification—the grape-form turn
of the lower holes. Good, mostly red varnish. Sought for as
concert-violins. Their value rapidly rising, particularly fine
examples have sold at over 40,000 Marks. Also sought for
are the Violoncelli because of their remarkable tone although
they measure but 73-74 cm in body length.

"GUADAGNINI, JOANNES BAPTISTA, PIACENZA,—TURIN 1711-1786.
(Son of Lorenzo Guadagnini.) Was the worthy pupil of his
father and seems also to have been taught by Stradivari,
whose pattern he preferred to follow. His works are mostly
flat modelled instruments. Broad purfling, yet nicely developed edge. The sound holes also have the characteristic

grape-formed lower openings while they are in general more rounded. The scrolls are often somewhat large and not of true form. He employed mostly handsome wood and had a fine golden-yellow to dark-red varnish. On his more ordinary instruments he applied a hard brown varnish. The majority of his works are highly regarded and sought for as concert instruments and are hardly less valued than the works of the aforementioned J. B. Guadagnini, of Milan. I hold it as false, when authorities class these two Guadagninis as one,* because the characteristics of certain examples vary so much that they cannot be from one hand. The archives will soon find this matter clarified and furnish a true family-tree of the Guadagninis, a task which up to the present time is engaging the thought of the violin craft."

The foregoing excerpts require no discussion, but the author of the closing remarks could hardly have foreseen at the time of their writing that he was to contradict his own pronouncement. Fridolin Hamma was one of the judges at the Stradivari Bicentenary observance at Cremona in 1937, elected to be the chairman of the international board of experts who passed on the authenticity of instruments tendered for exhibition in connection with the event. Acting in collaboration with others, he was primarily responsible for much of the text which appeared in conjunction with the illustrations of fine instruments in the brochure issued to commemorate the celebration. Four examples of the work of J. B. Gaudagnini are pictured therein, violins produced, respectively, at Piacenza, dated 1744, Milan 1757, Cremona 1758, and Turin, the date as 1770. Of these, the violin of 1758 (to be particularly mentioned later) is noted in

---

* It is this statement of opinion, unequivocal here, which was to be subsequently retracted by its writer.

the text as "one of the few works which were made by this master in the violin-making city of Cremona." The sentence carries
double significance: written by Mr. Hamma, it emphasizes the
fact that J. B. Guadagnini did not work, or at least did not sign
any works, in Cremona before 1740, and secondly, that there
was but one maker of the name, thus opposite to his previously
recorded opinion on that point. This reversal of opinion is more
emphatically stressed in the "Preface" to the Cremona book
(which, oddly, forms the last section of the work), in the following manner (translated):—"We take this opportunity to
assert that there was but one Joannes Baptista Guadagnini, who,
certainly, was a wanderer during his lifetime. His work periods
may be designated as follows: Piacenza 1740-50, Mailand
(Milan) 1750-58, Cremona 1758-60,* Parma 1760-1770, and
Turin 1770-1786.

MILAN

The city of Milan, the scene of disastrous visitation within
recent years, presently had a population of about a million, the
second in size in the land. To moderns it would involve less
than an hour's motor trip from Piacenza. In Guadagnini's time,
however, a slower progress along the miles probably made their
frequent passage more or less trying to undertake. Parma, the
next city to which the master emigrated, is 75 miles southeast
of Milan; to reach Turin, his last abiding place, he had to re-
trace his steps, probably passing through Piacenza to arrive at
his final destination, a journey of somewhat less than 150 miles.

Other than the promise which Milan, a large city, greater in
importance than Piacenza where J. B. Guadagnini began his

---

* There seems no doubt that J. B. Guadagnini tarried at Cremona for only a few
months in the year 1758. Also, that he made his last change of locality in 1771, in
which year he arrived at Turin.

career, held out to an ambitious craftsman, no reason has been found to account for Guadagnini's choice there to continue the pursuit of his art. He had, no doubt, been aware of the activity of a number of instrument-makers in that city, and this possibly decided him that the locality required someone to tread the paths no longer followed by the Grancinos or the aging Testores. Furthermore, Milan itself, rich in art and music as well as in commerce, must have possessed a potent attraction. Great names were connected with it. Such a man as Leonardo da Vinci, although not a native of the city, had, in earlier times than those of violin-making, done much to add to Milan's glory. It is recorded that on the occasion of his first visit to Milan, about 1482, it was as the bearer of a gift from Lorenzo de' Medici of Florence to Lodovico il Moro, then the reigning duke. This present was a musical instrument invented by da Vinci himself, of a strange form and sounding, in tone, like a lute. It is said that he thus "sang his way" into the Duke's favor. Leonardo remained at Milan until 1499, or until the Duke was driven out by the French, and it was during those years that he did some of his best work.

For centuries a battleground of warring factions of different nationalities and religious beliefs, Italian cities have known many conquerors and many rulers. Thus, during the lifetime of J. B. Guadagnini, Milan was under Austrian domination, which, judging by the master's productivity during the period of his residence, suggests that the lot of the instrument maker must have been one of steady patronage and satisfying emolument.

The time of Guadagnini's arrival in Milan seems to have been during the later part of the year 1749, as instruments dated from both Piacenza and Milan are known bearing that date. The in-

ference is that he made the journey subsequent to working for
a time at his old bench, and immediately resumed work upon
entering his new domain. There seems no likelihood that he
paid a visit to Parma in the year 1750; a violin bearing that date
on a Parma label, long regarded as correctly designated as to
the period of its making, cannot therefore be included as a work
of 1750 as anything other than a Milan production. The prob-
ability is that, like other fine works of the maker somewhat resembling Cremonese character, the violin at some time had the
original ticket removed and one with a more famous name inserted, later to be again restored to its correct author and due
to the faulty records of the time, furnished with the aforementioned label.

One of the features remarked upon by early writers, as found
in divers excerpts throughout this review, was the red varnish
presumed to provide identification as between the erroneously
recorded dual personalities of J. B. Guadagnini, sometimes
spoken of as a brilliant red, again as glaring red, etc. It is true
that the maker changed his method of varnishing with each
change of locality; the first years at Milan gives us some gor-
geously colored varnish, which, without exaggeration, must be
termed of richest hues, mostly of orange-red to pure red. The
type persists more or less throughout his years at Milan and,
apparently from supplies on hand, carries over to the early
Parma period, used during his stay at Cremona in 1758 and
upon his advent in Parma. With the exhaustion of his materials
some time after locating at Parma a decided change in the texture and color of his varnish takes place; we must account for
this in the maker's inability to find required ingredients available at local Parma sources of supply.

A Violin by
J. B. GUADAGNINI
Milan, 1750 (Parma label)
ex Senkrah

TABULATION

VIOLINS

1749 Of the period, a fine work of the maker bearing a label of Milan, but probably a late product at Piacenza, is in the possession of Richard Burgin, concertmaster of the Boston Symphony Orchestra. This is one of three violins made by J. B. Guadagnini owned by this family of artists, two by Mr. Burgin, and one by Mrs. Burgin, who was Ruth Posselt, a concert violinist of national renown.

1749 *ex* Rauer. Erich Lachmann purchased this violin of Georg Rauer in Vienna, in 1932, and later sold it to Miss Broadbent of Los Angeles. It passed to Wurlitzer in an exchange, and was purchased by Mark Levant in 1943 through Faris M. Brown.

1750* *ex* Senkrah. Characteristic of the Milan period, this violin bears a Parma label dated 1750. It is referred to as the Arma Senkrah, having once been owned by the American violinist Anna Loretta Harkness who toured Europe under the professional name Senkrah, her family name in reverse spelling. After her tragic end in Germany, the violin passed to the possession of an amateur player of Chicago, the late W. H. Winslow, since whose decease it has had several owners. It was purchased from Wurlitzer by Mrs. Lutie Goldstein in 1937; since then it has been in concert use by the brilliant artist Isaac Stern (who also owns the Guarneri del Gesù of 1737 known as the *ex* Belâtre, sometimes referred to as the "Alard"). The Guadagnini is a strikingly beautiful specimen with varnish of a rich orange-red color. (*Illustrated*)

1750* At one time in the Friedrich Collection, later owned by Herbert Limberg, this violin passed to Wurlitzer in an exchange when he acquired possession of the Stradivari violin of 1718 known as the Benno Walter. The Guadagnini has a back in two pieces of matched wood, small curls descending from the left in both parts.

1750* *ex* Birkby. From the collection of George A. Chanot, famous dealer of Manchester, England, this violin passed to Wilhelm Birkby February 20, 1904. Birkby was a pupil of Sarasate and

A VIOLIN BY
J. B. GUADAGNINI
MILAN, 1751
Hill

well known as a concert artist on the Continent before he settled at Manchester. He left the violin to his niece at his death, and from her it passed to John M. Vernon of Southampton to whom a certificate of authenticity was issued by William E. Hill & Sons, dated April 17, 1946. In the fall of that year the instrument was acquired by William Lewis & Son and brought to Chicago. Oscar W. Jepson is the present owner. A handsome violin, flat arched, with deep red-brown varnish shading into a rich ruby red. The back is in two pieces marked by faint curls of medium width.

1750* *ex* Moulton. Sold by Hill May 28th, 1940, to Richard Moulton of Needham, Massachusetts. A very fine example bearing the original label. The back is in one piece of slab cut maple, the sides quarter cut, and the varnish orange-red in color. The violin measures 13-15/16 inches in body length, 6-15/32, 4-3/8, and 7-15/16 inches across the upper, middle, and lower bouts respectively. Lastly privately owned by a resident of Oak Park, Illinois.

1750 Sold by L. P. Balmforth & Son, of Leeds, England, within recent months. Previously sold by W. E. Hill & Sons in 1906. It bears the original label, has two piece back of curly maple of small figure, the wood of the sides and head plainer, and golden brown varnish.

1750 *ex* Wieniawski. Said to have been a favorite of the famous Polish virtuoso, Henri Wieniawski, this violin was a highly prized item in the collection of Albert Caressa. Last recorded in possession of Emil Herrmann.

1750* *ex* Flusshoh. Purchased in 1909 from Hill, by Mr. Flusshoh of Highbury, this violin at various times was in the collection of Nathan E. Posner, Erich Lachmann, and Wurlitzer. A fine toned concert instrument, it was used by the American violinist Marie Caslova, later by Manuel Compinsky of the Compinsky Trio. The violin is of a very flat model and has varnish of brown color.

1750* The Charles Reade. This violin, once owned by the famous English novelist by whose name it is recorded, is a magnificent work. The November 1925 edition of *The Strad* magazine carries

A Violin by

J. B. GUADAGNINI

Milan, 1751

ex Maurin

its story and portrait. It had been in the collection of George Hart; in 1925 it was in the possession of Señor Gustavo Herten, of Buenos Aires, whose name attaches to many fine Italian masterpieces. From him it again returned to British ownership in an exchange, subsequently passing to the Lyon & Healy Collection; plates show the violin in color in their 1929 catalogue. It had been purchased at that time by Ernest Walker of St. Louis, but again reverted to Lyon & Healy and passed to private ownership in California. Through Herman Walecki, representing Lyon & Healy, the violin was sold to the concert violinist Dorothy Wade (Mrs. Dorothy Wade Marsh) in May, 1947. It is distinguished by handsome maple in its two piece back and a rich orange varnish.

1750   Formerly in the collection of Ch. Enel and Chardon of Paris, this violin passed to Camille Couture of Montreal. In 1918 the instrument was sold by him, the purchase negotiated by friends for the French violinist Raoul Georges Vidas, now residing in Los Angeles, California. A typical work, with two piece back of small figured maple, the curls extending horizontally across its breadth.

1750*   From the collection of George Hart, this violin came to the firm of R. S. Williams & Co., of Toronto, Canada, in 1910. R. S. Bacon of Chicago purchased it in 1914 for John Hornsteiner, who sold it to Maurice Goldblatt. He retained possession until 1924 when it was purchased by the eminent Chicago violinist, Rudolph Mangold, who is the owner at the time of this recording.

1750*   ex Sinsheimer. A violin sold by Hamma & Co. to a violinist of Mannheim named Sinsheimer. It was subsequently acquired by Miss Helen Hesse, who came to the U. S. A. and became a resident of Chicago, where she is prominent in professional and teaching circles.

1750   Formerly in the Hamma Collection; sold to Dr. Schmidt of Darmstadt, Germany.

1750   Sold by Hamma & Company to Herr Siegler of Stuttgart, Germany.

A Violin by
J. B. GUADAGNINI
Milan, 1751
ex Zajic

118

1751* *ex* Birkigt. Once owned by Hugo Birkigt, a German violinist born
at Niederbronn, Alsace, in 1885, who was a pupil of Joachim and
Halir. The violin was acquired by Albert Caressa of Paris, from
whom it was purchased by Richard Burgin and brought to this
country. It has a fine covering of the original rich orange-red
varnish; the back is in one piece, the lower flanks with added
wings, original with the maker, the maple showing a broad figure.
It has been remarked that two other J. B. Guadagnini violins are
owned by Mr. and Mrs. Burgin.

1751 *ex* Leonard. Formerly in the Wurlitzer Collection, a catalogue
issued in 1925 informs that this violin, once owned by the famous
Belgian violinist Hubert Leonard, born at Liege in 1819, died at
Paris in 1890, was sold by him in 1876 to a pupil Gustave Sama-
zeuilh, who retained it until July, 1915. It was purchased by
Wurlitzer from Albert Caressa in 1916 and has since had various
owners.

1751* A violin characterized by the late Alfred E. Hill as "in fine state
of preservation and amongst the best specimens of the maker's
work" was sold in 1928 by Wurlitzer to Nathan Abas. It reverted
to Wurlitzer in an exchange and was subsequently returned to
Hill & Son. The plate shows the beauty of the wood employed in
its making. *(Illustrated)*

1751* *ex* Maurin. Possessed of outstanding tonal qualities, this violin was
once owned by the French violinist Jean Pierre Maurin (1822-
1894), who succeeded Alard as Professor at the Paris Conservatoire. It came to Wurlitzer from Albert Caressa in 1917. Later
American owners included Andre Polah, Dr. Eugenio Sturchio,
and John Hudson Bennett. Subsequent to the death of the last
named, the violin passed, again through Wurlitzer, to Mrs. Esther
Coplin, and more recently to other private ownership. *(Illustrated)*

1751 *ex* Brodsky. This violin is owned by Anton Maaskoff of Los Angeles. He is also the owner of the Guarneri del Gesù violin of 1735
which was once owned by the French virtuoso Lafont, who played
in public contest with Paganini in 1816. Both the Guarneri and

A VIOLIN BY
J. B. GUADAGNINI
MILAN, 1751
ex Sametini

the Guadagnini violins were acquired by Mr. Maaskoff from his professor, Adolf Brodsky.

1751* *ex* Zajić. A magnificent instrument, as the plate portrays. It was owned by the late Professor Florian Zajić, famous Bohemian violinist who succeeded Emile Sauret as professor of violin at the Stern Conservatorium in Berlin. In 1885 Zajić acquired possession of the "David" Guarneri del Gesù (c. 1742), now owned by Jascha Heifetz. The Guadagnini violin was brought to this country by Emil Herrmann and was sold by him in 1926 to the late D. H. Walton, whose entire collection was acquired by Mr. Herrmann subsequent to his death. The Guadagnini was purchased by Vladimir Resnikoff of the Boston Symphony Orchestra in 1944. (*Illustrated*)

1751* *ex* Sametini. One of the outstanding works of the year, this example is unique among the specimens illustrated in having a one piece back. George Hart sold, it to H. G. Walter of New York about 1900. It was later acquired by John Hornsteiner, of Chicago; Herman Felber, then a member of the Coolidge Quartet, considered its purchase but, called upon to enter the armed services, relinquished the instrument in favor of the late Leon Sametini, who became its owner and kept it until his death on August 20, 1944. Mr. Sametini related that one of the deciding factors which made him purchase the violin was the reaction upon auditors who were present on an occasion when he played the Bach Double Concerto with Eugene Ysaÿe (about 1918) and, particularly, his famous countryman's admiration of the violin. Wurlitzer acquired possession from the Sametini estate in 1948, and the violin is now privately owned. (*Illustrated*)

1751 A violin of 1751 was sold by Emil Herrmann to Wolfe Wolfinson, eminent New York violinist and chamber music player, member of the Stradivarius Quartet sponsored by the late Felix Warburg.

1752* *ex* Havemann. Gustave Havemann, German violinist and composer who had an interesting and varied career before he was appointed professor at the Berlin "Hochschule," once was the

A Violin by
J. B. GUADAGNINI
Milan, 1751
ex Kneisel

owner of this violin. In this country it was part of the Wurlitzer Collection, from which it was acquired by Bradley Nickerson. Now in private possession. The violin has a one piece back of broad figured maple, the wood of the sides and head matching, the varnish of a golden-orange color.

1752* *ex* Kneisel. A flat model, red varnished violin which belonged to the late Franz Kneisel, famed for long connection with the Boston Symphony as its concertmaster, his own string quartet, and during his late years as head of the string instrument department of the Institute of Musical Art in New York. The violin passed from Kneisel to his friend Felix Kahn, and in 1927 from him to Wurlitzer. Through an exchange of instruments the Guadagnini then became a possession of Hamma & Company. Present owner is not known. *(Illustrated)*

1752 *ex* Baron Kohner. Formerly owned by a titled music lover, this fine example was sold by Emil Herrmann to Professor Victor Popoff, of Moscow, U.S.S.R., who was a previous owner of the "Prince Khevenhüller" Stradivari violin of 1733, acquired from Mr. Herrmann by a New York banker and presented to Yehudi Menuhin. (See cello of 1743.)

1752 *ex* Hartmann. This violin provided the theme of certain reminiscences by the eminent Hungarian-American violinist Arthur Martinus Hartmann, presented in the columns of *Violins and Violinists,* issue of December, 1946, concerning the history of a Stradivari of 1735 surrendered by Mr. Hartmann to W. E. Hill & Sons, and in which transaction he accepted this Guadagnini as part of the sales price. At the time the article was written, Mr. Hartmann could not recall the date on the label, and the strong point of his narrative was that he had sold it to one Wagner, a concertmaster of Arnheim, Holland, by whom he was entertained and who was, in stature and appearance, the image of his famous namesake, Richard Wagner. A sequel to the story was not long in appearing; seemingly lost track of and last known to its former owner as in Dutch possession, the subsequent history was supplied by William Moennig & Son, of Philadelphia, as a result of

A VIOLIN BY
J. B. GUADAGNINI
MILAN, 1752
ex Hartmann

reading the story in the magazine. Not only was the violin located, but it had been in this country since 1925! The documentary evidence embraces the original Hill certificate issued to Hartmann on October 9, 1905, attesting that the violin, including the label of Milan, dated 1752, was original, the varnish of orange-red color, and all in good state of preservation. The back of the certificate is inscribed (translated): "This violin was from the year 1905 until 1925 in my possession, and I sold it this day to Alfred Lorenz, Arnheim (Holland). C. L. Georg Wagner." Mr. Lorenz came to this country in the same year he acquired possession, and sold the instrument to Mr. Beaumont Glass, further inscribing the Hill certificate to that effect under date of December 18, 1925. Mr. Glass is the present owner of the violin. *(Illustrated)*

1753* A fine example of the year is in the possession of Margaret Horne, long a prominent member of the musical fraternity of Pittsburgh, Pennsylvania. The instrument was presented to her, a native of Scotland, as a token of appreciation, the tender having been through the offices of the Mayor of Glasgow in the name of her many friends and admirers prior to her leaving for America. The back is in two pieces, of broad rather faint figure, sides and head of matching wood, the varnish of an orange-red color.

1753 A violin with one piece back, maple of broad faint figure extending horizontally across its breadth, was in the collection of Hamma & Co. It was pictured in a small plate in the January 1944 issue of *Violins and Violinists*.

1753 *ex* Rauer. Georg Rauer was one of the many fine violin makers of Vienna who attained prominence also as a collector of and dealer in the works of the old masters. Many famous examples found their way to his establishment; the "Mercury" (or "Avery" as also called by name) Stradivari of 1688, the "Liebig" of 1704, and the famous ornamented "Greffuhle" of 1709, are among instruments at one time or other in the Rauer Collection. The J. B. Guadagnini violin listed here was purchased from Rauer by Erich Lachmann and sold by him to the eminent violinist Naoum Blinder, in whose possession it remains.

A Violin by
J. B. GUADAGNINI
Milan, 1753
ex Skolnik

1753* The plates portray the features of this fine specimen. The violin
was purchased in London in 1920 by Miss Jennie Skolnik, from
W. E. Hill & Sons, whose certificate is dated August 31, 1920.
Miss Skolnik renounced a successful professional career and in
1925 she sold the violin to Mrs. Frank Buttram of Oklahoma City.
Mrs. Buttram (née Merle Newby) graduated from the Oklahoma
State University and also studied at the Conservatoire de Giuseppe Verdi in Milan, and under Jean Ten Have and Arthur
Hartmann in Paris. Mrs. Buttram was one of the patrons and
organizers of the first Oklahoma City Symphony Orchestra, and
has been a liberal supporter of the community's musical activities.
The Guadagnini violin is in excellent preservation; the varnish is
of an orange-red color. (Illustrated)

175?* Of the period 1750-58, a violin typical of the Milan epoch was
acquired from the Lyon & Healy Collection by Dr. Neal Davis in
1946. The varnish is of a red-brown color, the back in one piece
with a medium curly figure extending horizontally across its
breadth.

1753 ex Youngman. This violin was in the possession of a violin dealer
of Halifax, Yorkshire, M. Youngman, before it was acquired by
Mrs. Twist in 1933. No further particulars at hand.

c.1753 ex Ysaÿe. A typical work of Milan bearing a Turin label dated
1774. It was a favorite with the great Belgian violinist; he sold
it in 1895 at the time he acquired possession of his famed Guarneri
del Gesù of 1740. The Guadagnini is a magnificent instrument,
unfortunately not with the original head. The back is of handsome wood in one piece, the varnish of a deep reddish-orange
color. It is a full proportioned violin. Presently an American
possession, owned by Mrs. Edwin Harris.

The following anecdote concerning Ysaÿe's Guadagnini appeared early in the century in the magazine *Music*, which was
founded at Chicago about 1891 by W. S. B. Mathews, the last

issue December 1902. The item was reprinted in *The Etude* magazine of September 1909. I am indebted to Mr. Sigmund Beel for the clipping.

YSAŸE'S GUADAGNINI

From *"The Etude,"* September, 1909.

When Eugène Ysaÿe was young and poor he coveted a Guadagnini violin that he saw in a pawnbroker's window in Hamburg. Though he could not dream of purchasing it at that time, he went into the shop one day and asked the pawnbroker to keep it for him, as he might by chance be able to buy it at some future date, says *M. A. P.* The obliging pawnbroker agreed to lay it aside for a reasonable time.

All the way back to his lodging house Ysaye worried over his inability to appropriate the violin at once, but on reaching the house, to his great astonishment, he found an old friend from Belgium there awaiting him. Ysaÿe immediately told him about the Guadagnini, and begged him to lend him the money to buy it.

"It's a large amount to pay," was the friend's reply, "and I haven't as much money with me."

"Would you lend it if you had?" asked the budding violinist.

"Yes," said the friend, "for I believe in your future and in you; but, as I have said, I have not the money."

An inspiration seized Ysaÿe.

"Look here," said he, "you deal in diamonds, don't you? Well, then, just leave a few diamonds as security and get me the Guadagnini."

The friend was so taken aback by the proposal that at first he was speechless; then, realizing the life-and-death seriousness of the young violinist, he consented to leave a bag of stones as security for the instrument.

"In this way," relates Ysaÿe, "I was married to my first love among the fiddles—my beautiful Guadagnini."—*Music.*

          *   *   *

1753   A fine violin, certified by Hill, which was long owned by an Austrian of noble ancestry, Count Saruba, who died in Los Angeles, is in the possession of Jeanette Sonja Violin, formerly Mrs. Numi Fisher. It is a typical work of the period, the back in two pieces with the flames extending upwards from left to right, the varnish of red-brown color.

1753   A violin with one piece back showing broad horizontal curls, was in the Hamma collection prior to the last war.

1753* Contained in a catalogue listing the 1925 Wurlitzer Collection, this violin was acquired by Sol Nemkovsky, well known Chicago violinist. It is a strikingly handsome instrument, the back in two pieces being of maple showing strong medium curls slanting upwards from the center joint. The varnish is of reddish color.

1753   The Lyon & Healy catalogue of 1921 lists a J. B. Guadagnini violin of this date.

1753* A fine example certified by Hill, formerly in the possession of Feri Roth, of the Roth Quartet, who acquired it from the Wurlitzer Collection, is now owned by Eugene Kash of Toronto.

1753* *ex* Mlle. Flayelle. Marius Casadesus of Paris brought this violin to America. The two piece back is of curly maple showing broad faint figure and marked by a dark streak extending throughout the length of both parts. Further unique, the varnish is of a pale golden-brown shade, almost colorless.

1754* The violin illustrated was at one time in the collection of T. C. Petersen. Through the intermediary of Emil Herrmann, it passed to J. W. Ledoux in 1931. Within recent years it came into posses-

A VIOLIN BY
J. B. GUADAGNINI
MILAN, 1754
Zazofsky

A Violin by

J. B. GUADAGNINI

Milan, 1755

ex Wollgandt

sion of William Moennig & Son and was then sold to George Zazofsky, a member of the Boston Symphony Orchestra. The wood characteristics appear in the portrait and the beautiful figure is enhanced by a rich covering of orange-red varnish. (*Illustrated*)

1754   Formerly in the collection of Maucotel & Deschamp, Paris dealers, Charles Tunsch brought the violin to New York in 1928. It was acquired by Wurlitzer, later passing to private ownership.

1755   An excellent example, with golden-red varnish setting off its one piece back of rather plain maple, was in the possession of Mrs. Helen W. Smith of Stamford, Connecticut.

1755*   Brought to this country by Nathan E. Posner, this violin was shown in illustration in the May 1935 edition of *The Strad*. The back is in one piece, of broad flamed maple, the varnish orange-red in color.

1755   Brought from Paris by the eminent viola player Henri Casadesus, this violin was acquired by Wurlitzer and subsequently passed through the hands of Roger Chittolini to private possession.

1755*   From the collection of Erich Lachmann, this violin was acquired by Sydney Small of Detroit, Michigan. The back is in one piece of somewhat irregularly flamed maple, the varnish a rich golden-red.

1755   A violin of somewhat higher arching than general, was in the Friedrich Collection of 1923, acquired from a visiting foreign player. Other than naming the color of varnish as lustrous deep red, no description is available.

1755*   *ex* Lakatos. Thus titled when sold by Emil Herrmann to Alexander Murray in 1930, from whose possession this violin subsequently passed to Wurlitzer. It was then purchased by Charles Petremont of Boston, the last recorded owner.

1755*   *ex* Bailly. A certificate issued in August of 1929 by Maucotel & Deschamp of Paris to Louis Bailly, formerly of the Flonzaley

Quartet, mentions that this violin had been used by one of the players of the Alard Quartet. Bailly submitted the violin to Hill, and obtained their certificate dated September 3, 1929, attesting its authenticity in all essential parts including the label. Through William Moennig & Son, the violin passed to the possession of Harry Ellis Dickson, a member of the Boston Symphony Orchestra, in July of 1946. The violin has a two piece back of handsome curly maple, ribs matching, the wood of the head plainer. The varnish is of an orange-brown shade.

1755   A letter received by a now departed friend, Dr. F. F. Lyon of Patchogue, N. Y., referred to this violin. The letter was received by Dr. Lyon while a resident of Freiburg, Switzerland. Writing under date of June 6th, 1921, Caressa & Français advised that there were in their possession two outstanding violins by J. B. Guadagnini, one dated at Parma in 1770, the other the instrument here recorded as of 1755, in regard to which the letter stated it to be one of the finest specimens in existence. It was described as having a top of rather wide grained wood, the back in one piece of most beautiful maple, all in perfect preservation and covered with a rich golden-yellow varnish. The price asked was 45,000 francs, equivalent, at that time, to about $3,600.00.

1755* *ex* Wollgandt. This was the concert violin of Edgar Wollgandt, a pupil of Hugo Heermann. Wollgandt was a prominent artist who was concertmaster of the Gewandhaus Orchestra and leader of the Gewandhaus String Quartet of Leipzig. Emil Herrmann brought the violin to New York and sold it to Iso Briselli in 1925; reverting to him later in an exchange, Herrmann then sold it to the banker Alfred O. Corbin, and again, after the death of the latter, to John Corigliano. The handsome wood is evidenced in our portrait of the instrument; it is enhanced by rich varnish of golden-red color. *(Illustrated)*

1755   *ex* Stoessel. This violin has been referred to as the "Red Diamond" owing to its rich covering of red varnish. It had long been held in the private collection of the Parisian dealer Albert Caressa, as a show piece, before Emil Herrmann obtained pos-

A VIOLIN BY

J. B. GUADAGNINI
MILAN, 1755
ex Stoessel

A VIOLIN BY

J. B. GUADAGNINI
MILAN, 1756
ex Burmester

A Violin by

J. B. GUADAGNINI

Milan, 1757

ex Dr. Trechmann

session in 1937. He sold it to the late Albert Stoessel, eminent American violinist and conductor, who retained it through his lifetime. *(Illustrated)*

1755 Fritz Meyer's story of famous violins and their destiny includes mention of a number of Guadagnini instruments, many, however, incorrectly noted as regards dates and locality of origin. One violin, which appears to be correctly ascribed to the maker's Milan period, with date 1755, is described as of slightly high arching, with back of one piece and varnish an orange-red color. Meyer records its sale by Hamma & Company to concertmaster Nagel of Düsseldorf, Germany.

1756* *ex* Burmester. A magnificent specimen which for many years was owned by Dr. Toeplitz of Breslau, Germany, a noted amateur violinist and quartet player. After his death in 1918 the violin was purchased by August Herrmann passing eventually to the possession of his son, Emil Herrmann, who sold it to the famous Willi Burmester in 1924. From him it passed to Max Adler, Chicago music patron and philanthropist, who retained possession until 1944, when the violin was sold through Kenneth Warren to Arthur Grossman. The physical characteristics of the instrument and its fine head are shown; the varnish is of a rich orange-red color. *(Illustrated)*

1756 A fine work of the year was sold by Emil Herrmann to William McPhail of Minneapolis, Minnesota.

1757* *ex* Trechmann. A particularly handsome violin was acquired by Kenneth Warren in London in 1946. Wood of exceptional beauty and richness in varnish of an orange color, together with immaculate preservation, mark the instrument as an outstanding example. It was formerly owned by Dr. M. L. Trechmann of Eccleston Square, London, who purchased it at Hill's in 1905. Small added wings at the lower flanks of the back are original with the maker. Owned by Leon Lustig. *(Illustrated)*

1757 A violin sold by Emil Herrmann to Stefi Geyer of Zurich, Switzerland.

A Violin by
J. B. GUADAGNINI
Milan, 1757
ex Herten

1757   A violin in possession of the Royal Conservatory of Music at Milan, Italy. Pictured in the Stradivari Bicentenary Memorial.

1757* ex Pochon. Alfred Pochon, who was second violin of the Flonzaley Quartet, used this violin for many years. Through Wurlitzer it was purchased by Raoul Berger. It has a two piece back of handsome figure; the varnish is of a rich reddish color.

1757* ex Herten. An outstanding specimen. Through Wurlitzer it passed successively to Gustavo Herten of Buenos Aires, and in Chicago to Ralph H. Norton, then to R. C. Wiebold. In 1946 Kenneth Warren negotiated its sale to C. L. Mason. The varnish is of a golden orange color. (Illustrated)

1757   Purchased from William E. Hill & Sons in 1885, and for over twenty years in the possession of Fred Brough of Rusholme, Manchester, England. Details descriptive of the wood characteristics are not at hand further than that the varnish is of a dark orange-red color.

1757   ex Wirth. A very beautiful example. Some traces of worm ravage in no degree affects the tonal desirability of the instrument, as the long succession of eminent owners evidences. The history of the violin dates back to 1897; prior to then it had been used by Emanuel Wirth of Berlin who was long a member of the Joachim Quartet. In 1897 Wirth parted with it to his contemporary Carl Wendling, of the famous Wendling Quartet. He retained possession until 1922 when, through Hamma & Company, it was purchased by the frequently mentioned violin enthusiast Gustavo Herten. He made an exchange at Wurlitzer, and from their collection the violin passed to Harry Ben Gronsky of South Pasadena, California. Calmon Luboviski acquired it and played upon it from 1929 to 1945, when it again changed hands and since has been the concert violin of Joachim Chassman. The illustration provides an excellent likeness of the instrument.* (Illustrated)

---

* See remarkable similarity of violins of Turin, c. 1771-1776 ex Zimbalist, and 1775 ex Joachim; the latter was also once in the possession of Calmon Luboviski, one of the most brilliant violinists on the Pacific coast.

A Violin by
J. B. GUADAGNINI
Milan, 1757
ex Wirth

A Violin by
J. B. GUADAGNINI
Milan, 1758
ex Vieuxtemps

141

1758* *ex* Vieuxtemps. This is one of several J. B. Guadagnini violins recorded as having once belonged to Henri Vieuxtemps. It was acquired by one of his pupils by name Vaillard. Later in the Wilmotte collection it had passed to Albert Caressa in 1928, in which year it was purchased by Nathan E. Posner. He brought it to New York and it later was acquired by the collector, the late Alfred E. Corbin. Subsequently it passed through Emil Herrmann to a banker of The Hague, Holland, who bought the violin in 1934. The one piece back is of very handsome wood of broad figure and the varnish is golden-orange in color. *(Illustrated)*

c.175– *ex* Vieuxtemps. Previously mentioned in the text in comments on Fritz Meyer's book, this noteworthy example was once owned by Henri Vieuxtemps. About 1879 it passed to his pupil Madame d'Exarque, wife of a Bulgarian diplomat. From the latter it was purchased by the eminent pedagogue, the late Carl Flesch, who used the violin continuously until, in 1907, he acquired the famous "Brancaccio" Stradivari of 1725. About 1913, Flesch sold the Guadagnini to one of his pupils, Robert Pollak, in whose possession it remains. Mr. Pollak, now a resident of Los Angeles, was born at Vienna in 1880. His long career as a concert violinist was also one devoted to teaching; he held professorships in conservatories at Geneva, Moscow, Vienna, Tokyo, San Francisco, and at Chapman College, Los Angeles. At the time the violin was in possession of Vieuxtemps it carried a spurious label of Guarneri del Gesù, which was later replaced with a Guadagnini ticket, of Milan dated 1760, probably by the German dealer Eugen Gärtner of Stuttgart who issued a certificate, since lost.

VIOLA

J. B. Guadagnini evidently had little call for the making of violas during his years at Milan. A single specimen finds place for recording here.

1757* A viola of very excellent acoustic properties is owned by Keith Cummings, of the Blech Quartet of London, which toured America with the Royal Air Force Band in 1945. A Guadagnini violin

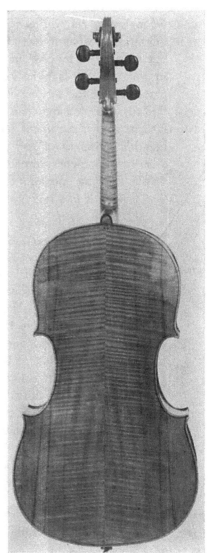

A Cello by
J. B. GUADAGNINI
Milan, 1754
ex Gerardy

143

belonging to Harry Blech has been mentioned. This viola is of unique interest as it was at some time reduced in its dimensions but restored to its original proportions in highly expert manner, so well, in fact, that the vandalism can hardly be detected. Replacement of the sections which form the extensions has been so skilfully executed that it is not apparent to the casual eye. The instrument has a present body length of 16-1/4 inches with the breadth across the upper, middle, and lower bouts 8, 5-11/16 and 9-15/16 inches respectively. The back is in one piece of maple showing medium curls slanting upwards from the left. The varnish is in a rich orange shade of color.

VIOLONCELLOS

1754   *ex* Gerardy. The famous cello virtuoso, Jean Gerardy, used this instrument with great success on his many tours. It passed to the collection of George Hart, who sold it to John Wanamaker on May 19, 1926, that being the date of his certificate issued at the time of its change to American ownership. The cello was part of the celebrated Wanamaker Collection at the time of its acquisition by the Wurlitzer interests. The well known cellist Michel Penha purchased the instrument in 1930. The varnish is of golden-brown color, the back in two pieces of small figured maple, the curls slanting slightly downwards from the center joint. The lower flanks of the back have added wings, original with the maker. The length of the body is 28-3/16 inches, widths 13-3/16, 9-3/16, and 16-1/2 inches at the upper, middle and lower bouts respectively. *(Illustrated)*

1755   A cello mentioned by Lütgendorff as in the Hämmerle Collection, of Vienna.

1758   A fine example long used by the eminent Hungarian cellist Imre Hartman, of the Lener Quartet. The instrument is mentioned in Max Möller's excellent work.

1758   The Hamma book shows two views of a handsome cello described as a Milanese work of 1758.

CHAPTER IV

J. B. GUADAGNINI AT CREMONA

There is a strong temptation at this point to digress from our topic of the violin maker Guadagnini and indulge somewhat in fantasy. The subject of Cremona having so often enthused violinistically inclined writers in the past, this one is mindful of the fact that it would be difficult to escape repetition of the words of other, more gifted scribes and, therefore, the urge to dwell at length on the topic must be curbed. However, it is one which offers opportunity to present certain facts concerning J. B. Guadagnini as having played some part ordained to bear fruit in the time of this generation.

The mere mention of the word "Cremona" carries with it implication of something beyond the pale of the commonplace and to those who understand its meaning epitomizes the romantic and significant in violin lore. As Mecca is referred to as *Om Al Kora,* "Mother of Cities," the most holy of all of Islam, so is Cremona now memorialized and revered as the mother city of the brotherhood of the *liutai,* and symbolic of the *ne plus ultra* in the world of violins. That the veneration held by modern generations of violin lovers for the old city as the home of the Amati, Ruggieri, Stradivari and Guarneri families did not similarly move those of its own citizens to respect their memory has been the subject of many narrators.

That the violin makers contributed mightily to the glory of Cremona seems also to have escaped the notice of general historians. Our encyclopedias tell of wonderful cathedrals—its Torazzo which with a height of 397 feet is the highest clock tower in northern Italy—its place in the arts, omitting to pay more than scant mention to its great violin makers, Stradivari alone receiving occasional casual notice. Propaganda material featuring the attractions of Italy and its cities exploit Cremona's specialties appealing to the gourmet, of very material consideration no doubt but failing signally to appeal to the higher tastes that would prefer to rate its historic significance to be resting at least in some measure on the lustre rightfully its heritage in having cradled a great art.

In his notice to Stradivari George Hart deplores the situation: 'It is somewhat singular that the Cremonese take but little apparent interest in the matter, and have expressed themselves as being astonished at the demonstrations of respect which their English and French visitors pay to the hallowed spot. The better informed Cremonese have some acquaintance with the name of Stradivari; but to create any enthusiasm among them from the fact of his having been a Cremonese, or from the historical associations which connect him with the city, would be difficult . . . The citizens of Cremona are, however, not quite singular in this respect. It has been remarked that our American friends show far greater interest in Stratford-on-Avon and its memories than we ourselves do. I must confess that I have great respect for the genuine enthusiast."

HUGH R. HAWEIS

The British writer, the Reverend Hugh R. Haweis, devoted many words to Cremona in his several works on musical subjects. In his "My Musical Life" (Third Book, titled *Cremona*), he wanders somewhat widely anent the subject, too lengthily to be quoted here *in toto;* some paragraphs, however, well bear reprinting. Regarding Stradivari, Haweis tells that: "A traveller who lately visited his house, still standing in the square of

Cremona,* remarked that it was heated through with the sun like an oven. He said you might sit and sweat there as in a Turkish bath. That was how the Cremona makers dried their wood, and so it was their oils distilled slowly and remained always at a high temperature, their varnish weltered and soaked into the pine bellies and sycamore backs beneath the tropical heat of those seventeenth century summers!" Bringing Guadagnini into the picture, Haweis wrote: "With Carlo Bergonzi . . . and Guadagnini (1710-1750) the great Cremona school comes to an end." Obviously, the short visit of J. B. Guadagnini to Cremona, in 1758, did not prompt that statement, nor does it appear that Haweis was aware of the actual circumstances. Haweis labored under misapprehension, most likely led astray by the writings of others, both in attributing the period 1710-1750 to Guadagnini, as well as in regarding him (as of 1750) among the last of the Cremonese school. Later in the book, under the theme "On the Oblivion of Great Men," Haweis tells of his visit to Cremona in 1880, and of his chagrin in finding small memory of the famous violin makers once resident in the city. Of Haweis' numerous literary contributions, that which is best known to violin fanciers is his book titled "Old Violins" (about 1898). In this book (Chapter IV, *Violins at Cremona*) two paragraphs, the second of which bears strongly on modern Cremonese indifference to its once famous violin makers, are well to quote here:—

"Cremona, ancient city of strife, which, owing to its very situation (Greek 'high rock' and 'alone'), was the battle-point of the middle ages from the days of the old Goths and Lombards down to quite modern times; Cremona, with its stately cathe-

---

* The houses, among which that of Stradivari was one, have been destroyed and replaced (1920) with a modern office building during the era of Mussolini.

dral so little known or visited, yet possessing two of the finest red lions couchant, supporting portico columns of one of the noblest cathedral façades in Italy; Cremona, with its antiquated back streets, its drowsy quiet life gliding on apart from the beaten thoroughfares of travel—truly, Cremona town is a place to set one dreaming!

"I have narrated elsewhere my pilgrimage to the place which so ungratefully forgets almost the very tradition of the Amati, Stradivari, and Guarneri, whose fabrics alone have given it a musical immortality, and whose names are hung up high like the stars, which no discords of the middle ages, sieges, or brawls can ever reach."

*   *   *

Alas, all that remained for the passing eye to see in Haweis' day was a small plaque marking the spot where the house of Stradivari once stood. Since the time of Haweis there has been an awakening and, belatedly it is true but nonetheless in effort to atone for the neglect of earlier generations, silent as well as material homage is paid, notably to Antonio Stradivari.

THE STRADIVARI PATRIMONY

It is a matter of violin history that Stradivari's direct descendants made unavailing efforts to have the city of Cremona heed the greatness of the deceased maker in fitting memorial, to which preservation and permanent housing of the many patterns, moulds, tools and other shop appurtenances that had been their father's and were their heritage would have contributed. Moved by the apathy of the town officials, Paolo, the last born son of Antonio Stradivari, eventually decided that nothing reminding of the master should remain in the city.

As a figure in the story of J. B. Guadagnini, Count Cozio di

Salabue was not to appear until years later; there is purpose in bringing him into this chapter about Cremona as he was destined to be the instrumentality through which the city was one day to lose and much later to recover the relics of their departed citizen, foremost among the great violin makers whose works have made Cremona a byword where fine accomplishment is topic for discussion.

During Guadagnini's short stay at Cremona in 1758, there can be no doubt that he tarried as a visitor at the home of Paolo Stradivari, who was established there as a merchant dealing in cloth. Nor was he forgetful of what he had seen or failed to dwell on his experiences during the many meetings with Count Cozio subsequent to his meeting with him at Turin in 1773. More will be said about the relations between the two in the proper place, but here it is fitting to introduce the subject of Cozio and the Stradivari relics because it bears directly on Cremona, and also, because Guadagnini deserves the credit of an early part in the developments to be related.

Whatever the thoughts may have been that motivated Count Cozio in his fancy for violins, there is the certain fact that his interest was quickened through his acquaintance with the violin maker. Thus, having learned from him of the precious things in Paolo Stradivari's possession, the Count desired much to become their owner, at first concerning himself with the acquisition of violins remaining unsold in the estate. This was accomplished in 1775, therefore about two years subsequent to his making the acquaintance of Guadagnini. In furtherance of a plan to found a school of violin making at Turin to revive the art in the tradition of Stradivari, Cozio then began negotiations looking towards the purchase of the various fittings that had been preserved from the deceased master's workshop. Some of the details appear in Hart's work (in the later editions), Federico Sacchi's "Count Cozio di Salabue," and of more recent vintage, Renzo Bacchetta's "Stradivari, vita e opere del celebre liutaro," published at Cremona in 1937, extracts from which appear in Georges Hoffmann's "Stradivarius l'enchanteur," published at Paris in 1938, reprinted at Geneva in 1945 with an edition in German following in 1947 published at Zurich entitled "Der bezaubernde Stradivarius," as well as in Franz Farga's "Geigen und Geiger," published at Zurich in 1940. In this connection, readers of the various books mentioned will note conflicting dates given as those of the correspondence between Cozio's agents Briatta & Co., and Paolo Stradivari and his son Antonio: Hart gives the year as 1776; in Sacchi's tribute to Cozio, we find the quoted letters dated 1775; a genealogical table in Hill's work on Stradivari gives the year of Paolo's death as 1776; in the Hoffmann original and subsequent editions both dates appear in conflicting sequence, while in Farga's book we read that Cozio was *born 1775* (1755 being the date). Such entries exhibit the danger of blind reiteration, error into which writers (this one not excepted) are prone to be led and to which none are immune.

Hart, in his fourth edition, relates the episode of the transfer of the Stradivari residue to Cozio in his beautiful phraseology and while kindly to the Count, does not evade that taint of commercialism was made apparent in the activities of his agents, Briatta & Co., the cloth merchants of Casale who trafficked in anything that promised gain. As said, some of the letters were presented by Hart, in English, by Sacchi in Italian, while in Bacchetta's book the entire surviving series is entered in their original Italian form. These letters will be discussed in another chapter.

GIUSEPPE FIORINI

Count Cozio's plan to found a school of violin making at Turin did not eventuate and though he gradually disposed of many of his large collection of instruments, he retained possession of all the varied complements of the Stradivari workshop. These passed intact to his heirs at his death and were guarded from the outside world until 1881, when the then owner, the Marquis Dalla Valle, permitted their exhibition at the Milan Music Exposition. At that time an Italian violin maker, Giuseppe Fiorini, made overtures looking to the purchase of the collection. Fiorini was born at Bazzano in 1861; he established himself in Bologna in 1881, later at Munich in 1899, removing his business to Zurich in 1915 for the period of the then raging war. Unsuccessful in acquiring the collection of Cozio at that time, he achieved his aim in 1920, having paid, it is said, the sum of one hundred thousand lire for all that was contained in the collection, including besides the tools, patterns, forms, etc., the entire records of the Count pertaining to violins —his diaries, inventories and a vast number of other documents said to exceed fifteen hundred items.

His investment brought Fiorini many disappointments and much grief, and contributed to an almost complete financial ruin. He tried in vain to have the collection placed in various Italian cities, which he was agreeable to effecting if a school of violin making would be founded with him as the directing head. Towards the end of his life his vision became affected and Fiorini finally gave the collection to the city of Cremona in 1930, where the city fathers, belatedly moved to grant homage so long withheld from their illustrious citizen of an earlier day, later established the *Sala Stradivariana* to house the historic relics. Further, with the celebration of the Stradivari Bicentenary in 1937, a master school of violin making was established, thus realizing Fiorini's dream, too late, however, to be known to him as he had passed away in death at Munich in 1934.

Thus it came to pass that Cremona regained possession of a long lost treasure and now honors a great name and an important art.

A brochure of more than a hundred pages was published in 1937 by the *Comitato Celebrazioni Bicentenario Stradivariano,* "Archivio Storico Cremonese—Antonio Stradivari, Notizie e Documenti," in the compilation of which Carlo Bonetti, Agostino Cavalcabo and Ugo Gualazzini collaborated. Illustrations include among its numerous plates, four showing the very considerable number of items comprising the Cozio collection in their glass enclosed exhibition cases.

Although Guadagnini finds no mention in the pages last mentioned, his shade pervades the Sala Stradivariana of the Cremona Civic Museum as once knowing and handling the mementos of his great predecessor and as having been close to their one-time possessor both in personal relation as well as the subject of some of his writings.

GUADAGNINI AT CREMONA

Violin historians have recorded, whether rightly or not, that Lorenzo Guadagnini .and his son Joannes Baptista worked in Cremona, some contending that both, some only that the latter was born there. As regarded today, and by virtue of the evidence of signed works, there is little to support the first and less to confirm the second premise. Yet, as the spirits of the great of that city must have then remained, as they do now, to beguile those who followed in their wake, we can imagine that J. B. Guadagnini's thoughts were not infrequently of Cremona, and that the exploits of its violin makers were never completely absent from his mind. So that, when compelling urge caused him to quit Milan, it is not strange that Cremona beckoned strongly. The shortness of his stay there can be accepted as definitely establishing that Guadagnini did not plan to settle in the city, but was on his way to Parma where, if oft repeated statements hold truth, there was a demand for a violin maker with promise of support by the ducal court.

If, on the other hand, it had been his thought to establish a permanent abode at Cremona, the situation there at that time, as we can regard it now, would seem to have made it an auspicious move. The great masters of Cremona had ceased their labors—the last of the Stradivarii had passed away in 1743; Guarneri del Gesù in 1744. Carl Bergonzi died 1747, his sons were still working, but could have offered no obstacle to deter a worthy and aggressive competitor from successfully carrying on in their vicinity.

Before leaving Milan in 1758, Guadagnini had completed a number of instruments, as shown by our tabulation; it is obvious that he could not have arrived at Cremona until during the later months of the year. No chronicle records his coming, nor where he chose to abide, and there can be no knowing what greeting awaited him there. If his visitation was in the nature of exploring—an investigation occasioned by a desire to acquaint (or re-acquaint?) himself with the city, he did not find that which he sought for his stay was only for a few months at most. Short as this working period at Cremona was, he was not idle, as attested by several fine works existing at this time.

Regarding Guadagnini's length of stay in Cremona, an article, connected with the illustration of the Milan work of 1755, then owned by Mr. Posner, in the May, 1935, edition of *The Strad* (author not named, but in the style of Mr. Arthur W. Dykes) mentions, in the course of outlining the periodic changes in the maker's habitat: "He is next found at Cremona where he stayed apparently for two years (1759-60)." The error of this is clear in the fact that we have definite knowledge of works at Parma during the year 1759, with none at all dating from Cremona in that year. The quoted article continues: "It would seem that he only visited Cremona for the short period previously mentioned and to have made very few instruments whilst he was there. These Cremona productions are consequently rarely met with but a very fine violoncello made there and dated 1758 was at one time in the possession of a well-known artist in the North of England."

Guadagnini's work style shows no radical departure in the instruments produced at Cremona. With regard to labels used during his period there, that which marks the *ex* Bazzini violin is unique in departing from the maker's accustomed practice of having the sign of the cross to the right of the text, in this instance being at the left extremity. Its authenticity is quite dubious, but genuine or otherwise, the wording points clearly to Piacenza as J. B. Guadagnini's origin: whoever designed it followed the general form of wording—"Placentinus fecit Cremona, 1735."

The dating is palpably wrong, presenting as it does predating by five years the beginning of the maker's epoch at Placentina. There seems no question of the authenticity of the instrument and that it is a work at Cremona produced in 1758. This has confirmation, established by the judgment of a number of experts: firstly, it will be found pictured in the Stradivari bicentenary memorial volume, named as a product of 1758 and so adjudged by the Messrs. Fridolin Hamma, Max Möller, and

Emile Français, who were the judges that passed on and certified to the authenticity of instruments accepted for exhibition; mention of the instrument occurs in Max Möller's book, attributing the origin to 1758. Other authorities who know the instrument, agree with the correctness of the date as 1758, notwithstanding the label nor the existence of a certificate issued in 1943 mentioning that the violin was produced in Cremona "about 1735 as indicated by the label it bears."

The violin has the following history; it was acquired by Mario Frosali in Florence, Italy, from the eminent violinist Bazzini (mentioned previously in connection with a violin of Piacenza of 1742). Frosali loaned it for exhibition at the Stradivari bicentenary at Cremona in 1937, as said. Included in the comment on Guadagnini's stay at Cremona, Max Möller's book, published subsequent to the Cremona affair, contains, in romantic strain: ". . . did Guadagnini revisit the city of his birth to look up old friends, or perhaps mix with old fellow-workers; and did their jealousy prohibit his staying?" Obviously, Herr Möller accepted the theory that the maker was Cremonese, notwithstanding the fact that even on the label of the violin in question it is plainly stated that he was of Piacenza! Mr. Frosali brought the instrument to this country about 1943, and after its return from the Cremona exhibition, took it to California where he sold it in 1947 to Francesco Mazzi, concertmaster of the San Francisco ABC broadcasting chain, a former pupil of Adolfo Betti of Flonzaley Quartet fame.

A beautiful work is one that was acquired by Nathan E. Posner at Beare's in London in 1929. The story of its purchase as told by Mr. Posner has peculiar interest. As related by him he had previously bought a Guadagnini dated at Milan in 1758 while in Paris, and upon arrival in London visited the prominent

A Violin by
J. B. GUADAGNINI
Cremona, 1758
ex Bazzini

dealers, John & Arthur Beare, and showed this lately acquired 1758 Milan work. Mr. Beare then produced the Cremona example and Posner immediately purchased it. Then he showed both to Alfred E. Hill, who remarked on the rare occurrence of meeting two works of the maker, both produced in the same year yet each in a different city. The violin had previously been in the possession of a well known Scottish maker and dealer, J. W. Briggs, Glasgow.

TABULATION

1758* *ex* Bazzini. An excellent example attributed to Cremonese origin and as a work of 1758. The wood characteristics show in our plates; the varnish is of an orange-red color. (*Illustrated*)

1758 *ex* Briggs. A lovely instrument as evidenced by our illustration. Brought to this country by Nathan E. Posner in 1929, and now in private possession. The back is of maple cut half-slab, the varnish of soft texture, of orange color. (*Illustrated*)

1758* *ex* Thomann. Formerly owned by Karl Thomann, a Bohemian violinist who had been a pupil of Ottokar Sevcik. It was brought to this country by Emil Herrmann and sold to Walter Ury of San Francisco, after whose death it passed to Erich Lachmann. It is now privately owned in Santa Barbara. The physical characteristics of the violin are similar to those of the *ex* Bazzini example.

1758* *ex* Knapp. This violin has been in America many years; it is in the possession of Isadore Gralnick. It was purchased for Joseph Knapp, whose father was one of the founders of the Metropolitan Life Insurance Company, when the young man was a student in Germany. He discontinued playing in 1923, since when the instrument remained unused until Gralnick acquired it in 1944. The violin bears the original label of the maker. Its physical characteristics so closely resemble the ex-Briggs violin that it might be regarded as a companion-work. The wood of the two

A Violin by
J. B. GUADAGNINI
Cremona, 1758
ex Briggs

piece back has almost identical figuration. A slight difference exists in the classification of the color of the varnish, which, in the case of this violin, is described as of a pink-orange color. The violin is of 14 inch body length, widths across the bouts 6-3/8, 4-3/8 and 7-7/8 inches.

1758 Daniel Kuntz, long member of the Boston Symphony Orchestra, owned a violin said to be a work of Guadagnini at Cremona in 1758. The information was recorded by me in 1932. Present owner is not known to me.

1758 A Cremona work of Guadagnini was contained in the Hamma Collection prior to the outbreak of the last war.

1758 A fine work of the year was in the collection of Roger Chittolini at the time of this recording. Described as having a one piece back of broad flamed maple, the figure slanting downwards from left to right, with matching wood in the ribs, the varnish of orange color with reddish tint. Measurements: body length 13-15/16 inches; across the bouts, upper 6-1/2, middle 4-1/2, lower 7-15/16 inches.

A VIOLONCELLO

1758 Mentioned in *The Strad* in the edition of May, 1935, this cello was referred to as having been in the possession of a prominent artist in the North of England.

PART V

J. B. GUADAGNINI AT PARMA

The Parma epoch in the career of J. B. Guadagnini has been variously approached in the works of early historians. From what is known to have been the political situation in the city at the time of Guadagnini's advent, it is difficult to place faith in much that has been written to suggest a reason for the violin maker to locate there. A pawn of rival factions, the Duchy of Parma, like other provinces of northern Italy, was long exploited by its rulers, puppets under the sway of higher powers whose personal interests generally superseded those of the state.

If we refer to John S. C. Abbott's *Italy* it will be read, embracing a period anterior to that of J. B. Guadagnini:—"The little duchy of Parma had a succession of dukes, whose lives were shortened by their dissipation, and not one of whom merits any notice except for his crimes. During their short reigns they rioted in all licentious indulgence which their limited incomes and their obscure courts could afford."

An item in an encyclopedia edited by Lloyd Edwin Smith has:—"There were eight dukes of Parma from 1545 to 1731. The duchy passed and repassed alternately into the hands of Spain and Austria till 1860 . . ."

Count Cozio put on record that "Guadagnini received employment from the ducal court at Parma," perhaps because the maker so informed him. It is true that labels he used during the period support the claim in having been imprinted "serviens C. S. R.", with probably an intent similar to that found on labels used by makers in other countries—an old custom carried on to this day in England, proclaiming favor of royalty or nobility.

It may be assumed that the abbreviation, C. S. R., was used to designate the court at Parma, and not, particularly, service for any member thereof, hence the Latin *curia signa regis* (seal of the royal court) is the most plausible interpretation. Whether Guadagnini's labels, or Cozio's remarks prompted later enlargement on the point is not for this writer to venture. It will be recalled that Yusupov erroneously connected the Guadagninii with Milan; other writers followed suit. Hart repeated the error, placing the maker's Piacenza period after that at Milan and telling that he went to Parma where he became instrument maker to the duke. Lütgendorff endeavored to provide some historical background to account for Guadagnini's removal to Parma and presumed service to the duke; unfortunately, he built his story according to periods wrongly assigned to Guadagnini, thus to fit a time previous to the maker's arrival at Parma! Quoting from his survey of the craft, we read (translated):—

"A really outstanding master was first to appear in Parma in Giambattista Guadagnini who probably, like his younger brother Lorenzo, was trained at Cremona. He was called from Piacenza, where he is said first to have shared Lorenzo's shop, by Antonio, the last Archduke of the House of Farnese, or by Don Carlos, to Parma, and seems to have remained in the service of the Court after the duchy passed to Kaiser Carl VI. If Parma occupies good repute in the story of violin-making, it is to be thanked primarily to the fact that Giamb. Guadagnini worked there until 1750."

HISTORICAL

There is no cause to point out the recurrence of the disproven "younger brother" myth, but it must be noted that Lütgendorff does not account for the maker's period at Milan, previous to that at Parma; this is understandable as his biographical note alloted that period to the by him named Giambattista II. In laboring under the belief that Guadagnini worked at Parma until 1750, we may find the reason why his research into the history of Parma, devoted to a period anterior to 1750, caused him to err and write as he did. Thus, his reference to Antonio, the last Archduke of the House of Farnese, who died in 1731, as well as possible service under Don Carlos of Spain or the court of Kaiser Karl VI, (Charles VI, Emperor of Austria) who died 1740, is not historically correct as related to Guadagnini's Parma period. Neither of the monarchs mentioned could have in any manner been influential in attracting Guadagnini to Parma in 1758. Happenings at Parma subsequent to the death of Charles VI and the succession of his daughter, Maria Theresa, to the throne of Austria were of little concern, musically, to the harried empress.

What seems to have been the situation is to be read in various encyclopedias, as follows: When Charles VI of Austria died in 1740, the three branches of the House of Bourbon, ruling in France, Spain and the Sicilies, joined with Prussia, Bavaria and the Kingdom of Sardinia to despoil Maria Theresa of her heritage. In 1748 the treaty of Aix-la-Chapelle formed Parma, Piacenza and Guastalla into a duchy for Don Philip (Felipe) brother of Charles III, both of whom were sons of Philip V of Spain. Philip, with a Frenchman, Guillaume Du Tillot, as his able minister, brought about a condition of prosperity and culture in Parma that caused it to be called the Athens of Italy. Du Tillot instituted a series of reforms, in some restricting the privileges of the clergy which brought him the disfavor of the church. He continued his work after the death of Philip in 1765, in the service of the Infanta Ferdinand who continued to reign as duke at Parma until his death in 1802. However, after Ferdinand married Maria Theresa's daughter, Maria Amelia, who was hostile to all innovations, he, incapable and corrupt, fell entirely under her domination and in 1771 obliged Du Tillot to resign, and many of the reforms which had been instituted were abolished. These facts, if correctly recorded here, suggest a reason for Guadagnini's decision to quit Parma. Whether he was originally attracted to the city by promise of commissions from the ducal court, or obtained work in its service after his arrival cannot be stated but there is support for the first premise in the adoption of the C. R. S. notice on his labels. If another form without the designation was in use at Parma, no example has come before me and the conclusion is that he went to Parma on summons from the court.

Another point of interest and of peculiar significance in connection with these Parma labels is that soon after Guadagnini's arrival at Parma, he incorporated mention of Cremona. Some writers have found reason to support the theory that this was the maker born at Cremona, as separate from another born at Piacenza! Guadagnini, although deleting reference to Piacenza on the Parma labels, did not remove the letter "P" from the monogram and while it might be argued that it designates Parma it is more likely that he meant by it to avow allegiance to Piacenza.

TEMPER—JEALOUSY

The English writer Haweis made free with Count Cozio's remark concerning Guadagnini's irascibility; in his "Old Violins," he tells:—"He was always changing his place of residence and wandered from Piacenza to Milan, and at last to Turin, where he died. His own explanation was that the envy of rivals made each town too hot for him, but his neighbours said that his frequent migrations were due to his own hot temper." Imagination works wonders to inspire the pen, but when a writer so far injects fantasy as we find it here, he goes beyond the bounds of fair reason. With so little that is definitely known about the man, how could Haweis give us "his own explanation," or tell what "his neighbours said"?

Hart had remarked that Guadagnini was "said to have excited the jealousy of other makers, which caused him to remove so frequently, but most likely he offended chiefly with his hasty temper." Such remarks may be regarded as allowable, if Cozio's are literally taken. However, criticism is justified, on several grounds:

Direct descendants were not able to provide reasonably definite information of their famous antecedent, hence, Cozio's reference to an aging man's testiness seems to have been ample reason for almost all writers to attribute a hasty temper as governing Guadagnini's entire career; had that been so, and detrimental to his cordial association with others, it would seem unlikely that he would seek other spheres of action where to vent his spleen. Granting that he was highly emotional, a not unusual trait of the Latin people, jealousy would hardly have aroused competitive workers, of whom few existed—in his time—as will be shown. Had that actually been the situation, a natural reaction would appear to have been to bolster the pride and morale of a craftsman possessing Guadagnini's fitness.

COMPETITORS

If we review conditions as they were at the various times of the maker's epochs, we will find that at Piacenza, the only local competitor was his own father, Lorenzo; at Milan, during his second period, the Testore and Grancino families had ceased their labors before his coming. If we remark the presence there of Carlo Ferdinando Landolfi and his son, Pietro Antonio, the evidence of their productions, although many are highly meritorious, has not accorded them eminence comparable to that achieved by Guadagnini, so that if jealousy motivated unfriendly feeling at Milan, it can be taken to have existed only on their part. Further, a far more numerous production of finished works emanated from Guadagnini's workshop than the combined output of the Landolfis. The locality of Milan, as remarked by Hills in their characterization of its violin makers as "Milanese cheapjacks," had been a center which catered to a less exacting clientele than that which patronized Cremonese makers. The uncomplimentary title thus bestowed, was not directed to Guadagnini, but had reference to the earlier makers of the area. Milan, therefore, provides no ground to support the theory that jealousy of other makers prompted Guadagnini to seek other environment. Max Möller's query—why did the maker visit Cremona?—cannot be answered, although I have remarked on that subject. If Parma held out great promise and Guadagnini seriously considered the locality to offer him fertile ground for cultivation, it may well be that he had considered the value of a claim to Cremonese background, which could not be contradicted if he tarried there even for a short period of time. I do not intend, in advancing the thought, to question any asserted Cremonese influence exerted on the early life of the maker.

Again referring to Hart, he remarked that Guadagnini left Parma after the ducal favors were "discontinued in 1772." The maker had already quit the city before that year, as is reliably proven by authentic labels dated from Turin in 1771. As it is the belief that his arrival in Turin with his family was under conditions of financial stress, there is good reason to believe that his labor at Parma had not been sufficiently rewarded, whether by duke or citizenry, notwithstanding numerous product during his last years at Parma, as the tabulation of his works will indicate.

Following the line of argument here presented and discounting various theories advanced to account for J. B. Guadagnini's meanderings, the subject can best be regarded as closed on the assumption that his was a nature possessed by a craving for change and a continual belief that improved conditions might be found elsewhere than where he was located. A similar wanderlust seems to have been inherited by his first born son, Giuseppe, who was born 1736, or in that period during which J. B. Guadagnini is believed to have been working at Cremona; Giuseppe did considerable roaming but, like a rolling stone, gathered no moss, and died in poor circumstances at Pavia about 1806.

PARMA

Notwithstanding many vicissitudes which retarded normal development and growth, Parma has many monuments to its culture in the arts and sciences. Fine churches and institutions of learning attest century-long devotion to the higher aims of life: as examples, the University of Parma was founded in 1512, and the Teatro Farnese, one of numerous contributions of the powerful Farnese family, dates from 1618. Although a school of music and an active traffic in musical instruments existed, there had been no violin maker of note working at Parma prior to the arrival of J. B. Guadagnini in 1759.

Soon after Guadagnini's advent at Parma, a distinct modification of his work style becomes apparent. With a few exceptions during his first years there, when his material, work-manship and varnishing continued much as before, we find a change of pattern and arching, and the employment of varnish that lacks the richness of coloring found in those instruments of any of his other periods. This varnish, unlike that previously used, is found to be generally of a yellowish brown shade, most-ly of light tint, less often darker, more resinous in its texture and inclined to chip or peel. Where this condition is strong, modern application of colorless varnish has generally sufficed to protect the original covering without an appreciable effect detrimental to the tone which, in these Parma instruments, is usually in no wise of less desirable character than that produced by those of Guadagnini's other periods. As a class, the tone of Parma violins may be said to lean toward brilliancy. The wood is always excellent; the tops of straight even grain and the backs often of wood cut from a log of small tight curl, a log of maple evidently of local purchase which served in the making of many instruments, and being a strong feature of identification of his Parma works. The typical pear shape design of the sound hole terminals continues as does also the method of setting his pins at the extremities of the plates, large, and well inside the pur-fling. The heads show the marks of the implement with which he stippled out the outlines of the spiral, the latter often ter-minating in small extremities at the boss of the helix. It is not to be wondered that writers of earlier times found it difficult to reconcile these instruments as the works of the same hands as found in the maker's other periods.

Illustrations depict both types of wood above described. Con-cerning the broad flamed type of maple, Arthur W. Dykes, in the October, 1927 issue of *The Strad*, remarked it to have been "the matured choice of the Cremonese giants," but whether this can be accepted as final must remain a matter of opinion. Surely, the maple of small figuration, such as will be found depicted in the *ex* Hamma violin of 1765, the *ex* Millant of 1770, and the *ex* Zamustin of 1771, loses nothing by comparison nor does it in acoustic properties. The three examples mentioned clearly show cuttings from the same log. Others, in which some of the same wood was employed, show less even distribution of the curls, an instance being found in the *ex* Brusset violin of 1770; this has the further characteristic of a sap line running lengthwise along the middle joint, a fault in growth which has been remarked in certain of the instruments produced by Stradivari, as well as by Guarneri, Bergonzi, and others of the classic school of Cremona.

TABULATION

VIOLINS

1759*   *ex* Merton. This violin passed from the possession of H. B. Merton to W. E. Hill & Sons. Later in the Wurlitzer collection it is described in the 1925 catalog as "one of the finest examples we have seen by this celebrated maker. It is without a crack or a blemish, almost like new." The instrument bears out the quoted words, and recalls the style of the maker at Milan. It has a two piece back of handsome figure; the varnish is of a golden-orange color. Joseph Gorner, of Chicago, is the owner.

1759*   Originally inscribed with the date 1759, the figure "5" was altered to read "3," probably to bring it in accord with erroneous recordings. American owners were Otto K. Baumann, and later Dr. Eugenio Sturchio; present location not known.

1760*   *ex* Hoevel. This violin was long in the possession of the late Heinrich Hoevel, who was born at Bonn on the Rhine, June 22, 1864. After study at the Cologne Conservatory, he came to the United States and settled in Minneapolis, where he joined the

A Violin by
J. B. GUADAGNINI
Parma, 1760
ex Wanamaker–Caressa

Minneapolis Symphony and became a faculty member of the MacPhail School of Music. This famous school was founded early in this century by William McPhail, a Scottish violinist, pupil of Sevcik. Hoevel also wrote on subjects pertaining to the violin, including such works as "The Cremona Violin," "Bach's Violin Music," "Modern French Chamber Music," etc. This violin was bought from him by the renowned Richard Czerwonky, of Chicago, whose death occurred April 16, 1949.

1760* A large half-size violin, an original work of J. B. Guadagnini with the exception of the head. It was formerly in possession of the late Vatelot-Hekking, a dealer of Paris, and was acquired by Erich Lachmann who brought it to this country where it passed to Wurlitzer. Authentic works of small size by the great masters are very scarce.

1760 Plates in *The Strad*, issue of March 1918, with an accompanying article by Towry Piper, picture this attractive violin. At that time it was owned by Mr. A. Tibble, who had purchased it from the dealer Arthur Beare, of London. The instrument has a two piece back of broad figured maple, and the varnish was described as a lustrous red.

1760* *ex* Keller. Once in the possession of the English dealer Hesketh of Manchester. In 1923 it was acquired by Wurlitzer. Through the intermediary of the late O. H. Bryant, of Boston, Harrison Keller of that city became the owner. In 1947 he sold it to Alfred Krips, of the Boston Symphony Orchestra. It is a handsome specimen, with two piece back and orange varnish.

1760* *ex* Wanamaker. An amateur player of Paris formerly owned this violin before it passed to Albert Caressa, from whom it was acquired for the Wanamaker interests. It was one of the items of the collection at the time it was purchased by Wurlitzer. The present owner is Charles Jones, of Oakland, California. *(Illustrated)*

1761* *ex* Hart-Wanamaker. The second of two quite exceptional works of the maker contained in the Wanamaker Collection when it

A Violin by
J. B. GUADAGNINI
Parma, 1761
ex Wanamaker–Hart

passed to Wurlitzer. It had been acquired from Hart & Son, in 1927, by Wanamaker. In 1943 Jay C. Rosenfeld, of Pittsfield, Massachusetts, purchased it from the Wurlitzer Company. *(Illustrated)*

1761 *ex* Aranyi. Emil Herrmann sold this violin, an outstanding example of the period, to Francis Aranyi, in 1930. It passed later to Max Möller, of Amsterdam, Holland. This present location is not known.

1761* This fine concert violin, formerly owned by Benno Rabinof, was acquired by him from the Wurlitzer Collection, to which it was subsequently returned. It is listed in the 1937 bulletin of that collection.

1763* *ex* Lamiraux. This violin was formerly owned by Madame Helene Lamiraux. Emil Herrmann acquired possession in February, 1930, and sold it to L. H. Maywood, of Suison, California, in April, 1931. It has a two piece back of small figured wood, with sides and head matching. The varnish is of dark brown color.

1765* A violin of the Milan type was owned by the late Bernard Sinsheimer. The two piece back shows broad figure, and the varnish is of deep red-brown color.

1765 *ex* Hamma. The plates evidence the remarkably fresh condition of this specimen. It was purchased and brought to this country by N. E. Posner. The small figured maple, to be found in many of the later Parma violins is here used, and a daintier pattern is also shown, as well as the protruding finale twist of the scroll. *(Illustrated)*

1765 At one time in the collection of Lyon & Healy, and listed in their catalogue of 1913-14, this violin is described as in exceptional preservation, with rich red varnish.

1766* *ex* Krasner. This typical example with back of small grained curly maple, and varnish of reddish brown color, was once owned by

A Violin by
J. B. GUADAGNINI
Parma, 1765
ex Hamma

174

Louis Krasner, and passed to Royal K. Johnson of the Chicago Symphony. It is now in the possession of Leo Michuda of Chicago.

1766 The Lyon & Healy catalogue of 1929 lists this violin as in their collection at the time; it is described as having a handsomely figured one piece back and golden brown varnish.

1766* Formerly in the possession of Maucotel & Deschamp, Parisian dealers, Wurlitzer sold this specimen to the late Roderic Meakle, of Ridgewood, New Jersey, in 1926. Emil Herrmann sold the violin subsequently to Harold Ayers. The back is of small figured curly maple, and the varnish is reddish-brown in color.

1767 Mentioned in a brochure published by Wurlitzer in 1917, and according to the information contained therein, this violin was formerly in the possession of Count de Joybert, a famous art collector of Paris (1857), some of whose paintings are said to be hung in the Louvre.

1767 Bought from W. E. Hill & Sons in 1928, this very fine example was brought to America by Wurlitzer. The varnish is of golden-brown color, and the two piece back is of slab cut maple showing broad flames extending downwards from the joint.

1767 Wurlitzer sold this violin in San Francisco in 1935. It also came from Hill & Sons. The two piece back is of curly maple of somewhat irregular figure, the wood of the sides and head of similar character, and the varnish is of golden-brown color.

1767 ex Corbin. A violin that was in 1930 in the collection of Alfred O. Corbin of New York. It was later in the possession of Philip Williams and lastly C. M. Carlson.

1767 The Lyon & Healy catalogue of 1921 lists this instrument as then in their collection, and describes it as having wood of handsome figure and varnish of orange-red color.

1767* ex James. Illustrated in The Strad, issue of July, 1945, this work was then owned by Eric R. Dale of Nelson, Lancashire. A cer-

A Violin by
J. B. GUADAGNINI
Parma, 1767
ex James

tificate issued by W. E. Hill & Sons to Miss Ethel James of Oxford, dated December 12th, 1938, attests the authenticity of this finely preserved specimen. The varnish is of a dark nut-brown color. In the Lewis Collection at the time of this recording. *(Illustrated)*

1768   A violin formerly in the collection of Lyon & Healy, and listed in their catalogue of 1913-14, described as being made of choice selection of wood, the varnish a rich brown color.

1768   *ex* Posner. Pictured in four views in the Hamma book. Nathan E. Posner acquired possession during one of his trips to Europe, and while there, sold it to Hamma & Company, from whom it passed to Georg Rauer of Vienna. *(Illustrated)*

1769* An excellent specimen, illustrated in *The Strad,* issue of November 1938, at which time the violin was owned by Ralph P. Powell. It was subsequently sold by him in this country. The back is in two pieces, the wood marked by a figure of medium width of grain, and the varnish is dark red-brown.

1769   The Möller book illustrates a violin of this date, typical of the period in form and arching. The small figured curly maple used in the back shows some of the grain in each side slanting upwards from left to right, in the same direction. It was in the possession of Ferdinand Helmann at the time of Möller's writing.

1769   This instrument is pictured in the Herrmann catalogues of 1926-27, and 1927-28. It offers interesting comparison with the aforementioned Helmann example; the maple is of similar grain, with the difference that in the back the figure slants downward from left to right in each of the two parts of the back. Erich Lachmann acquired the violin in 1922 from a retired army officer, Hauptman Merter, and it was subsequently chosen by Professor Willy Hess for his then pupil Tossy Spivakovsky, who retained it for several years.

1769* *ex* Kingman. A fine specimen which was purchased in 1922 of Hills by A. Kingman of Montreal. It has a two piece back, and

A Violin by
J. B. GUADAGNINI
Parma, 1768
ex Posner

178

a fine covering of red-brown varnish. The violin was brought to Chicago and eventually was purchased by William Lewis & Son in 1939. Milton Cherry acquired possession in 1940.

1770* This violin, formerly in the early collection maintained by Erich Lachmann, was brought by him to America in 1925. The following year it was purchased by Mrs. E. W. Wescott.

1770* *ex* Caressa. Erich Lachmann bought this violin of Albert Caressa and sold it to Dr. Fischer at Berlin in 1927, subsequently regaining ownership through an exchange of instruments. He brought it to this country; through Wurlitzer possession has passed through several owners and at the time of this recording the violin is in the collection of Rembert Wurlitzer.

1770* *ex* Millant. This violin, which was once in the collection of Roger and Max Millant of Paris, was brought to America in 1939. It is a typical work of the period in form of sound holes and scroll, as well as in the golden-orange varnish which plentifully covers it. William Lewis & Son sold it in 1944 to Nathan E. Posner, from whose possession it passed to Theodore Marchetti, in 1947. Now owned by George Brooks. *(Illustrated)*

1770* *ex* Silvestre & Maucotel. In many respects, this violin is a counterpart of the "Millant" specimen as to model, sound holes, varnish and figure of the maple in the two piece back. Margaret DeLong Tearse owned it prior to its sale by Kenneth Warren to Edward E. Cramer. In the collection of Frank J. Callier at the time of this recording.

1770* *ex* Brusset. This instrument is shown in two views in the Wurlitzer catalogue of 1931. It was formerly owned by Mr. Brusset of London, and through Hills passed to Wurlitzer, who then sold it to Gaylord Yost in 1944. In 1946, through the intermediary of George Humphrey of the Boston Symphony Orchestra and John A. Gould & Son, Mr. Yost disposed of the violin to Willis Munro of Boston. *(Illustrated)*

A Violin by
J. B. GUADAGNINI
Parma, 1770
ex Millant

A Violin by
J. B. GUADAGNINI
Parma, 1770
ex Brusset

181

A VIOLIN BY

J. B. GUADAGNINI

PARMA, 1770

ex Chappey

1770° *ex* Kochanski. One of two Guadagninis once owned by the eminent violinist, Paul Kochanski, this fine example was sold by Emil Herrmann to the Juilliard School of Music. It has been heard in concert by many of our American audiences when played upon by the brilliant young artist, Carroll Glenn.

1770   A fine violin of this date is in the joint possession of Mrs. Nellie W. Olds and Miss Mary Baack. It was acquired from private owners through the intermediary of Oswald Schilbach of New York. The back is in one piece of handsomely figured maple, and the varnish is of a golden-brown color.

1770* *ex* Madame Chappey. This violin was formerly in possession of a Parisian player of the name; certified by Vatelot-Hekking and Maucotel & Deschamp. Erich Lachmann bought the instrument in 1930 and sold it to Dr. Wolfgang Schütt in Berlin, regaining possession in an exchange. He brought the violin to the U. S. A., where it was acquired by Wurlitzer, and was illustrated in their 1931 catalogue. Roger Chittolini owned the instrument in 1944, and in December of that year, through Frank J. Callier, it was sold to Allen Wertz. *(Illustrated)*

1770   A characteristic work of the period this violin was sold by Hill to G. F. H. van Kooten Kok of Zeist, Holland, in 1920. Rembert Wurlitzer bought it in 1947 and through Kenneth Warren it was sold to A. A. Ward. It bears the original label of the maker, the terminal figure of the date apparently faded out. It has a back in two pieces of small figured wood and deep red-brown varnish.

1771° *ex* Steiner-Schweitzer. One of the last violins of the Parma period, and as the illustrations show, strikingly like the *ex* Posner of 1768, as well as the *ex* Millant of 1770. It had been once in possession of the Hills, passing to Hamma, to be then acquired by the late Dr. Steiner-Schweitzer of Zurich, Switzerland. Erich Lachmann brought it to America, and through Wurlitzer it was purchased by A. Zamustin in 1926. Subsequently it was again in Lachmann's possession through an exchange of instruments, and, taken by him to Vienna, it passed to Georg Rauer. The violin was

A Violin by
J. B. GUADAGNINI
Parma, 1771
ex Steiner—Schweitzer

brought back to the U. S. A. by K. Donald Hopf about 1940. It
is now owned by Robert Quick, formerly of the Chicago Symphony Orchestra, and at the time of this writing with the WGN
Symphony. *(Illustrated)*

VIOLONCELLOS

1759* A magnificent instrument which was for some years in the possession of Professor Lennart von Zweygberg, this cello was owned
by Ludwig Schneider of Zurich, Switzerland.

1759 This cello, formerly in the collection of Emil Herrmann, was purchased by Mrs. Cameron Baird.

1760 Previously in the Wurlitzer Collection, this cello is now privately
owned.

1760 A cello of the period was sold by Emil Herrmann to Max Baldner
of Berlin.

IGNAZIO ALESSANDRO COUNT COZIO DI SALABUE
*A portrait painted by an artist of Casale named Morera in 1831
when the Count was seventy-six years of age.*

PART VI

COUNT COZIO DI SALABUE

As it concerns Giovanni Battista Guadagnini, this narrative remains to be concluded with the telling of his career at Turin, where the remaining years of his life were to be passed. The epoch stands out as one of extraordinary significance in violin chronology as it introduces a personality ordained to intrigue the fancy of historians to this day.

Remarked upon at various points previously in these pages, this was the wealthy young Italian nobleman, Count Cozio di Salabue whose early fondness for the violin was accelerated during his acquaintance with Guadagnini to a degree which made of him an enthusiast, an avid collector and at a later day, the subject of encomium which, it is regrettable to note, has been attacked as not completely merited. His private records, long held safely immune to public eye but now known in their entirety, tell all the little that may be said against him. To him, whose love for fine violins moved him to accumulate them and write about their makers, our debt is considerable.

As the author of certain biographical sketches of Cremonese violin makers, he deserves recognition as having been one of the first to apply himself to that field, of such engrossing interest to votaries of the instrument. For reasons of expediency those paragraphs concerned with the Guadagnini family have been recorded earlier in this review. As has been there remarked, the notes were indited in 1823, many years after the death of his erstwhile protégé, Giovanni Battista Guadagnini, and though the Count kept meticulous records it is quite possible that in dictating the mentioned notes he depended on his memory, which, as he was at that time of age sixty-eight, may not have served him rightly or fully, therefore lacking much that he might have told about the maker had urgency required it to be ascertained.

Count Cozio apparently was not well known outside his Italian environment until in the later half of the last century. In the first edition of his work on the violin, George Hart, who had been gathering data for some years prior to its appearance in 1875, evidently was not informed of the Count's activities. His name does not appear in a long discourse on Luigi Tarisio, nor does Hart refer to him in mention of the famous "Messie" Stradivari violin of 1716, which had been one of Cozio's most cherished possessions while his enthusiasm for fine violins ran high and which Tarisio purchased from the Count's banker Carli in 1824. Hart mentions the violin only in relating the circumstances of Tarisio's death at Milan in 1854. Subsequent editions make amends for the omission with a lengthy tribute, sections of which lauding Count Cozio have since been quoted by later writers, notable by Federico Sacchi in his biography of the Count. I have previously remarked—in speaking about Cozio in our chapter on Cremona—that Hart was not unaware of the fact that the noble Count, at least as judged by the conduct of his agent Briatta, was at once earnest in the pursuit of his wishes as well as canny in his dealings to realize them, which neither Yankee nor Scotsman would find reason to cavil at.

The information thus given by Hart was obtained from documents which passed at the time, of which parts were also quoted in Hill's work on Stradivari. It appears that other matter existed of which much remained undivulged as Cozio's heirs, the Dalla Valle family, were unwilling that their relative's affairs, as noted in his voluminous records and diaries, should be exposed to public notice.

Among the records so preserved by the Marquis Dalla Valle, many had reference to his connection and dealings with Guadagnini, to which access was not permitted even to Cozio's ardent admirer and biographer Federico Sacchi as late as August, 1891. Before going more into detail on that topic, we should consider first the words of some of those who voiced approbation, appreciative of what Cozio stands for in his connection with our literature—a personality to whom we are indebted far more for what he did to enrich our story of the violin than, if censure is called for, the manner of its accomplishment.

FEDERICO SACCHI

Federico Sacchi's tribute to Count Cozio has been mentioned, which, edited by Towry Piper, was published at London in 1898. Piper wrote in his preface, directed to Count Cozio: "Had he done nothing else, his encouragement and support of the now world-famed Giovanni Battista Guadagnini—to whose rare merits such tardy recognition was accorded in other quarters—should be amply sufficient to preserve his name from oblivion." Sacchi quotes Hart relative to his remarks on Cozio as a collector of violins "which should be the representative of the work and character of each maker, and serve as models to those seeking to tread the path of the makers who made Cremona eminent as a seat of violin manufacture. Virtuosity emanating from a spirit of beneficence is somewhat rare. When, however, utility occupies a prominent place in the thoughts of the virtuoso, he becomes a benefactor. The virtuosity of Count Cozio was of this character." The notes which Count Cozio placed at Lancetti's disposition in 1823 did not reach the public until many years subsequent to their writing. They, among other papers, were left by Lancetti to his daughter, passing about 1845 (quoting from the Sacchi work) "into the hands of the learned historiographer of Cremona, Dr. Francesco Robolotti, who gave them unconditionally to us in 1867, to use as we deemed proper for the special illustration of this interesting chapter of Cremonese artistic history . . ."

The Sacchi memorial includes the following:—"It is not known whether young Cozio began the study of the violin during his college education, but it is certain that while still a young man he showed great interest in it; and in 1773 began to patronize Giovanni Battista Guadagnini.

"This excellent, and now famous maker, after working for many years in Piacenza, Milan, and Parma, had established himself, in the year 1772, in Turin but owing to his numerous family, and the competition and jealousy of native makers, his slender resources were soon exhausted, and the worst might have befallen him had not his critical position been brought by some charitable person to the Count's knowledge. . . . Count Cozio states that between the years 1773 and 1776 he constantly supplied Guadagnini with work, and he adds that at the time of writing (in 1823) he had still in his possession all the instruments made by his protege, in their original condition. . . ."

We have here reiteration of the competition and jealousy theme, but, it should be noted, only as affecting the maker's first period at Turin. Strangely, nothing was contained in the Sacchi biography to tell of Guadagnini's *numerous* family. His first son, Giuseppe, born 1735, had long gone his own way; Gaetano, the second son, born 1745, therefore at Piacenza, is presumed to have been with his father at Turin and to have been his assistant during previous years, remaining at Turin and carrying on his work subsequent to the father's death. A third son, Lorenzo, recorded as Lorenzo II, evidently did not exert effort to follow his father's vocation. Other than these sons no mention is to be found about other members of the family in any notice known to this writer.

TOWRY PIPER

In addition to his able work as editor of the Sacchi memorial to Count Cozio, we are indebted to the late Towry Piper for numerous articles on the violin. One of his many contributions to the columns of *The Strad* was titled "A Famous Collector," and had as its theme Signor Sacchi's biographical sketch of Cozio; this was a feature article in the November, 1920 edition. As bearing on that period of J. B. Guadagnini's life involving the first years at Turin, I quote the following extract:

"Count Ignazio Alessandro Cozio di Salabue . . . succeeded to his father's title and estates at an early age, and was a mere lad of eighteen or so when in 1773 the case of Giovanni Battista Guadagnini was brought to his notice. Guadagnini, after many vicissitudes, had finally taken up his abode in Turin in the previous year, 1772. Things did not prosper with him there, owing if report says truly, to his quarrelsome nature; but whatever the cause it is certain that when introduced to Count Cozio the famous fiddle maker was reduced to the direst straits. Thenceforward, until sometime in 1776 the Count kept Guadagnini in constant employment, bought all or most of the instruments, and many years later had them still in his possession—about fifty of them—in their original state. The collection included violins, tenors, and violoncellos, and the Count, writing in 1823, described these instruments as being fit to compare, for tone and power, with the best Cremonese masterpieces. . . ."

COUNT COZIO DI SALABUE'S ANNOUNCEMENTS
OFFERING HIS COLLECTION OF INSTRUMENTS FOR SALE
(Reproduced from the original edition of Hill's book on Stradivari)

ADVERTISING

In Hill's work on Stradivari (1902), directly following the remark that many violin fanciers must have indulged the hobby of collecting fine specimens and the statement that "unfortunately no one deemed it worth while to chronicle their existence," we read: "Count Cozio di Salabue appears to have been the first really ardent admirer of Stradivari's works, and we learn from his correspondence that in 1775 he purchased *en bloc* from Paolo Stradivari no fewer than eleven violins—in fact, all that remained in the hands of the family of those left by the great maker at his death. From an inventory of the Count's instruments made in Milan in 1808, we learn that he still retained, among other violins, five by Stradivari, including the 'Messie.' The troubled times in Italy, caused by the French invasion, had in 1800 forced the Count to realise some of his possessions; and his printed announcement in both French and English, which we give,* will be read with interest. . . ."

The printed announcements mentioned are reproduced herewith and it will be noted that there were included instruments by "John Baptist Guadagnini" (in the English), "Jean Baptiste Guadagnini" (in the French), thus using the Anglicized and French forms of the Italian "Giovanni Battista Guadagnini."

As will be divulged by the correspondence of Cozio's agents Briatta & Co., a campaign of advertising had been conducted as early as 1775!

It is fitting at this point to recall that in our chapter concerning Guadagnini's period at Cremona in 1758, there was mention of an article that appeared in *The Strad,* issue of May, 1935. Al-

---

*The words "which we give" are found also in the 1909 reprinted edition of the Hill book, but the plates illustrating the announcements, here pictured, are not included.

though the extract from the said note previously quoted was directed to the maker at Cremona, there was more in another paragraph, directed to his Turin epoch, the reputed connection with the workshop of Stradivari, and Count Cozio; this reads as follows:

"Towards the end of his life J. B. Guadagnini describes himself on his labels as a pupil of Stradivari; this in the strict sense of the term is inaccurate as there is not the vestige of evidence that he ever worked or had received instruction from the master at Cremona. Possibly owing to the help and assistance . . . that he received through the good offices of Count Cozio, who was his friend and admirer, he considered himself entitled to add this qualification to his labels. It is quite certain that had he at any time been a personal pupil of Stradivari that Count Cozio would have left us record of the fact, and again as additional evidence against this it would surely not have been necessary for his patron to have handed him information regarding Stradivari's working methods."

FRANZ FARGA

In our chapter devoted to Cremona extracts from Renzo Bacchetta's book on Stradivari were mentioned to have appeared in the writings of Georges Hoffmann in French and German versions, and Franz Farga's in German. The last mentioned composed a well presented story, attractively put out by Albert Müller at Zurich, Switzerland, in 1940, under the title *Geigen und Geiger* (Violins and Violinists). It contains some excellent illustrations among which a violin by J. B. Guadagnini, Piacenza, 1744, another by Lorenzo Guadagnini, Piacenza, 1743, and one named as a work at Cremona, no date mentioned. However, the text remarking these makers is faulty, reiterating errors such as: "From Piacenza Giambattista removed to Milan. To him and his brother Lorenzo, together with the dynasty Testore, is the distinction of having made the best Milan violins." Farga also exhibits delinquence in telling his readers that Guarneri del Gesù was a son of Giovanni Battista (a brother of Andrea), and only *possibly* a pupil of Giuseppe (son of Andrea), who it is now conceded was actually the father of del Gesù, but to whom Farga refers as his uncle. In the face of such and other misstatements contained in a present-day treatise it would seem permissible to question the reliability of such published matter therein that pretends to throw discredit on Count Cozio, although what he relates in that connection originated with Bacchetta.

Signor Bacchetta may be depended upon to have closely studied the documents contained in the Dalla Valle collection of Count Cozio's residue. His book of 1937 must therefore assume a place of great importance in the literature of the violin. Indicating the scope of the work, various letters that passed at the time Count Cozio acquired possession of the equipment of Stradivari's shop are presented, translated from the originals as transcribed for publication in his book.

CORRESPONDENCE BETWEEN PAOLO AND ANTONIO STRADIVARI AND
COUNT COZIO'S AGENTS

It is a great misfortune that we cannot know what actually transpired during those first years of Guadagnini's acquaintance with Count Cozio. The latter was a young man of seventeen when they met: it has been said that he was already possessed of a desire to collect violins and that his agents (Sacchi wrote "some charitable person") directed his attention to the precarious situation of the aging violin maker. How much truth there is to be granted that assertion must remain a matter for theorists to ponder.

It has been variously written that Count Cozio acquired the remaining number of Stradivari violins in Paolo's possession in the year 1775. Federico Sacchi stated that Cozio's ambition was ". . . to collect masterpieces which might in some measure be the means of recovering a lost art. With this end in view he began, in 1775, with the assistance of a Casalese firm of cloth merchants, Messrs. Anselmi di Briatta, to form his collection, and in a couple of years had succeeded in obtaining from Stradivari's son Paolo, and from his grandson Antonio, over ten violins, together with the moulds, forms, models, and tools still in the possession of the great master's family; also instruments by Francesco and Omobono Stradivari, and violins belonging to various private persons in Cremona. These masterpieces formed a nucleus of the great store of instruments which, after a few years of continuous labour and research, he contrived to bring together. The number of violins, tenors, and violoncellos alluded to in Count Cozio's Memoir . . . furnishes ample evidence of the magnitude of the collection, and though the death of Guadagnini in Turin in September, 1786, may have deprived him of an able adviser in the acquisition of further treasures, he seems to have never ceased from making additions to his specimens whenever an opportunity presented itself."

RENZO BACCHETTA

Renzo Bacchetta's study of documents preserved at the Civic Museum in Cremona found nothing to substantiate claims that Guadagnini worked for Stradivari. There is said to be evidence that Count Cozio first entertained the idea of founding a school of violin making at Turin in 1773 and that already in that year had acquired through his agents, the cloth dealers Anselmi Briatta & Company, nine violins by Antonio Stradivari and three by Francesco Stradivari. Signor Bacchetta has transcribed a number of letters of a period from 1775 and 1776 (others of earlier dating probably no longer available) which exhibit shrewd business procedure, pertaining in their content to a great extent with the purchase of Stradivari's shop equipment, showing that consummation of the transfer was many months in fulfilment.

Some parts of these letters have appeared in earlier books. Sacchi's work quotes several, transcribed for him, as said, by the Marquis Dalla Valle who wrote under date of November 30th, 1883, that according to promise he did so, but only in furnishing simply the gist of their contents. These will appear in the letters numbered 3, 7, 11, 14 and 22 to follow. It should be noted that several historians have erred in quoting the letters under the date of 1776, as well as naming that year as the one in which Paolo Stradivari died (an error to which I must confess in the narrative "How Many Strads?"). Comparison of the earlier quotations from the correspondence under discussion with that of the version here to be given will show many variations in telling, due no doubt to Dalla Valle's more modern construction when copying from the originals. A striking inconsistency will be found in the third letter as here presented: Dalla Valle no doubt correctly named the figure *ventotto* giliati, whereas Bacchetta has it *centotto,* a seemingly simple error but as in the Italian the first named means 28 (as quoted in earlier works) and the second means 108 giliati, the vital significance of the use of the *c* instead of the *v* becomes apparent. It will be noted that two versions of the Briatta firm name appear, sometimes in that form and again as Briata.

$$\left[\,1\,\right]$$

Reading the first of the letters, we find that Count Cozio had, through Guadagnini, been carrying on negotiations for the acquisition of several instruments. Expressed in the vernacular of the time we find oddities of speech, given here as nearly true to the original as translation permits. It should be noted that Paolo Stradivari demands payment in giliati "of the correct weight," indicating that the value of the gold coin varied according to weight.

To Gio. Batta Guadagnini, maker of instruments, Turin:

March 2, 1775. Cremona

In regard to the viola d'amore, I cannot let you have it for the price that you have offered me, while if I ever decide to give it to you for 12 giliati, there is a person in Cremona who would pay me the money for a nobleman of Parma, who, three months ago was in Cremona to see it and try it, and tried to pay it to me. In a letter after going back home, he wrote to another nobleman, friend of his, that he would try again with me if I would finally consider letting him have it, but I told him no; finally two weeks ago he came back to find out if I had the notion to give it to him, but I would not want to accept, as it is a most beautiful and most perfect instrument, and before leaving, he told me that at any time that I took a notion, I should bring it to him and he would promptly pay the 12 giliati, nevertheless I could not possibly consent. In respect to the two violins of Father S. Sigismondo, again I have had a conference with professors of the violin, and particularly Galli, a man of complete honesty and a true Christian, and everyone of them assured me that both of those came from the Amatis. . . . Finally he accepted 3 giliati as a deposit in escrow, on account of 40, and a contract was made showing that such violins have their protective cases, which he did not want to include, but finally he released them also in that contract; therefore, you will favor me to pay out 40 giliati of the correct weight to sig. Domenico Dupuy & Sons, our correspondent, and he will give us credit for it, and when we hear from sig. Dupuy himself that he has given us credit, we will get the two violins with their boxes, and then you will pay over 2 giliati more which will serve for the extra expenses which occur when shipping the same.

PAOLO STRADIVARI.

$$[\ 2\ ]$$

This letter, dated April 22nd, 1775, suggests that Count Cozio had at about that time decided to enlarge his activities in the violin field by engaging, through Briatta, in selling as well as accumulating. Capable of differing interpretation, the allusion to the young "professor" whom they could not "find," might well indicate young Count Cozio whom they could not designate.

To Paolo Stradivari in Cremona:

April 22, 1775.

You shall receive here enclosed a list of merchants in Turin, just as I promised you in my last letter. In regard to the professor who has left me the commission to enter the market, it has not been possible to find him, being yet too young, but otherwise, if you happen to have the occasion, I will do all that is possible, and therefore, before you undertake obligations to some other dealer, let me know it first. I beg you again for a ready answer to what I wrote you in my letter of April 1st, and to do me also the favor to tell Father Ravizza Sicismondo that I expect an answer from him to my last letter. Then, I am awaiting some of you to reply. I declare myself respectfully at your disposal.

GIOVANNI MICHELE BRIATTA & COMPANY.

$$[\ 3\ ]$$

The following letter is one that was quoted in part by Hart and others as containing Paolo's wish that no part of his father's shop residue should remain in Cremona; what he writes in this letter infers that for 28 (*ventotto*, which Bacchetta read centotto) giliati "all," including the forms etc., etc., was available provided everything was removed from the city. A subsequent letter indicates that the amount demanded by Paolo for the parts was in the sum of eight giliati and it seems, therefore, that the larger sum here mentioned included some other items, perhaps violins, as reference is made to two letters written in November, therefore in 1774. It should be remarked that the allusion to "dutchmen" was not in a manner intended as offensive or derogatory but as a common expression of the time applied to residents of the northern low countries of Europe. Paolo's reference to "quite a few" instruments by Stradivari should have caused him to recognize the "young fellow" as Count Cozio unless he remained uninformed of the identity of the actual buyer of his father's instruments, which appears highly improbable.

To Giovanni Michele di Briatta & Co., Casale:

Cremona, May 4, 1775.

Of my two letters (of November), I told you in the first that all those forms and measures and utensils and tools which I happen to have, I would have no difficulty at all to give to you, providing they are not present in Cremona. You will recall the tools I let you see and also the box of measures, in any event, all that I find will be at your service, and I will give you everything for centotto giliati.* A few days ago there happened to come to see me two dutchmen, who wanted two violins from Stradivari, and on hearing from me that I did not have any, they left very disappointed. In the meantime I mentioned you to them, and I took note of their name, surname and town, but they would not say anything else to me. I told them that you could furnish them with instruments of several makers, and those of Stradivari you had quite a few. In regard to the second letter, I did not find enclosed any list of mer-

---

* Early excerpts, as supplied by Dalla Valle, end at this point. The same portion as well as other short excerpts appear in Alfonso Mandelli's "Notice to Antonio Stradivari," published at Milan in 1903.

*chants. I have already told signor Morandi all that you had written
to me for the young fellow whom you say is to conduct [business?]
at Turin. I have spoken to signor Stefanoni to whom I sold my viola,
but he would not deprive himself for any kind of price.*

PAOLO STRADIVARI.

$$[\,4\,]$$

In the following letter it will be noted that Briatta mentions
a sum of *otto* (8) giliati and as this letter was not, apparently,
released by Dalla Valle, Sacchi and others naturally concluded
that the sum of twenty-eight giliati mentioned in letter No. 3
had reference only to Stradivari's shop residue and thus remarked upon, leaving the inference that Briatta made an offer
of five for property priced at twenty-eight giliati. We read,
also, that the firm was henceforth to be regarded as sellers as
well as buyers of instruments and that it should become so ad-
vertised in order that, as the letter closes, "we can find some
sales."

To Paolo Stradivari:

Casale, May 15, 1775.

*In the absence of G. M. di Briatta, my companion, I have received
on the 1st of the current month, by which having understood that
you would return [deliver] to me all of the forms, both those of the
violin and violoncello, being four of the first and three of the second,
and of the violas, which your deceased father had been using. Also
those which he had loaned to the Bergonzis, with all of the tools
and measures through the payment of 8 giliati. So, if you want to
release them to me, I offer you 5 giliati, at your order, providing
that you have them packed and ship them to whom I shall indicate
later. In regard to the two dutchmen who desire some of your violins, it will be a pleasure to me if you will send their names and country. Pardon me for not sending to you the list of merchants, but I
left it in error on the desk, and now you shall receive them. Do me
the favor to let your best correspondents know of our business
location, assuring them of the perfection of these instruments, so
we can find some sales.*

G. M. DI ANSELMI BRIATTA.

$$\begin{bmatrix} 5 \end{bmatrix}$$

According to the following letter, Paolo Stradivari still had a violin of his father's work in his possession.

Sig. Michele di Anselmi Briatta. Casale.

S. Sigismondo Cremona, May 15, 1775.

> *I have received the various letters of your honor of the tenth current month, from which I learn that you had never received my letter of April 25th, sent to Turin. Nevertheless, I reply in the present by telling you that Sig. Spagnoletti, for his violin of Nicola Amati, represents as his best and last price 35 Giliati. The merchant Righetti, for his violin of the Amatis, with a scroll by another artisan, wants 16 Giliati. The violin of Stradivari which Sig. Paolo Stradivari owns, I can assure you at the price of 10 Giliati, and not 12 as you have written me. The violin of the painter Boroni, which is from Nicola Amati, I can guarantee for 12 Giliati, so that you may dispose for the two violins one of Stradivari and the other of the Amati. Two of the violins which I have acquired from Andrea Guarneri, the first for 10 Giliati and the second, because it is a most perfect instrument that sounds like a trumpet, they want 18 Giliati as the least they will take.*

DON IDELFONSO RAVIZZA.

$$\begin{bmatrix} 6 \end{bmatrix}$$

Here we find signs of an expanding activity in the sale of instruments. It has not heretofore been recorded that Cozio had caused Briatta to advertise and the effort to dispose of some was no doubt to rid himself of specimens not found of sufficient interest to retain in his private collection. Elsewhere I have included advertising mentioning him by name, of a later period.

To Signori Boch & Gravier, merchants in Dora Grossa in Turin:

Casale, May 23, 1775.

> *I have reached Casale; I will write you again to recommend the business of which we had an understanding on my departure from*

*Turin, that is to say for you to write to all your best correspondents
in foreign cities, especially Paris, London and Vienna, and send the
advertisements I sent you, and ask them, these merchants, to take
an interest in disposing of my merchandise. And also inform them
to facilitate in everything the means and security for the purchasers
in their respective cities. I hope you will take this trouble and shall
be very grateful to you; and as I have already told you before my
departure, if someone wishes to be served with the instruments he
keeps in his shop, advise the price and I will refer to them without
a corresponding assurance, and in case they shall ask for other
manufacturers, you shall write to me and we will be able to supply
them.*

GIOVANNI MICHELE DI ANSELMI BRIATTA.

$$\left[\; 7 \;\right]$$

An excerpt from the letter here quoted was one of Dalla
Valle's transcriptions published in Sacchi's work. Of particular interest in this letter is Paolo's reference to recent acquisition by Briatta of a number of his father's instruments, suggest-
ing that he was not informed that Cozio had been the actual
purchaser.

To Signor Michele Anselmi Briatta:

*Turin, near Casalmonferrato.
June 4, 1775, Cremona.*

*I see from your acceptable letter of the 13th past the offer of 5
giliati for all the forms and models which I have including those that
I have loaned to Bergonzi, and also the precision tools of my deceased father; but it is too little; nevertheless, to let you see the
eagerness which I have to serve you, and so that nothing may be left
in Cremona, not a thing of my father's, I will let you have them for
6 giliati, on condition that right away you will pay into the hands
of sig. Domenico Dupuij & Sons, makers of silk stockings, and I
will ship all those things on condition that I will retain the 5 giliati,
and for the other one make use of it for the expense of the cases
and baling, and payment of tariff for the shipping which is necessary to send the merchandise to you. And what will be left over, I
shall return it by sig. Dupuij, or if you wish, you may pay sig. Dupuij
7 giliati and I will stand all of the expense and besides I will send*

you two bows of serpentino [snakewood] *which I have.** Sig. Boroni has come to see me while Father Ravizza was in Venice, but
he had to leave very soon and he told me to write to you that the
contract for his violin has already been established, and for it he
will not accept a reduction in 11 giliati, but that if you will pay
that to sig. Dupuij, he will promptly consign the violin to him on
your order. And so I will address and consign the above things
just as your order was. There has come through Cremona an English person of rank who wishes two violins of Stradivari. I did not
have the heart to ask his name and surname, but I told him of you
and that you play [handle] as an amateur instruments of all of the
most renowned makers. Having given to him your name, surname
and town, that is, Casale, and he inquired of me if you had those
of Stradivari, and I told him that you have many of them, as it is
a very short time since I sold them to you. And he said that he was
soon to be in Turin, and he will be looking for you and ask directions of sig. Dupuij, I having mentioned to him that I would write
to you.*

PAOLO STRADIVARI.

$$\left[\; 8 \; \right]$$

Pertaining to advertising and circulars, posting of announcements to proclaim Briatta's purpose to sell to amateurs and at
the same time asking for information where violins both old
and new could be purchased!

To Padre D. Sicismondo Ravizza in Venice:

Casale, June 10, 1775.

*Having an understanding with sig. Paolo Stradivari to whom I
have given commission to answer my last letter of May 25th past
because of his leaving for Venice right away, I send here enclosed
those circulars in order to make known in that city the nature of
my business, which announcements I beg of you to expose in the
most public places; also I beg of you to notify in person those prac-
ticing the art as amateurs, in order to obtain some sales. Will you
do me the favor to inquire regarding old violins of good makers, or
if not old, modern ones, and in everything give me a list of these
new ones, and when you come back, make a complete answer to my
last written letters.*

GIOVANNI M. BRIATTA.

---

* Dalla Valle's excerpt ends at this point.

$$\left[\; 9 \;\right]$$

A letter indicating that the deal for the Stradivari shop residue had not been completed. Also expressing desire to make
further purchases of instruments.

To Paolo Stradivari.

June 10, 1775.

    *I understand from your last letter of the 4th current month that
you have been satisfied with the 6 giliati for all of the forms and
tools which belonged to your father. The money will be paid by
the 15th of this month to the Signori Dupuij, and you will send to
him in Turin the case with my address. In regard to the Amati violin
of sig. Boroni, the painter, I answer that if he is not pressed for the
money that about the end of the month it shall be paid, otherwise
right away, and then get a receipt for the money, so send the violin
on in its case as quickly as possible for a safe delivery. For all the
rest, I thank you, and you will also communicate with all the foreigners and give them my name, and as I explain this enclosed bill . . .
from sig. Dupuij.*

    *Do me the favor to write to your correspondents in Mantua to
find out if they can find some violins of Stradivari or Amati, or any
other good maker, or if any of them would be willing to buy, and
also inquire if in that city there is to be found a certain signor cavaliere Fondu who has a famous violin of Stradivari, and that of Mauro
d'Aloy, and find out if he wants to sell and for what price, and the
quality of the instrument.*

GIOVANNI ANSELMI DI BRIATTA.

$$\left[\; 10 \;\right]$$

Briatta, as found in this letter, has appointed an agent to
handle the sale of instruments at Turin.

*To Signor Domenico Luigi and son Anselmo
under the porches of the Fair of Torino:*

Casale, June 11, 1775.

    *I gather from signor Paolo Stradivari, of Cremona, your corre-
spondent, and mine also, that an Englishman came to see him look-*

ing for two violins by Antonio Stradivari, his father, and who not having any, had this Englishman to pass by Turin and gave him the address of this shop as it is easier to find there at Turin, as I am not to be here, having business in another city. That Englishman or any other person who might ask for me, can spend time with pleasure in the Dora Grossa with Signori Boch & Gravier, with whom we are still maintaining instruments which are ready to be sold.

G. M. DI BRIATTA.

$$\left[11 \right]$$

Another of the letters from which an excerpt was furnished by Dalla Valle for Sacchi's tribute to Count Cozio. The larger portion of the message from Paolo, not transcribed by Dalla Valle, presents an unmistakable feeling of doubt and distrust of Briatta's methods of procedure.

To Signor Gio. Michele Anselmi di Briatta & Co.
Turin, near Casale Monferrato.

June 25, 1775. Cremona.

In answer to your acceptable letter of the 10th past, sig. Boroni says that when he hears that the money has been paid to sig. Dupuij according to our agreement, that he will give me the violin, so I shall not have difficulty to accommodate it in the same box with the forms, utensils and other gadgets left by my father, and tools and measures which I happen to have,* according to our understanding. But you will have to consider how much expense I will be obligated for in consigning that violin, and it will cost me much more for a secure baling that must be done in order to insure the safety of this instrument, and although you may complain of it, this baling must not carry the forms. The reverend Father Ravizza tells me that he has not received any of your letters, although he has made a contract for the violins, and says that he is out the escrow money because of your order. But he would not like to make a bad impression by questioning your honorable contract made by your order; also that the other violin of Stradivari, I am having a little trouble in getting it for 10 giliati with an escrow of giliati in

---

* Dalla Valle's excerpt ends at this point.

order to keep our word. And therefore, this Father tells that after having given you a favor, he doesn't think that he should sacrifice any of his own money or put himself to any inconvenience. I have received on the 4th a printed receipt which explains much, but it fails to state the most necessary things, the address, the country and city where he lives, and might be the store of Boch & Gravier. Sig. Fondu, cavaliere which you mentioned to me, I believe he lives in Parma and not in Mantua. While when I sold him the violin he was living in Parma, he gave me an order for another one, and later on I learned that he acquired also the one of sig. Ranvino Dalaij which had been sold years before by my brother Francesco. I also will write to Mantua in order to get information, and will later let you know by letter.

Stradivario Paolo.

P. S. I shall await your meeting the major expense which will bring the case of baling in order to put together the forms and tools and models; and the violin of sig. Boroni I will put with the other one which has been held in escrow by your order to Father Ravizza.

$$\left[\,12\,\right]$$

Again pertaining to the purchase of the Stradivari shop fittings, including also instruments, bringing a total of twenty-seven giliati, six of which for the fittings, the balance for two violins, thus approximating the sum previously subject of remark.

To Pavolo Stradivari:

Casale, July 4, 1775

In answer to your last letter of the 25th, having to put the violins in the case with the utensils will cause a larger expense. For that reason you will have to make a case for the purpose, and put in the violin of sig. Boroni and the Stradivari for the merchant Righetti, well made, strong and sealed, and you will put them in the case with the utensils, and you will also allow for the expenses to me. I write on this subject to Father Ravizza, not knowing whether he has returned from Venice. I am sorry that in the receipt that I sent you for my store they forgot the name of the city and the store in Torino. At any time I can get this order, sig. Dupuij will be paid 6 giliati for the utensils, 11 giliati for the violin of sig.

Boroni, and 10 giliati for the violin of sig. Righetti by Antonio Stradivari, which makes the sum of 27 giliati. As soon as you receive this, send quickly all of this with my address to sig. Dupuij.

GIOVANNI MICHELE DI ANSELMI BRIATTA.

P.S. The money for the two violins I shall pay to don Ravizza.

$$\left[13 \right]$$

An Amati violin is brought to the attention of Briatta. More in connection with this instrument appears in subsequent correspondence.

To Signor Gio. di Anselmi Briatta & Company, Casalmonferrato:

Cremona, July 6, 1775.

We have come across a violin of the Amatis of large form, intact as if it were new, without fault, and very well polished and tight, of a beautiful tone of ready response, and with an original label: "Nicolaus Amatius Cremonien Hieronimi fillij Antoni Nepos fecit anno 1656" for which is asked 40 giliati with its own box. It is beautiful and well made.

GIUSEPPE MORANDI.

$$\left[14 \right]$$

This letter is the fourth found in Sacchi's work, presented in full without substantial change. Paolo has been paid twenty-seven giliati but finds that he had underestimated the number of things he had to pack and therefore found it best to use separate casing. He asks for shipping instructions.

To Signor Giovanni di Anselmi Briatta,
Turin, near Casalmonferrato:

Cremona, July 10, 1775.

From sig. Dupuij we have received the 27 giliati paid by you on my account as you told me in yours of the 4th current month, and therefore we shall advise Father Ravizza, and have already fixed up everything with sig. Boroni, only I shall tell you that I did not know that I had so many things as I found, and they would make the case very heavy by reason of the quantity of the forms and tools, and therefore I am not putting them in the same case with the violin. I fear that because of the weight, they might carelessly throw the box on the floor without realizing that the violin in the case might suffer. And again I advise you beforehand that on these instruments and tools I will have to pay tariff, not very much, but will have to pay something, but this does not affect me, so you will advise the way of shipping, whether by Favarini of Piacenza or by waiting for the boat on the Po. According to your orders, I await your service.

PAOLO STRADIVARI.

$$\left[\ 15\ \right]$$

More about shipping instructions: also exhibiting concern regarding authenticity of the Amati violin mentioned in letter No. 13, also as to its qualities. Briatta evidently expected Paolo Stradivari to furnish names of potential customers for violins.

To Paolo Stradivari, Cremona:

July 16, 1775.

I have received yours of the 10th in which you tell me you have received the 27 gigliati from sig. Dupuij and that you will dispose of the money according to my past order. I understand that you hold things in readiness for the baling, but that your sentiment is not to put the two violins inside the case, so you will do well to make for them a strong box. If you wish, pay the charges, for which you will be reimbursed, and after all at most they come to very little, or almost nothing because these things are not new. In regard to the shipping, make the case for the two violins well sealed, and send by some reliable agent of the stagecoach, mentioning it in one of your letters so we may agree together on the port; the other case being much heavier, you could ship by boat. I beg you to go to sig. Morandi and let him show you a violin of the Amatis which is labeled "Nicolaus Amatius Cremonien Hieronimi Filii ac Antoni Nepos fecit an 1656" which violin he has shown to me, and let me know if some other, intelligent and well informed, believes it a legitimate work of the maker. Also, what virtues it has, and what price it may be worth. Again, remember to write to all your correspondents especially in Spain for my business.

G. A. BRIATTA.

$$\left[16 \right]$$

Briatta's doubts concerning the Amati violin mentioned in the letter of July 16th, 1775 were evidently made known to Guadagnini who thereupon communicated with Paolo Stradivari, to receive from him the following reply:

To Signor G. Batta Guadagnini, Turin:

July 17, 1775. Cremona.

I answer your last letter of July 14, which was gladly received only yesterday, from my bed, being very sick. So I will tell you that sig. Andoli cannot deny that for the entire payment of our contract it is not I who is the main creditor of the three-fourths giliati, although I sent you the entire receipt on the word of a man of honor. And in the last letters that I wrote to the same, I told them that in order not to retard the expedition because of the three-fourths of zecchino, he should go and pay it to sig. Domenico Dupuij & Sons, as he confirmed it must be paid to him. In respect to the violin shown to me by sig. Favenza, I tell you that the instrument has been handed for judgment to the first violin of the orchestra in Cremona, and as is known to us, he arrived at the exact conclusion we had, and said that it seems to him really one of the Amatis, as I see in his certificate here, and after that he wanted to see it again. I had it in my room over where I was staying in bed, and I had it played by sig. Calamani, known to us, in such a way that it shows good quality. Although he expressed later to sig. Spagnoletti that it lacks a little on the third string, but this might depend on its not being supplied with a softer string, which observation I make, or it is the soul which is out of place. The violin is in the accustomed form neither small nor too large, the back is of the wood called curly maple, in two pieces and not in only one, the top has several breaks but they are well fixed and this should not be any detriment to the tone. Also, a small piece has been put back in the top. The scroll and peg box has been put together again. This is as much as I can tell you; at the same time I tried again another violin provided by sig. Morandi of Vienna, the past month, and sent to Cremona, and which was handled by your father,* and which is the work of Nicolaus Amati, and equally beautiful in form and condition, and of particularly good tone in my poor understanding, and when played by sig. Calamini, they wanted to sell it.

PAOLO STRADIVARI.

---

* Reference to Guadagnini's father is not easily understandable unless Paolo had knowledge of some document executed by Lorenzo that accompanied the violin.

$$\left[\,17\,\right]$$

Evidencing some bickering concerning three-fourths of a giliati (or zecchino) mentioned in Paolo Stradivari's letter of July 17th, 1775. Briatta mentions that owing to the new appearance of the violins by Antonio Stradivari it was difficult to dispose of them to prospective buyers and demands certificates in a form prepared for Paolo's transcription.

To Signor Paolo Stradivari in reply to one of yours of
the 17th to Guadagnini for certain business of his
following in the same strain as our other business.

Casale. July 30, 1775.

Giovanni Guadagnini on coming to Casale let me see this one letter of yours of July 17th, and gave me permission to write for the residual of three-fourths giliati due you. . . . The violin of sig. Favenza, not being in perfect condition, which is not good for our own business. Nevertheless, send me the request for the same, and we will let you know how much we could get for it.

The violin of sig. Guarangni I found to be very good in tone, and of a good maker, and therefore, let him write to me and give his price, and his good will, and if he wants me to facilitate the contract. There being many a person who doesn't know much about instruments, they doubt the authenticity of your father's instruments, because they appear to be completely new. Therefore I beg you to write a certificate on carta bollata *according to the custom of the country with your signature as a testimonial in the following form:*

"I attest that having been left in my care by my deceased father, Antonio Stradivari, were a few of his true violins intact, yet never having been played, with red varnish, and some with a little lighter red varnish. I have disposed of all, and never kept any, but sold all to sig. G. M. di A. Briatta, excellent dealer in instruments. In good faith of which I sign my name."

It will be your pleasure then to send me such certificate right away, with one of your letters recommending the two violins.

This letter sent August 3rd.

G. M. Briatta.

[18]

The Amati violin of Signor Boroni has been acquired. Paolo is not unwilling to declare the shipment of the heavy box of tools etc., as containing only old, second-hand stuff!

To Signor Gio. Michele Anselmi Briatta & Company,
Casalmonferrato:

July 31, 1775. Cremona.

To your welcome letter of the 20th, in regard to the two violins which will be shipped, I believe I will be able at the most to effect in the next week via the stagecoach to Piacenza, directed to sig. Michel Angelo Tabarini, who is a shipper to sig. Domenico Dupuij. I am not able to tell you the expense of the post, or signify to you any except that between Cremona and Piacenza. But whatever is the baling up to there sig. Tabarini will assign to sig. Dupuij, and he can remit for these expenses. I will tell you that the violin of Sig. Boroni has its own case, which in travel will give good service, and so it is more convenient to put one on mine, and for this you will see there is extra expense to pay, but it will not cost you anything on account of the box. And at least the violins will not suffer which might happen if I wait to put them with the other things and make a heavy weight. And these others I believe cause the tariff, being wood and iron. Although I think it will be rather light weight, I will try to tell them that the box contains only old secondhand stuff, and maybe they will not exact anything because of this trickery. I will remain attentive and when some of the boats come back from Venice going to Turin, if the captain is Gobis or another, we will make the consignment by warning him.

PAOLO STRADIVARI.

[19]

Paolo voices his opinion of disbelievers who condemn the fine works of masters because they have a "new" appearance. He refuses to furnish certificates attesting the authenticity of the violins sold by him to Briatta. Sig Morandi's violin is again brought into the correspondence, with the remark that "some" attributed it to the hands of Stainer.

To Signor Michele Anselmi Briata & Company,
Casalmonferrato.

August 20, 1775, Cremona.

I am forced to remain in bed while I answer yours of the 3rd of the current month, and shall tell you that the violins left by my father, and also from my brother Francesco, total ninety-one besides two violoncelli and violas, and the concerto sold to the Court of Spain, all new, and those who wish to criticize saying that they should have been used beforehand and played, I will say that they are crazy, because had those been used and played, it could not be said that they were violins inherited by me from my father and brother as it would seem as if I had bought them for sale. I could not have done such a thing because I did not then, neither do I now, have any knowledge of it. So, I cannot give you the certificate you wish on carta bollata *because here we have none. In regard to the violin of Signor Favenza, you may write to him yourself, saying that inasmuch as said violin had been broken and then repaired several times by different professors, you feel you now should spend only what I think it is worth. In regard to the one of Sig. Morandi, notwithstanding that it has the label of Amati, some think that it is from Stainer, but it is more probable that it is by Amati according to the label; be as it may, the violin has neither defects nor breaks, and the players Spagnoletti, Calamani and Mariotti declare it to be an instrument of fine quality, but I have no knowledge of it. Therefore, as to the price, you may offer only what you think is right, and what you are able to pay for the same.*

PAOLO STRADIVARI.

$$\left[20\right]$$

This excerpt clearly exposes the connection in which Briatta acted as agent for Count Cozio in the violin business. Advertising was to be carried on in Madrid, Spain.

Excerpts from a letter written by Giovanni Reggio, companion of Count Cozio, in Madrid, to signor Giuseppe Faitelli, professor of music and playing the violin.

Casale, August 30, 1775.

Signor Count Cozio, my employer, having had a commission to have the advertisement here enclosed exposed in public places in Madrid, and not knowing to whom he would better address it than to you, as being of the profession and enjoying here a great reputation and very well known, I beg you, on his behalf, to make several copies and have them put in the best public places of the city, and to take the trouble to notify him and his son of the ensuing requests by writing to Turin to Signor Giovanni di Micaele di Anselmi Briata, and those will be complied with.

GIOVANNI ANSELMI BRIATTA.

$$\left[\, 21 \,\right]$$

The following letter presents an enigma in bearing the date November 8th, 1775, if Signor Bacchetta transcribed it correctly from the original, as Paolo Stradivari's death is recorded to have occurred on October 19th, 1775. Several important works record the year as 1776; Mandelli correctly names 1775, yet the Notice to Stradivari prepared and published at Cremona subsequent to the Stradivari Bicentenary again presents the figure 1776!

To Gio. Batta Guadagnini of Turin:

Cremona, November 8, 1775.

I have just received two of your welcome letters on the same day, and I note that you wish two violins of my late father, as you told me some time ago in another letter, with the understanding that Sig. Spagnoletto Francesco Diana, virtuoso player of the violin, shall make the choice, and accordingly I shall comply with your request. I have received another letter from Sig. Pietro Andoli with an enclosed letter for Sig. Bartholomeo Gianetti & Company to whom you will consign same; moreover, I may tell you that regardless of all their correspondence to me, it shall be sufficient that the money shall be paid in the hands of Sig. Domenico Dupuij & Son on my account, and that, after I have received credit from him, I will promptly ship it in only a single traveling case, but will use also a good wrapper to avoid deterioration in travel, so much so because we are in a humid and rainy season, therefore, also, such things will incur expense, and I will add also some mustard.

PAOLO STRADIVARI.

P. S. Without your writing me on this subject, you will explain to Sig. Andoli all that I have suggested to you.

$$\left[\, 22 \,\right]$$

Antonio Stradivari, grandson and namesake of his famous ancestor, here announces the death of his father Paolo in a letter to Briatta. Antonio makes it clear that he was a sterner business man than his departed parent. He resents certain insinuations and also insists that certain payments shall be made. Two receipts for payments were made by Antonio Stradivari, one dated December 3rd, the second December 5th, 1775, according to Sacchi's work, but strangely as done in 1776 in Bacchetta's transcription. 1775 seems to be the correct interpretation.

To Signor Giovanni Michele di Anselmi Briata & Company, Turin:

Cremona, November 21, 1775.

After the death of my father, I received your welcome letter of the 8th of October, in which I take notice of the complaint you make on the violin I have sent you lately which was in the keeping of the merchant Righetti, and of which you cannot give me proof that the contract was made with my father, because this has been a contract made by Father Ravizza from whom my father did not learn anything except that you gave instruction that he should obtain the expert opinion of Sig. Righetti, together with that of Sig. Boroni, and I remember that the last time, you went to Sig. Righetti to see it, therefore about this you cannot complain of my father, whom I do not believe would deceive you, because he had seen this and had had sufficient experience in the sale of many other violins, and besides in this he had never had occasion to deal with any but Father Ravizza, and so in this business you will have to deal with him, as we have not had anything to do with it. With Gobbi I will send the case with the forms of instruments and tools of my late grandfather, Sig. Antonio Stradivari, which case was closed and packaged before my father came to his last illness, and which you will find are well adjusted, with marks on the case which is sealed just as on the violins which we have already sent you; you shall favor me to pay to Sig. Domenico Dupuij s. g. 10 di Milano for the already mentioned case and baling, and pay this extra expense into the hands of the above mentioned man, as it is just. If after then we can make another contract for the viola which is still in my possession, and also for several models of instruments found enclosed in a casabanco after the death of my father. I think he did not know that he had them, and about this we should make another deal, and in case you happen to come to this part of the country, we should be able to work out a good understanding concerning these other pieces. Besides, I will send to you the certificate which I shall make in my name and hand and subscribed as it here is. I beg of you for a ready answer to this so that I can settle this matter.

ANTONIO STRADIVARI.

[23]

Briatta invites the friendship of Antonio Stradivari and brings up the subject of delivery of the collection of utensils etc., from the shop of his grandfather, not with any display of tact, nor without a distinct flavor of commercialism.

To Antonio Stradivari grandson of Antonio Stradivari of Cremona:

Casale, December 18, 1775.

With the greatest sorrow I received the news from your letter of the past November of the loss of your father which I regret very much, because he had been a man of honor and my good friend, although I had never dealt in person with him. And I hope that you will be a deserving son of such a father and never reflect unfavorably on his memory. We shall be good friends, and I begin right away leaving aside the ceremonies. I understand also from your letter that you were considering sending me, through Gobbi, the case of utensils and measures and forms which were used by your grandfather and later owned [?] by your father. I have not been able to give you ready information on this, and during my absense from here you notified me that you found new models of instruments which were in a cassabanco, and certainly your father must have forgotten them, because when we closed the contract with your father, he wrote in his letter: "I resolve that for the price that you offer I will give you all the measures, models, utensils and tools and others which Antonio, my father, may have used. Enclosed also are those which I have loaned to Bergonzi, and I shall ship them to you as you advise me. . . ." *So, having said that you are not less a man of honor than your father, you should have no difficulty to put them in the same case, or any other one, and you shall ship it to me as soon as you can at my address. I have not paid yet the 9 lire 10 centimes of which you write me. In regard to the viola d'amore, I have no good prospect of sale here, having already several of the good ones, nevertheless, write me in regard to it in case I might be able to sell it. I am awaiting with great anxiety for the certificate which has been promised to me for the violins of your grandfather, in good form and specified as I advised in my last letter to your father. I tell you again what I did sometime ago that if some foreigners come to you to buy some violins of your grandfather, you will give them my address in Turin at the store of Boch & Gravier in Dora Grossa, telling them that I already have an option on all those which are the true and real ones. And also tell them that I have some from any of the best makers. Besides that, make sure to take the name and surname and country of such foreigners and let me know please as before, so that I may serve them as they deserve.*

G. M. A. DI BRIATTA.

[24]

The following letter refers to an inlaid set of instruments said to have been made by Stradivari for presentation to the King of Spain, a purpose not carried out. The "concerto" of instruments—two violins, viola, tenor and violoncello—remained in the maker's posession until death; it was sold by Paolo Stradivari to the Spanish priest Padre Brambilla, with two other violins, here stated to have been in 1772 but in the writings of others as 1775. Hill's *Antonio Stradivari* mentions: "We learn . . . that in 1776 Antonio, the son of Paolo Stradivari, at the instigation of Count Cozio di Salabue, tried to repurchase the instruments, but without success." Whether the salutation beginning Antonio's letter was directed to Count Cozio in person or to Briatta, it expresses a warmer regard than its writer seems to have held for the latter!

Dearest friend:
                                        January 16, 1776. Cremona.

In answer to your last letter of December 7th of last year, which I have received only on January 6th, this year, I tell you that the concerto which is in Spain is with Father Brambilla, and which was sold to him in the year 1772, consists of a violoncello, two violas and two violins, all polished to perfection, and with their protective cases, and besides, two other violins, altogether costing 124 giliati zecchino and 5 for expenses. And if you can get them all for the same price, I shall be glad that you have acquired a good concerto. The cases are all lined outside with red calf with handles and locks of brass, and inside lined with mocagliata a fiamma. I am expecting you to attend this carnival time in order to make another contract for the two violas and also the remaining items without fail.

                                        ANTONIO STRADIVARI.

$$\left[\,25\,\right]$$

This letter praises the work of Guadagnini and recommends a concerto, a set composed usually of two violins, two violas (contralto and tenor) and a violoncello. Briatta has engaged the interest of Carlo DeMarchi to aid in the disposal of instruments. The price set on violins by Amati almost double the amount asked for Strads!

To Monsieur Giuseppe DeMarchi, first violin of the
  concerto in Genoa:
Dearest son:
                                        April 1, 1776, Vercelli.

Gian Michele di Anselmi Briata, dealer in good violins of the Amati and Straduario, true and real, of the above mentioned makers, has also those of Stainer, true and real also, has come to beg me to help him to dispose of some one of them, which he will not fail to furnish you at your convenience. For all the Antonio Stradivari violins the price is 600 lire, those of the Amatis 1000 lire in Piemonte coin. If sometime you would like to have a violoncello of the same makers and violas to make a concerto, there are those some instruments by Gian Battista Guadagnini which are also a concerto, violin, viola and violoncello. For the celebrated maker Guadagnini, therefore, do your best possible, to show that I wrote to you to do me a favor for my friend.

CARLO DE MARCHI.

[26]

Briatta again refers to certificates with which to assure the authenticity of Stradivari violins, reiterating that he had received none from Paolo.

To Signori Domenico and Pietro Mantegazza, makers of instruments in Milano:

Torino, April 9, 1776.

I have reached my country, thanks to heaven, and leaving aside all ceremony, I will write to you in the mercantile style, and after some gracious offers from you, I take the liberty to put you to some inconvenience. I will begin by begging you to look around to see if you can possibly get from Father Galarati his violin of Antonio Stradivari of 1702 for 12 giliati, as I have decided to pay in the presence of Sig. Bianchi, watchmaker. And if it is possible to have the violoncello by the same Stradivari which is in the hands of the marchese Peratta of the year 1700, for another 12 giliati, or less if it is possible. And if you can get them for me, promptly advise, and I will let you have the money immediately.

I beg you in the meantime to let me have a certificate for the violin of Stradivari never having had a certificate from Paolo Stradivari's son, but only for three violins of Francesco, two of which are sold and the other one is one of the two which he holds with him because they were made with his own hands* and marked with his own seal, just as Stradivari did himself . . . that it is hard for the buyers to believe they are genuine, although they are still new like the violins of Antonio Stradivari.

I beg you that if some foreigner comes to you, let me sell him some instruments, and try to hold back until the last the Stradivari of 1730 for it is the best. And give me the information to whom you sell, and to whom the violins will eventually go.

G. M. A. BRIATA & Co.

---
*Meaning Francesco?

$$\left[27 \right]$$

The shipment of the Stradivari relics is still the subject of correspondence. Briatta continued to stress the matter of certificates. The situation here presented is not unlike one 'faced in our day in which antipathy works against the maker of *new* instruments. Briatta also make an age-old request to inform and answer the query—"How Many Strads?", a demand probably no less possible to satisfy by Antonio Stradivari II than has been for writers of later generations!

To Signor Antonio Stradivari:

Casale, April 12, 1776.

I have been waiting up to now for the information which you had promised to give me, but until now it has never reached me. Therefore, I come to solicit you. You will ship me at your first opportunity when a boat passes there the case of utensils, and you shall be careful to pack the whole properly, and I will ask for the receipt from the skipper of the boat when the consignment arrives at this end, so as to make it secure. I am awaiting also with great anxiety the certificate for the violins of your grandfather which were bought by me from your father, and made in the following form, written by your own hand and with your seal, as follows: "I attest that I am the writer, Antonio Stradivari of Cremona, and that I have seen sold by my father Paolo to Signor Giovanni Michele Anselmi Briatta of the city of Turin the remainder of the violins, still new because they had never been played, and having always been taken care of as rarities by my father, having gotten them in inheritance from his father, Antonio, and my grandfather, as violins that my father assured me several times he had seen in the making, all by my grandfather, and therefore being the truth, I have subscribed with my hand and my seal this present attested certificate."

And this affidavit you will make in all in the letter and send it to me as soon as you can find it practical to do it. And if you are

*going over the books you will do me the favor to make an estimate
and note of how many violins your grandfather had made, and to
whom he sold them and at what price. You will also take the inconvenience to send me the particular description for every one of the
violins, violas and violoncelli which might be found in Cremona,
true and real, of your grandfather, and those who probably own
them, and in which year they were made, and at what price it would
be possible to buy them, but I know without asking that they command a high price.*

G. M. A. BRIATTA.

An interval of time passes; in the meantime shipment of the
cases containing the subject of previous letters evidently had
proceeded. George Hart, in the Popular Edition of 1887, although wrong as to the time of delivery, spoke in romantic
vein concerning the transport of the cases over the sixty-mile
route between Cremona and Casale via the river Po:

"It is by no means uncommon to discover the memories of
men kept green in our minds from causes strangely curious and
unexpected. Many seek to render their names immortal by
some act the nature of which would seem to be imperishable,
and chiefly fail of their object; whilst others, obscured and un-
thought of, live on by accident. Imagine the paints and brushes,
the pencils and palettes, the easel and the sketches of Raffaele
having been given over to a Po barge-master, and that chance
had divulged his name. Would he not in these days of micro-
scopic biography have furnished work for the genealogist, and
had been made the subject of numberless pictures? Hence it is
that admirers of Stradivari cannot fail to remember the name of
honest Gobbi, who carried the chest wherein the tools with
which the Raffaele of Violin-making wrought the instruments
which have served to render his memory immortal."

$$\left[\, 28 \,\right]$$

Antonio Stradivari's letter makes it clear that he will not bide
delay in collection of monies due him, in fact that his legal advisor has instructed him not to make any deliveries before having been paid in full of all claims.

To Signor Giovanni Michele di Anselmi Briata, Turin:

Cremona, June 31, 1776.

> *The violins of the Amati, as well as those of Stradivari are gone
> after as if they were bread; three weeks ago there were two English
> lords lodging at the Colombina who were looking for eight violins
> of ours; they sent persons to ask me if I had some, and I answered
> to them no, that I did not have any more, but I gave them the ad-
> dress of your house, saying that I had made only one contract, with
> you; I warn you if you want the violins, do it quickly, as they are
> sought by several crowns; about what you are saying that I make
> a shipment of the case, I have to tell you that my solicitor doesn't
> want me to ship anything outside my house until the time that I
> receive the other 2 giliati for those models which you have sold, and
> you pay to Sig. Dupuij the same as we have an understanding with
> your store, and that Sig. Dupuij give an explanation if he has not
> deposited one giliati of the remainder for the cases, and that he
> come to our store and pay the 3 giliati.*

ANTONIO STRADIVARI.

This concludes the quotations of letters pertaining to the
transfer of the Stradivari relics to the possession of Count Cozio
di Salabue.

BACCHETTA'S "COZIO DI SALABUE"

Bacchetta's new book, soon to appear, is the result of further
study of the Cozio document collection now preserved in the
Civic Museum at Cremona. Titled *Cozio di Salabue, Carteggio,*
and to be in four parts: Storiografia, Liutologia, Catalogo, Epis-

tolario (Historical, Technical, Catalogic, Epistolary Evidence),
some advance publicity has been provided in a colorful story
from the pen of Joseph Wechsberg which appeared in the columns of *The New Yorker* magazine, issue of July 10th, 1948.
This tells, under the title "No Weeping Tonight, Bacchetta," of
a visit to the home of Antonio Stradivari's descendant, the *Av-
vocato* Mario Stradivari at No. 4, Via Settembre, in Cremona.
Written in whimsical narrative style, Wechsberg describes the
home and person of the attorney and his introduction by the
latter to Renzo Bacchetti. During the ensuing session of con-
versation, in which wine and cheese had frequent part, Bacchetta bewailed the fact that although three big halls of the
Civic Museum were devoted to the exhibition of medieval coins,
only one room was given to house the souvenirs of Stradivari
and the other violin makers and angrily exclaimed (quoting
Wechsberg), "Why, the museum people didn't even want to
lend me the diaries of Cozio di Salabue, which I have edited."
Bacchetta had with him "Two thousand pages" of manuscript
which took him "nine months, sixteen hours a day, two magnify-
ing glasses, and three secretaries to edit. . . ." Bacchetta also
showed Wechsberg proofs of his work claimed to prove that
Stradivari Was Not Born in 1644, which is the title. It was explained that Count Cozio had himself inscribed notes on some
of the labels contained in Stradivari violins, thus making the
famous little "d'anni" notes meaningless. . . . Wechsberg's story
goes on telling incidents of the night's passing and at the end
recounts that while standing at the spot where a stone marks
the location where the violin maker's tomb had once been located, disturbing the quiet of an early morning with loud con-
versation and singing, the party attracted the attention of two
caribinieri at which Bacchetta is quoted as saying, "I bet you

my manuscript of Cozio's diaries that they don't know what this stone here stands for."

And so, we are to be convinced (?) that J. B. Guadagnini's patron was not a saint, but at worst, only very human! Whatever prompted the withholding of Cozio's documents in full in the past, if some parts contained matter derogatory to the good name of an antecedent, such sense of loyalty that possessed the keepers of that trust in defense of a respected name seems alien to a younger generation which not incorrectly holds that history demands truths and feels no pangs of remorse in destroying old ideals. Weighed in the balance against Count Cozio's notable achievements his mortal failings can perhaps be overlooked and pardoned.

Some of the details accusing Cozio do not agree with what we have believed to be true in the past: we read in Hoffmann's work (and its subsequent re-issues) that he had taken "new violins which emanated from Guadagnini's shop and used them as exchange for old instruments in poor condition" whereas it has been recorded that at the time Cozio prepared his notes he had still in his possession *all* the instruments made for him by his *protégé*, in their original condition, etc. The new version presented would, if correct, place Cozio as mentor to Luigi Tarisio, whose trading of new instruments for old has been made one of the features of his story—a revival of the older fable of trading new lamps for old from the Arabian Nights!

It has been said that Count Cozio entertained an idea to establish a school of violin making at Turin, and that it was his belief that the acquisition of the historical equipment would provide a background of inestimable value affording prestige in such a venture. If such had been his plan, it was not carried out, but there can be no doubt that Guadagnini was allowed every opportunity to derive such benefit as the study and use of his illustrious predecessor's materials permitted. It is attributed largely to the influence of Cozio that Guadagnini experimented in the preparation of his varnish; that the true methods of Stradivari seem not to have been known at that time, any more than we know them today, must not be overlooked. Nevertheless, it was at this period, about 1775, that Guadagnini presumed to introduce the name of Stradivari on his labels, thus encouraging historians to assert that he had been a pupil of Antonio Stradivari, a myth well disposed of by the author of the article previously quoted from the May, 1935 issue of *The Strad*.

Dismissing for the moment the subject of Cozio and his place in violin history, we should consider the reference, contained in his notes, to competition and jealousy of local makers at Turin. To properly evaluate their significance it would require that something be known of those local makers, but the effort to name them would be largely negative to their virtual nonexistence.

Before his acquaintance with Cozio began, other problems undoubtedly troubled the master; the removal of family and household possessions must have presented a matter of no little concern. Methods of travel and the transport of family goods in his day precluded the carriage of little other than essentials; the equipment of a violin-maker's shop may not have involved an insurmountable problem, such tools, patterns and minor utensils required by a workman in the craft being possible to pack amongst the sundry items of the household. Bulky, weighty materials, such as a stock of wood, were probably left behind, for we find a different type in use at Turin, particularly noticeable in the maple of which the maker formed his backs and ribs, as well as heads.

PART VII

J. B. GUADAGNINI AT TURIN

A brief review of the history of Turin and its place in the story of violin making and playing should be introduced here. The city was originally inhabited by a tribe of Ligurians, the Taurini, and became a Roman colony under Augustus. After the fall of Rome, Turin became the capital of one of the Lombard duchies and in later centuries was under the rule alternatively of France and the House of Savoy. There are numerous churches; the famous University of Turin was founded in 1405. Violin making was practiced long before the time of Guadagnini, though not of notable importance. The fame of Turin as a violin making locality was achieved at a late day in the history of the art and can be attributed to J. B. Guadagnini, sustained by Joannes Franciscus Pressenda and Joseph Rocca, as well as in minor sense by Guadagnini's descendants. Players of the instrument prior to Guadagnini's era included Giovanni Battista Somis, solo violinist and conductor of the court chapel, a native of Turin, born in 1676, who died there in 1763. His pupils included many who gained fame in Turin and abroad, among them such as Jean Marie Leclaire, of Lyon, France, who was engaged in Turin for several years prior to 1723; Felice de Giardini, born at Turin in 1716, who after study under Somis left to embark on a remarkable career in various European countries, and later became prominent in London where he styled himself "Music Master to the Duke of Cumberland"—his death occurred at Moscow in 1796; and Gaetano Pugnani, born Turin 1732, pupil of Somis and Tartini, first violinist at the Sardinian Court in 1752, later prominent in Paris and London, finally returning to Turin about 1770 where he died.

Having in mind the reputation of such performers on the violin may have been one of the compelling reasons that led Guadagnini to venture there to again tempt fortune. The evidence of his first works produced at Turin are the best proof that he had entered upon difficult ground. Biographers have stressed the belief that he arrived at Turin in an unhappy state; it may be to such a condition that he was forced by circumstances to turn out hurriedly constructed violins to sell for what they would fetch, with apparently small regard directed towards the selection of material employed or particular care in details of finish. While instruments displaying such character may be counted among his Turin works, dating from different years, it cannot be denied that even they, as compared with the product of many other makers, possess admirable acoustic properties and are generally no less desirable, judged from a tonal viewpoint, than others made in his best style of finest choice of materials.

Illustrations of Guadagnini's Turin works will show that the maker made use of woods varying much in type, in no manner resembling that which mark his instruments at the closing of the Parma epoch. Thus, we find many examples showing backs of lightly figured or almost plain maple, of which a goodly proportion are slab cut. These instruments, showing a character so at variance with his late Parma works, both as to wood and pattern, were in no small measure responsible for the confusion of early historians who failed to discover any affinity of work methods with his earlier productions, and unhesitatingly ascribed them to different hands. The altered character, so sharply offering a line of demarcation to separate Guadagnini's Parma and Turin periods, would make one believe that he had a definite purpose in view to discard previous concepts and turn off to follow an entirely new path. More likely, however, he lacked a supply of handsome maple and worked such wood as limited resources permitted. Broader patterns of sturdier form, flattened archings with an almost complete absence of channeling in the plates, wider rims, and notably, varnish of a different texture, sometimes almost colorless, mark the first Turin works of the maker, comprising a type quite different from that of the daintier, more effeminate creations of the late Parma period. However, try though he may have to disguise the identity of the fabricator of this newly evolved style, if that was his intention, he could not entirely break with long practiced procedures; details of workmanship peculiar to him persisted and provide unfailing marks of identification, unmistakably his and immediately recognized by the trained eye.

It cannot be stated with any degree of assurance that the maker marked each one of his early Turin works with his label. If in this he failed, the reason is not hard to find: like artists of the brush who turn out unsigned "pot-boilers" when in need of quick funds, hastily constructed instruments were probably made to sell for what they would bring rather than for the glory of his art, and went out unsigned. For them labels have been supplied in more recent times, not always correctly and in some cases bearing dates earlier than his Turin epoch began. In other cases, dates on genuine labels have been tampered with due to the confusion attributable to erroneous division of the maker's periods, and terminal figures originally inscribed by the maker were altered to make them conform with those found in text books. In defense of those who were guilty of such vandalism, it must be explained that they did so in mistaken efforts to rectify seeming inconsistencies. It is apropos to remark that the labels of other makers have suffered from like cause; as an instance, those found in many violins by Nicolaus Gagliano exhibit flagrant misdating; Lütgendorff recorded his death to have occurred in 1740, whereas the maker was still working in the 1790's. As a consequence many of Gagliano's figures have been altered to read earlier by a full half century or more. We find less tampering with the labels of Guadagnini's Piacenza and Milan periods than with those of Parma and Turin.

To specify, a number of representative Turin works are known dated 1770; as Guadagnini did not leave Parma until 1771, the inconsistency is obvious. As applicable to labels which are otherwise genuine, we may assume that the terminal figure "0" was originally "6," and the expedient of removing the upper scroll of the last named figure was employed to produce the cipher. Although unable to offer this surmise as a definite assertion, and as the instruments in question are authentic Turin works of the maker, it is preferable to regard them as of the early Turin period, and certainly not as produced in the year 1770, notwithstanding their having been so listed and described elsewhere.

Of such incorrectly dated examples, several will appear in this recording. The first to be remarked is in the maker's finest style, a type which in every detail shows Guadagnini a great artist at his best. Next to follow, three violins lack the magnificence of the aforementioned specimen; they represent his work of the early Turin epoch in workmanship and varnishing. All four definitely exhibit the Turin style with no similarity to that of the late Parma years.

Taking the four violins in the order here to be recorded, the first may be found portrayed in color in catalogues of Lyon & Healy; it is titled the "Salabue." It is of the high excellence spoken of by the Count in his notes and obviously was produced with the most painstaking care. Thus, the dating of 1770 is clearly inconsistent both as to the time of Guadagnini's arrival at Turin and the period in which he became a purveyor to Count Cozio. This second example was formerly in the possession of the English violinist Frank Thistleton, and in this country of Gaylord Yost who acquired it from Wurlitzer, later exchanging it for the 1770 Parma violin recorded as the *ex* Brusset, subsequent to which the Turin work was returned to England. Illustrated here, we see the style of its modeling and the type of wood employed in the making of the back, in one piece of slab cut maple which in figuration is similar to others attributed to Guadagnini's early Turin period. The varnish is thinly laid on, is of a dark brown shade and the texture is in no manner like that of the final Parma epoch. The third of the four violins under consideration is illustrated in the Stradivari Bicentenary commemorative brochure; the plates are poor but depict Turin characteristics. The varnish is described as of a yellow-brown color. The fourth violin will be seen illustrated in the Hamma book, the one piece back of maple apparently of the same variety as the two last mentioned examples.

Obviously impossible to tabulate instruments bearing questionable datings among others of a certain year, works such as these mentioned must be recorded as of a period.

A fine work of Guadagnini to be so recorded is the violin owned by Michael Rosenker; although it bears a false label dated from Milan, it is a typical Turin production. Several others of this class will be recorded in the tabulation to follow. Particularly notable as open to question concerning the true date of origin, is a magnificent work which at one time was in a collection of violins owned by Efrem Zimbalist. Bearing date of 1771, this violin does not conform with others of the early

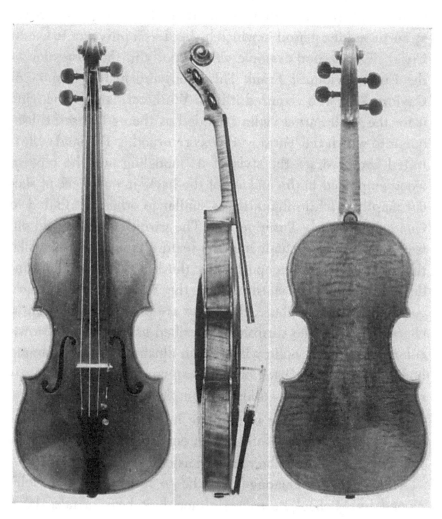

A Violin by
J. B. GUADAGNINI
Turin, Circa 1771-76
ex Thistleton

Turin epoch, being made of wood of fine selection, the back formed from maple of handsome figure. Comparison of the plate which illustrates this violin, with that portraying the work of 1775 recorded as the *ex* Joachim as well as another of 1757 at Milan exhibits such a close affinity that they might be regarded as sister-works, produced at the same time and their backs and sides from the same log of wood.

Aside from its visual attractiveness, the Zimbalist specimen is noted for outstanding tonal beauty. Erich Lachmann bought it in 1925 from Albert Caressa, in Paris, parting with it the following year when he gave it as part payment in an exchange involving the purchase of the "Duke of Cambridge" Stradivari violin of 1725 (a violin which later became known as the "Bott"), from the late A. Zamustin. Subsequently, this Turin Guadagnini once again was Lachmann's possession when he made another exchange with Zamustin, who then became the owner of the Parma Guadagnini now recorded under his name. Efrem Zimbalist then purchased the Turin specimen; from him it passed to Wurlitzer to be acquired by the present owner, the brilliant American violinist, Louis Kaufman, in 1928.

TABULATION

VIOLINS ATTRIBUTED TO THE PERIOD 1771-1776

1771-1776* *ex* Salabue. Bearing a label dated 1770, before spoken of, (1776?)   this is a handsome violin of broad pattern, fine wood and rich red-brown varnish, remarked in a catalogue of Lyon & Healy as a work especially made for Count Cozio. The dating recorded is obviously incorrect, as the violin maker had no acquaintance with Cozio until several years later. The violin has a recorded background dating from 1902 when it was certified by Silvestre & Maucotel, Caressa & Français in April 1916 and Lyon & Healy in December 1916. It was subsequently in the possession of

A VIOLIN BY
J. B. GUADAGNINI
TURIN, CIRCA 1771-76
ex Meinel

234

Mr. Chapman of Long Beach, California, who parted with it to Mr. Roy Gronsky of Westwood, California for the use of his highly talented son Harry Ben Gronsky, a pupil of Efrem Zimbalist. A brilliant talent, the boy had an untimely death. Count Cozio's name has been connected with a number of Guadagnini violins of the period; this specimen has actual proof that it was made for him, as the label, a type rarely seen, bears evidence in the words: "directione D.I.A. Cotti."

1771-1776* *ex* Thistleton. An authentic Turin work of the maker, bearing a label dated 1770. For some time in American possession, the violin was subsequently returned to English ownership. (*Illustrated*)

1771-1776 Milan Conservatorio. A possession of the institution named, this violin was exhibited at the Stradivari Bicentenary and illustrated in the Cremona book. The Royal Conservatorio of Milan is the outgrowth of what is said to have been one of the first public schools of music founded in Italy, having been opened in 1483 by Lodovico Sforza, Duke of Milan. A school of Bologna is one year older, having been founded in 1482 by Pope Nicholas V.

1771-1776 Hamma & Company. Pictured in the large Hamma book, this violin shows wood of similar character as the aforementioned examples.

1771-1776* A fine example, falsely labeled, which once belonged to Lidus Klein von Diltey, a Hungarian violinist, from whom it passed to Professor J. Gigor, of Rorschach, Switzerland. The violin was later in the famous collection of Dr. Steiner-Schweitzer from whom it passed to Erich Lachmann who brought it to this country, later to sell it to the eminent violinist Michael Rosenker.

1771-1776 Sold by L. P. Balmforth & Sons, of Leeds, England, to L. Tompkins of the same city. Described as a robust work, slightly deep model, the back in one piece of handsome wood showing a sap mark extending the full length. A Hill certificate describes the violin as a characteristic example of the maker's work of the

A Violin by
J. B. GUADAGNINI
Turin, 1772
ex Wishart

period with a head from the hand of Felice, son of Gaetano Guadagnini. The varnish is a golden color.

1771-1776   *ex* Meinel. Balmforth & Son acquired this violin from the widow of the late London violin maker Gustav Meinel. The back, in two pieces, is marked by a faint, irregular horizontal curl. The wood of the head is plain. The varnish is of an orange-brown color. *(Illustrated)*

1771-1776* *ex* Green. Formerly owned by the late violinist and conductor Louis Green, of New York, this violin passed from him to the Friedrich Collection, then to Lyon & Healy and was listed in catalogues of 1917 and later. It was correctly named a Turin work but erroneously dated 1751. The model was of higher arching than general with the maker, and the varnish of a purplish-brown color.

1772* Scipione Guidi acquired possession of this violin in Turin, Italy, in 1930, while on tour with the New York Philharmonic-Symphony Orchestra, of which he was then the concertmaster. It had long been owned by a family of the Austrian nobility, passing to Italian ownership after the ending of the first world war, and was in the possession of one of Mr. Guidi's old colleagues when he acquired it. Guidi later became concertmaster of the St. Louis Symphony, subsequently resigning the position to join the California colony of musicians. The violin is built on a broad pattern, the back in one piece and the varnish of golden-brown color.

1772* *ex* Wishart. Purchased at Hill's by Miss Margaret Wishart in 1902, and certified authentic including the label, this violin has its two piece back formed from small figured maple cut on the slab. The varnish is red-brown in color. Acquired by Max Pirani of Vancouver, British Columbia, from Miss Wishart, it passed to Louis Krasner, presently head of the string instrument department of Syracuse University. The violin had as subsequent owners Theodore Marchetti, and lastly Dr. James Sutherland. *(Illustrated)*

1772* *ex* Culbertson. Sascha Culbertson, noted violinist now deceased and brother of Eli Culbertson, exponent of the popular card game

A VIOLIN BY
J. B. GUADAGNINI
TURIN, 1773
ex Toedt

of bridge, acquired this violin from Emil Herrmann in 1908. Reverting to the latter's possession, it was sold in 1922 to Ralph Lewando, prominent Pittsburgh violinist and teacher.

1772 ex Carti. So recorded by the name of a former owner, this violin was in the collection of Emil Herrmann and was sold by him to Bela Szigeti in Lucerne, Switzerland.

1772* ex Friedrich. A fine example, once in the Friedrich collection, was sold to Nathan E. Posner. Alexander Cores bought it and retained possession until recently. The violin has a one piece back and red-brown varnish.

c.1772 ex Wilmotte. Bearing a label dated 1779, this violin passed from the possession of Charles Wilmotte, famous for his collection of violins, to Albert Caressa. Acquired by Wurlitzer, this specimen then was owned successively by Adolph Hahn, Jack Jellison, and latterly, sold by Rembert Wurlitzer to private possession. It has a one piece back and red-brown varnish.

1773* ex Morny, of Paris. Royal K. Johnson, member of the Chicago Symphony, acquired this violin from the Wurlitzer collection, and it remains in his possession at the time of this recording.

1773 ex Rappoldi. Once owned by Eduard Rappoldi, famous Austrian virtuoso who for a time was violist in the Joachim Quartet. After his death in 1903, the violin passed to his son Adrian who was eminent as a performer and teacher and who eventually became Director of the Dresden Conservatory.

1773* ex Toedt. Purchased by Robert Toedt of New York in 1916 from George Hart, and certified to be entirely authentic. The instrument has a rich varnish of bright orange-red color and is unique in exhibiting what appears to have been an experiment on the maker's part in raising the height of the ribs gradually from 29 mm. at the upper to 32 mm. at the lower right, and $34\frac{1}{2}$ mm. at the left (chin rest) side, thus $5\frac{1}{3}$ mm. higher than at the upper

A VIOLIN BY
J. B. GUADAGNINI
TURIN, 1773
ex Kosman

end of the instrument. Hart was authority for the information that the violin had been in the possession of a French gentleman "an amateur of great taste and a fine player," previous to his acquisition of it. Now owned by Harry Farbman, concertmaster of the St. Louis Symphony Orchestra. (*Illustrated*)

1773* Certified by Hill as a thoroughly characteristic work of the maker at the period, and bearing the original label, this violin was acquired in the 1930s by Miss Cecelia Van Atta from the Wurlitzer collection. It passed to William Lewis & Son in an exchange involving the purchase of a Stradivari violin and is now in the possession of Alfred Schade.

1773* *ex* Kosman. From the collection of H. C. Silvestre of Paris, this violin passed to a Dutch violinist, Elkan Kosman. Kosman, born at Rotterdam February 12, 1872, was a pupil of Massart, and after touring in England and Scotland, settled at Glasgow where he became leader of Mr. Mann's orchestra and the Glasgow Choral Union, also forming a string quartet. He later came to this country (about 1902) and in Philadelphia was head of a string quartet with Edwin Brill, second violin, Howard Rattay, viola, and Rudolph Hennig, cello. Before coming to America, Parisian dealers had made overtures to purchase the Guadagnini, but it was eventually acquired by Max Möller & Son of Amsterdam, to be subsequently sold to William Moennig & Son of Philadelphia. (*Illustrated*)

1773 Collection of Rembert Wurlitzer. A fine example with one piece back of small figure and golden varnish, the violin was sold by Hill to a private English player from whose possession it passed to Wurlitzer.

1773 A characteristic work of the period, this violin bears an original label of the "typis Antonii Stradiuari" form. Owned by Nicolai Berezowski.

1774* *ex* Beel. Sigmund Beel, presently a resident of San Francisco, who was born at Oakland, California, in 1863, and a child prodigy

A Violin by
J. B. GUADAGNINI
Turin, 1774
ex Beel

of the violin, acquired this instrument in London in 1900. Mrs. Phoebe Hearst, mother of William Randolph Hearst, arranged the purchase at Hill's. The history of the violin, as related to Mr. Beel by the late Alfred E. Hill, was that the instrument had been in an English collection for over sixty years at the time it was acquired by his firm, and had had no practical use since the time of its making. Beel toured extensively and during a subsequent visit to London, sold the Guadagnini to Joseph Read of Leicester for the use of his son. Subsequently the instrument came into the possession of the firm of Dykes & Son, and Harry Dykes, its senior member, brought it to this country where, in San Francisco, he sold it to T. C. Petersen. Erich Lachmann then acquired the violin and from him it passed in 1940 to Louis Kaufman, from whom it was more recently purchased by Dr. William C. Clough of Long Beach, California, for the use of his daughter. The physical characteristics of the instrument are illustrated in our plates; the varnish is of an orange-red color. *(Illustrated)*

1774° *ex* Kochanski. The late Paul Kochanski, who was well known to American audiences, purchased this violin at Hill's July 24, 1925. After his death, his widow left the instrument to be sold at Wurlitzer's in New York, and through Faris M. Brown it passed to the possession of Henry Schwab of Ventura, California, on September 5th, 1946. It is a superb work, as the plates indicate, and is described in the Hill certificate as bearing the original label dated 1774, and in an excellent state of preservation. The varnish is of a red-brown color. *(Illustrated)*

1774 A characteristic example was in the Wurlitzer Collection. After having been in the possession of Brainard Thresher, it passed to private ownership.

1774 *ex* Blinder. Also from the Wurlitzer Collection, a fine violin of this date was acquired by the eminent violinist Boris Levitsky. It had previously been owned by the eminent violinist Naoum Blinder.

A Violin by
J. B. GUADAGNINI
Turin, 1774
ex Kochansky

A VIOLIN BY
J. B. GUADAGNINI
TURIN, 1774
ex Ullmann

1774* *ex* Ullmann. This violin presents one of the many enigmas connected with the career of J. B. Guadagnini. Although considered to be without question a work at Turin, it shows certain characteristics reminiscent of his Parma style, possibly a work of previous years finished at Turin. It was in the possession of George Ullmann of Zurich, Switzerland, purchased from W. E. Hill & Sons November 11th, 1927; a letter from that firm reads:

> "The J. B. Guadagnini, certificate for which accompanies this letter, is typical of the Parma rather than the Turin type of the maker's work, and, although of new appearance, is untouched and has not been even over-varnished, as one might be led to assume. We have seen eight or ten similar examples in the course of our experience.
>
> (Signed) W. E. Hill & Sons."

The writer well recalls that when, in 1928, during his earlier connection with Wurlitzer, he sold the instrument to Miss Jane Dudley, then of Madison, Wisconsin, and a student with the late Professor Leopold Auer, the latter expressed his opinion that he doubted the violin could be an authentic work of the master, judged by its remarkably clean and fresh condition and appearance! The varnish is of an orange-brown color. Miss Dudley, who is now Mrs. John Hawkins, sold the violin to Dezso Szigeti, uncle of Joseph Szigeti, in 1946, from whom it was purchased by Mr. Thomas L. Fawick, the present owner. *(Illustrated)*

1774* From W. E. Hill & Son, this excellent violin was brought to this country; it was bought by Wurlitzer and was listed and pictured in the 1931 catalogue of their collection. It is a typical work of the period, the back in two pieces. It was purchased and remains the concert instrument of Roman Prydatkevytch, Ukranian violinist.

1774   The Lyon & Healy catalogue of the collection of 1916-1917 records a violin of this year. Later whereabouts unknown.

1774   A violin of the year with a top made by Joseph Rocca in 1836, was acquired in Italy many years ago by Erich Lachmann. He retained it in his private collection until 1941 when he sold it to Joseph Achron, since deceased.

1775* *ex* Maud Powell. A very interesting story is connected with a fine
red varnished violin of 1775, which was a favorite of our renowned
American violiniste, Maud Powell. Regarding the famous player
herself, it is not generally known that she was a pupil of William
Lewis, the founder of the firm which sponsored the publication
of this book. The fact that Maud Powell owed her early training
to Mr. Lewis is recorded in standard biographical works and
musical encyclopedias. What is not recorded is that at a certain
period of her progress, Mr. Lewis personally accompanied the
then already excellent player to Leipzig and placed her under the
tutelage of Henry Schradieck. The history of the Guadagnini
violin as known to me dates from a time when it was in the possession of the late Oswald Schilbach, long prominent in violin
making circles in New York. Many fine instruments passed
through his hands. As I recall the facts as they relate to this
Guadagnini violin, it had been sold to a prominent woman player
who had, however, not taken possession and having absented
herself from the city for a few days, left it for Schilbach to make
some adjustments desired by her. It so happened that Maud
Powell was a caller at the Schilbach shop and saw the instrument. Her interest was immediately aroused and after playing
on it she insisted upon taking it with her. Schilbach's explanation
that it had been sold was of no avail, and his expostulations in
vain—Miss Powell (afterwards Mrs. Turner) carried the violin
away with her, and in due time tendered payment for it in the
amount which had been stated as the price quoted to the original
but absentee purchaser. I believe a process at law ensued, but
in the end, ownership was acquired by Maud Powell. After her
death, the violin was purchased from her estate by Nathan E.
Posner, and shortly afterwards the writer, in his then association
with John Friedrich & Bro., sold it to Henry Ford, whose estate
retains possession.

1775 *ex* Partello. According to information supplied in 1916 by Dwight
J. Partello's son-in-law, Arthur M. Abell, this violin had been
owned by a Russian nobleman. Passing to Lyon & Healy with the
purchase of the Partello Collection, the violin was sold to one of
the late Leopold Auer's assistants, Lacey Coe.

A Violin by
J. B. GUADAGNINI
Turin, Circa 1775
ex Zimbalist

248

c.1775 *ex* Zimbalist. An outstandingly fine work with varnish of reddish-brown color, bearing the date 1771 on its label but of a type distinctly related to a later period. From what is known, the maker's output in the first years at Turin is not marked by the employment of handsome wood and this particular example will be found to possess characteristics, in the design of the sound holes and general appearance of the top as well as in the figure of the maple which forms the back, which have such close affinity with the violin of 1775 once owned by Joachim as well as the *ex* Wirth specimen of 1757 which is recorded as a work at Milan but might well be of Turin, that they might be called sister-works, produced at the same time from the same patterns and log of wood. The plainer type of maple, fine in acoustic properties, of which Guadagnini apparently acquired a generous supply in his early Turin years, will be found to have been used by him in the making of violins up to and for some time after his acquaintance with Count Cozio, subsequent to which his improved financial situation permitted the employment of more expensive woods. The *ex* Zimbalist violin has been owned by Louis Kaufman since 1928, and has been used by him since then in his concert performances and in the recording of numberless sound tracks for famous motion picture productions. *(Illustrated)*

1775* Illustrated in a catalog of the Emil Herrmann collection, this violin was for a time in the possession of Edith Lorand, passing later to Jascha Selwitz.

1775 *ex* Bisiach. Acquired by Lyon & Healy from Leandro Bisiach in Milan in 1911, this violin was purchased by Maurice Joseph the following year. He retained possession until 1946, when it passed to Emil Herrmann.

1775 This violin was sold in 1908 by Hill to J. Giger, musical director in Rorschach, Switzerland. It is unique in being in condition like new. The back is slab cut, in one piece. T. C. Petersen was for a time a later owner. Erich Lachmann acquired possession and sold the instrument to Felix Slatkin in March, 1942. In the fall of that year the violin was stolen from his parked car at Santa Ana camp, and no trace of it has since been found.

A VIOLIN BY
J. B. GUADAGNINI
TURIN, 1775
ex Joachim

1775* *ex* Joachim. A violin which at one time belonged to Joseph Joachim was in the possession of the late Oscar Wasserberger of Los Angeles. Joachim sold it to a pupil, N. Loesser, a wealthy art dealer in Berlin, who loaned it to a talented violinist named Mischa Reppel, eventually making an outright gift of it to Calmon Luboviski, who was studying at Berlin with Franz Von Vecsey. Mr. Luboviski is prominent in Los Angeles musical circles. In 1945 he sold the Guadagnini to Joachim Chassman who in turn shortly sold it to his friend Wasserberger. A striking similarity exists in the wood of the back of this violin and that of the *ex* Zimbalist, as well as that of the Milan violin of 1757, also once owned by Mr. Luboviski. Both the 1757 and 1775 specimens were purchased from Luboviski by Mr. Chassman in 1945. *(Illustrated)*

1775* Formerly in the collection of Maucotel & Deschamp, this violin was brought to our country by Wurlitzer and sold to Rudolph Bukeley, an amateur player then residing in Honolulu. In exchange for a Stradivari, the Guadagnini reverted to the Wurlitzer Collection; it was purchased in September of 1929 by Paul Bernard of the formerly well known Musical Art Quartet, who is at this time conductor of the Bridgeport (Connecticut) Symphony Orchestra. In the recent acquisition of a Stradivari violin by Mr. Bernard, the Guadagnini violin reverted to Rembert Wurlitzer. It is now the concert violin of the Brazilian virtuoso, Oscar Borgerth of Rio de Janeiro.

1775 Contained in the collection of fine instruments bequeathed to the city of Buenos Aires by one of its illustrious citizens, Isaac Fernandez Blanco. This valuable collection is maintained in fitting manner in fine galleries and under the expert care of a curator. The instruments are permitted to be used on occasions by artists for concert purposes.

1775 A violin of the year is illustrated in a catalogue of the 1912 Hamma Collection. The back in two pieces is of uneven wide curl, wild growth maple. The varnish deep orange red in color.

A Violin by
J. B. GUADAGNINI
Turin, 1775
ex Eisenberg

252

1775* *ex* Eisenberg. Described in a catalogue of the 1926 collection of John Friedrich & Bro., from whom David Eisenberg of Denver purchased it. It was acquired at Hill's by Nathan E. Posner, who brought it to this country. Fine broad pattern of flat arching, brown varnish of excellent soft texture and a handsome one piece back distinguish the violin. Deszo Szigeti became the owner in 1948 and sent it to London for adjustment. A letter received by him from Mr. Hill remarked the fact that the inside was still in its original state, untouched, and (quoting): "It is to be wondered that the violin has been in America so long and has survived the temptation of having a stronger bar fitted." (*Illustrated*)

1775 Once owned by Emil Herrmann, he sold this violin in Paris to Charles Muench, famous orchestra conductor.

※   ※   ※

STATE OF THE VIOLIN IN THE U.S.A. IN 1776

Before taking up comment on Guadagnini's works of 1776, mention of that year brings to mind that events of great importance affecting the destiny of our own great country were then in the making, of a nature vastly different from that which concerned the making of violins in far-away Turin!

That vocation, as far as I know, had then as yet not been practiced in America, although of players (of a kind) there were undoubtedly a number. It is said that George Washington owned and played upon a violin. Thomas Jefferson did, likewise, and it is recorded that he obtained an Amati violin from an officer of the British army. With that exception we find no records that violins of material value became American possessions until almost a century had passed. The earliest recorded work of Cremona purchased by an American was a violin by Giuseppe Guarneri del Gesù, in 1868, by John P. Waters of Brooklyn, N. Y., from George Hart. This instrument was later to be named the "King Joseph" by Royal de Forrest Hawley of Hartford, Connecticut, who probably brought the first Stradivari violin—the one known as "The Earl" of 1722—to this country in 1877. There is no record to tell when the first work by J. B. Guadagnini was brought here to become an American possession.

At the time Guadagnini was working at Turin, an American market for fine violins did not exist. Taking the island of Manhattan as an example by which to gauge the state of music in those times, we find recorded that the early Dutch settlers faced conditions which permitted them little or no opportunity to follow artistic pursuits; in fact, that music in their native land was at that time a sadly neglected art. Later, with the coming of the English, the social life of the colony gradually embraced forms of communal gatherings in which music had a part. As serious music-making spread in the colony, its advancement was furthered largely through German musicians who came to this country; their influence was felt not alone in New York, but also at Boston and other large eastern cities. Amateur orchestras were formed prior to 1800; one, called the Euterpean, was founded 1799. By the time this musical society celebrated its fiftieth anniversary, others had come into existence at New York, such as the Concordia and the Philharmonic.

There are no records available to the writer (although such probably exist) to indicate the nature or number of the instrument divisions; certainly, they included the string family, probably both of the plucked and bowed varieties. With regard to the latter, although values in Europe (from where many of the players came) had not reached any great height, there is no record to indicate that the players of violins, violas and violoncellos brought with them examples of fine Italian make. However, the fact that the violin and virtuoso performers were then truly appreciated can be judged by the fact that the first honorary member of the Philharmonic was Henri Vieuxtemps, elected in 1843, one year after the founding of the Society. Vieuxtemps was then twenty-three years of age, and had returned to Brussels after a long European tour, coming to the U. S. A. in the late months of the year. He remained in this country for two years, leaving then to accept an appointment by the Czar of Russia as soloist to the Court and Professor at the St. Petersburg (Leningrad) Conservatoire.

From the foregoing remarks it will be seen that long before the time of Waters and Hawley, string instruments and symphony orchestras were functioning. Although a country young in music, the founding of the Philharmonic Society of New York in April, 1842, made it the first symphonic orchestral group in America and the third oldest in the world! Boston had its Germania Orchestra in 1850 (the Boston Symphony was not organized until 1889); in New York, Theodore Thomas formed an orchestra to present "Symphony Soirees" in 1864, and in Chicago he directed concerts on the lake front from 1869; the Chicago Symphony, or Chicago Orchestra as then called, began to function under Thomas in 1891.

With the growth of orchestral activity, it is logical to suppose that the players who formed the personnel of the strings must, at least in part, have owned good instruments, some of better than nominal value. Yet, as I recall the period of fifty years ago, even then, in 1894, genuine Italian instruments were a great rarity, especially among the body of professional players. It remains impressed upon my memory that while attending the Louisiana Purchase Exposition at St. Louis in 1904, in charge of an exhibit of instruments produced by the late John Friedrich (who, by the way, was accorded highest honors there, as he had previously at Chicago in 1893), I received a letter from my then employers, John and William Friedrich, announcing with frank pride that a violin by J. B. Guadagnini had been sold—the first in the history of that firm. Unfortunately, details regarding the instrument are no longer recalled.

It will be noticed that our recording is deficient in specimens in American possession during years much earlier than the turn of the century. Undoubtedly there were some; the very first important move in the direction of cataloging rare violins in this country, to my knowledge, was when Lyon & Healy, in 1890, distributed a brochure, a copy of which is before me, bound in real leather, gilt edged, and imprinted with the name of John Friedrich. In this there is described, as No. 52 of the collection, a violin stated to be by Giovanni Baptiste (*sic*) Guadagnini, Cremona, 1776, with the remark that it is "one of the few genuine instruments by this noted maker to be found in this country." I refrain from quoting what follows and mention the item merely as being coincidental, as to the date, to the period of the master's work now under consideration. The error of attributing a work of Cremona to the year 1776 and the quoted sentence indicate difficulties which beset the best intentioned recorders of the time.

Three years later, in 1893, at the World's Columbian Exposition, Dwight J. Partello's collection of violins was placed on display. Among the instruments there were two Guadagnini violins of Turin, one dated 1775, the other, which had been in the Hawley Collection, of 1780.

Over fifty years had elapsed since the New York Philharmonic Orchestra was founded; violin playing had spread far and wide and among all stratas of society, and the importation of fine old instruments had begun to assume real importance, although a

duty of forty per cent acted as a deterrent. When this was removed as applied to artistic antiquities in 1909, the movement
of masterpieces to this country was accelerated. However, dealers' offerings for some years subsequent to 1909 were surprisingly small and catalogue listings included only an occasional
J. B. Guadagnini violin, in fact, works of Stradivari seem to have
been available in greater number, a situation which has not
changed very much to this day. A plausible reason may be advanced in that fine Guadagnini violins rarely remained long in
dealer possession. More within the reach of the purse of professional as well as the majority of amateur players, they found
ready takers and this condition exists as well at this age and
day. It is no exaggeration to state that a demand for Guadagnini
instruments exceeds the limited supply.

TABULATION

1776* *ex* Van Veen. Sold by George Hart in 1905 to J. Van Veen of
Holland. It was brought to this country by Emil Herrmann who
sold it to Stefan Sopkin. From Sopkin the violin passed to Wurlitzer in an exchange. The violin bears the original label, has a
back in one piece with figure slanting slightly upwards from the
left and varnish of a reddish-orange color. Now owned by Albert
F. Metz.

1776* A violin, in condition virtually as it left the maker's hands, with
the original neck and inside blocks, the upper or neck block still
intact with its three original hand-forged nails, is in the possession
of Erich Lachmann. This specimen has thickly laid on varnish of
vivid orange-red color. Available data is that from the collection
of Emil Herrmann the instrument passed to Roger Chittolini, from
whom it was acquired by Mr. Lachmann. (*Illustrated*)

1776* *ex* Bower. A typical example characterized by Hill as such, and
described as in an excellent condition. The varnish is of a light

A Violin by
J. B. GUADAGNINI
Turin, 1776
Lachmann

brown color; the back is in one piece of maple of small figure cut on the slab, and the sides, cut on the quarter, of a medium figure. Purchased from Hill by the well known London collector, R. A. Bower, in 1940. From the collection of William Lewis & Son this fine specimen passed temporarily to the possession of Albin Steindel. Present owner not known.

1776   A typical work was sold by Wurlitzer to Earl Pfouts, former member of the Philadelphia Orchestra, in 1940. The violin was recently reacquired by Rembert Wurlitzer.

1776*   Friedrich Collection. A violin of 1776 was described in a catalogue distributed in 1926 as having a back in one piece of maple of small figure, the varnish of golden yellow color. A distinctive feature of the instrument is that the purfling of the back does not meet at the upper end.

1776   A violin of the year in the possession of Harold Berkley shows the same feature remarked in connection with the above described specimen in the gap left by the maker in the purfling below the shoulder button. The violin has a one piece back of semi-slab cut maple showing small figure, the varnish of dark brown color.

1776   ex Hill. A violin of 1776 owned by Socatres Barozzi of the New York Philharmonic-Symphony, having the feature spoken of. The back is in one piece, the varnish of an orange-brown color.

The fact that Guadagnini failed to join the purfling below the shoulder of the backs in works of the period has been wrongly attributed to haste or carelessness. This, however, appears to be far from the truth, as the departure from customary methods was undoubtedly prompted by good reasoning. A frequent result of shock or strain at the foot of the neck causes it to break loose from the inside block, often fracturing the shoulder button and sometimes cracking the back in the region of

A Violin by
J. B. GUADAGNINI
Turin, 1779
ex Serdet

the neck insert. Guadagnini probably believed that the purfling channel weakened the wood at that vulnerable point, and for that reason left an adequate area of full thickness unbroken by channeling.

1777   Photographs furnished by Hamma & Company depict a handsome violin of the date formerly in their collection, the owner's name recorded as Falkenberg of Stockholm.

1778* *ex* Hart. A typical example of the maker's work of the period was acquired by C. M. Carlson in 1940 from the William Lewis & Son Collection. In the late fall of 1948, it passed to Philip A. Williams of Dallas, Texas. The violin was at one time sold by George Hart and was brought to this country by Ralph P. Powell. The back is in one piece of maple of small figure, with added wood at the lower flanks original with the maker. The varnish is of a red-brown color.

1778   *ex* Pochon. Alfred Pochon, who was a member of the Flonzaley Quartet, acquired this violin at Hill's in 1931. The head does not belong. The violin has a one piece back and red-brown varnish.

1779   *ex* Serdet. The story of this violin as reported by Erich Lachmann, is that he acquired possession in 1912 from the noted Parisian dealer Paul Serdet, who informed that the instrument had been entrusted to him by a descendant of a personality of note whose identity could not be divulged, but who, however, was said to have proffered the information that an ancestor purchased the violin in Turin from Gaetano Guadagnini, son and successor of J. B. Guadagnini, soon after the master's death in 1786. The violin was in condition, inside, as it had left the maker. In 1913 the late Professor Carl Flesch selected it for his then pupil, Sascha Jacobinoff, who continued to use the instrument constantly during his concert career until, in 1944, Mr. Lachmann repurchased it from him. In January of 1946, Robert Barene, of Sherman Oaks, California, acquired possession. *(Illustrated)*

1779   The Hamma Collection catalogue of 1901 showed two views of a violin of 1779. Back in one piece, medium curls descending from left to right. Brown varnish.

1779   The Hamma Collection catalogue of 1912 showed two views of a violin of 1779. Back in two pieces of broad figured maple. Varnish of yellow-brown color.

1779   *ex* Hill. The late Alfred Hill stated in a letter that he had purchased this violin about 1892 at Lyons, having been brought there to him from Turin. It was sold to a well known scientist, but reverted to Hill's possession. Later it passed to Samuel Crocker, who sold the violin to Alfred Vertchamp about 1936. In condition like new, the two piece back is marked by a faint small curl, light red-brown varnish.

1779   A pupil of Carl Flesch, Lisa Minghetti, of Vienna, now resident at Los Angeles, is in possession of this fine specimen. A concert violinist, she continues to use her maiden name professionally; in private life she is the wife of Anton Maaskoff, an artist with long European background before he settled in California.

1780* *ex* Spohr. The violin of 1780 which, about a century ago, belonged to the famed German violinist Louis Spohr was the subject of an article in the July, 1930 edition of *The Strad,* with accompanying portraits showing its front and back, the latter of one piece of richly figured curly maple. Having had close acquaintance with the instrument some years ago, I can vouch for the correctness of the details presented in the said article concerning the condition of the violin. Somewhat unusual in the works of the period, the varnish is of a very pale golden-orange color, of excellent texture. Subsequent to the passing of this violin to American possession, it was sold by Vincent Cardillo to John Corigliano, concertmaster of the New York Philharmonic-Symphony, who parted with it in exchange to Emil Herrmann, from whom it was then purchased by Kerr Atkinson.

The article referred to was from the pen of Arthur W. Dykes. Excerpts read:—

"I am fortunate in being able to introduce to the reader, by way of the illustrated plate which accompanies this issue, one of the very finest specimens of the Turin work of Guadagnini in existence. . . . There seems no reason to doubt that the magnificent varnish of Cremonese character to be found in abundance on this violin and some other specimens by Guadagnini, occurs as a result of Count Cozio's efforts to aid, and may have been based upon information received from Cremona.

"This instrument was privately possessed for many years, was formerly owned by Henry Holmes, the violinist, and is traditionally associated with the name of Louis Spohr. Henry, and also Alfred Holmes, both of whom are believed to have used the Guadagnini in turns, were pupils of Spohr, and when that is considered in connection with Spohr's association with the violin, there is every reason to believe that one or the other of the Holmes brothers may have originally acquired the instrument from his master. On a certain day in September of the year 1816, Spohr viewed and tested many violins of the collection of Count Cozio, and it is easy to discern, from the passage in the autobiography, that the great violinist was favorably impressed by the instruments of Guadagnini. Seven years later the information was given by the Count that Guadagnini violins had left Italy in large numbers, the direction of their journey being northward. The violin . . . is in an exceptionally intact and undisturbed state, being in possession of those rare survivals, the original neck and thrice-nailed top-block, whilst the frequently occurring modern addenda, peg-hole 'bushes' and under-edge strengthening of the table, are absent. . . ."

1780* ex Tarisio, ex Hawley. The violin now known as the "Hawley" has a background of eminent owners, including Luigi Tarisio as the first. As previously mentioned, Count Cozio informed Spohr that

A Violin by
J. B. GUADAGNINI
Turin, 1781
ex Remy

Guadagnini violins were moving northward out of Italy, and Tarisio was, as is well known, an active agent in the movement of Italian masterpieces. Tarisio sold the violin of 1780 to Vuillaume and he, in turn, sold it to George Hart. In the 1880s R. D. Hawley purchased it from Hart. The violin is pictured in color in the brochure "The Hawley Collection," a work published after the collection was purchased in its entirety by Lyon & Healy. It then passed to Dwight J. Partello and for his account was sold, again by Lyon & Healy, in 1914, when the late Franz Kneisel purchased it for the use of Samuel Gardner, well known violinist, teacher and composer. After several changes of ownership since that time, the "Hawley Guadagnini" was acquired by Dr. Barnet Fine, the present owner.

1780   *ex* Sennhauser. This violin is pictured in the Hamma book as the *ex* Joachim-Sennhauser. The last named was a resident of Saint Gall, Switzerland, and at various times owned fine instruments. The last recorded owner was a violinist of Leipzig named Wilfer. The violin has a two piece back of strongly figured curly maple of wild growth.

1780   Excellent reproductions of a violin of 1780 appear in the Möller book. The portrait indicates that the top is of fine grained spruce, apparently free from cracks; the back is in one piece, handsome maple of small fairly even figure forming the back.

1780   A handsome, dark red varnished violin dated 1780 was in the possession of Herbert Dunworth of Manchester, England, in 1946. It was certified in 1926 by Hill with remarks that it is a typical work of the master of the Turin period.

1780   A fine example of the year was in the possession of a Parisian violinist Gerard Velay at the time of this recording. Monsieur Velay was a pupil of Adolph Busch.

A catalogue issued by Lyon & Healy in 1909 lists a violin of 1780 as the *ex* Mme. Sancrah, intended to read Senkrah, the professional name of an American girl who has been recorded as the one-time owner of a Guadagnini of 1750. The descrip-

A VIOLIN BY

J. B. GUADAGNINI

TURIN, 1782

ex Chardon

tion as presented in the catalog item fits the Milan specimen perfectly—two piece back "of very handsome maple with a broadish figure, which is matched by the wood in the sides. . . . The varnish is of a beautiful, rich orange red tint and is of the finest quality." This is an instance where miscarriage of judgment prompted removal of a Turin label and replacement with another reading Parma, also incorrect as to period and date.

1781* This violin was contained in the Wurlitzer Collection and is described in the catalog of 1931. It has a one piece back of slab cut maple, well figured. The varnish is of orange color and remains in plentiful state. It was sold to Edwin Bachmann.

1781 A violin of 1781 described as a "twin of the Hawley" was acquired from Hill by Adolph Koldovsky, of Los Angeles, formerly of Vancouver, British Columbia, Canada.

1781 *ex* Remy. Samuel Dushkin brought this fine violin to this country, having acquired it from Professor Remy of the Paris Conservatoire, with whom he had studied. The violin was in the Friedrich Collection of 1924, illustrated in a catalogue of that year. It passed to the possession of Mr. Morris Nathan of Far Rockaway, New York, the present owner. *(Illustrated)*

1782* *ex* Chardon. Leonard Sorkin, former member of the Chicago Symphony Orchestra had owned this violin of 1782 in his connection with the orchestra and in his subsequent activity as head of the Fine Arts Quartet of the American Broadcasting Company, a quartet of young Chicago musicians which has attained an enviable reputation in concert appearances and on the air in broadcasts. Mr. Sorkin has acquired, through William Lewis & Son, the Stradivari violin formerly owned by Désiré Defauw, eminent conductor and fine violinist. The Guadagnini violin was in the collection of Chardon et fils of Paris; it bears a certificate issued by Hill dated July 3rd, 1935. It is a well preserved specimen, the varnish of an orange-brown color. Presently owned by Joseph E. Chapek. *(Illustrated)*

A VIOLIN BY
J. B. GUADAGNINI
TURIN, 1782
ex Maucotel

1782* *ex* Maucotel. Maucotel & Deschamp, dealers of Paris, had this violin in their collection in 1922, at a time Erich Lachmann then of Berlin was visiting there previous to his first trip to the U. S. A. It was his intention to acquire possession of the violin when he revisited Paris the following fall, but found that it had been purchased by a resident of New York. By an odd coincidence, the violin was offered to Lachmann at Los Angeles in 1941, was purchased by him, and in November, 1943 became the possession of Carol Louise Launspach. The instrument is in remarkably unworn condition, the varnish of a rich reddish-brown color. *(Illustrated)*

1782* *ex* Betti. A very fine toned instrument which once belonged to Adolfo Betti, who was first violin of the famed Flonzaley Quartet, and who latterly has been mayor of Bagni di Lucca, Italy, for some years. The violin is built on a broad flat pattern, the two piece back formed from handsome curly maple, the varnish red brown in color. Betti acquired the instrument from W. E. Hill & Son. It was in the Friedrich Collection of 1923, and was purchased by Maulsby Kimball. In 1937 it passed in an exchange to Emil Herrmann who sold it to Walter H. Trampler of the Boston Symphony Orchestra. Paul Ciani acquired possession in 1949.

1782* A very fine example was illustrated in color in the 1929 catalogue of the Lyon & Healy Collection. For a time in the possession of Ernest Walker of the St. Louis Symphony, it was purchased in 1931 by the late Miles Frank Yount. The October, 1927 edition of *The Strad* carried an article regarding the violin, which is reprinted here.

The writings of Arthur Dykes are never without a personal whimsy, and are always interesting. In the following article from *The Strad,* mentioned in connection with the violin of 1782, he went to some length in expounding his views on Guadagnini's varnishing. Quoting, we read:—

"'A Red Guadagnini.' This phrase has become almost a slogan with the younger generation of players and collectors, to describe the violin which is with most of them an ardent

want. A statement of the present day position of J. B. Guadagnini in the world of fine violins, will give us the reason. To
the owners of most purses, a fine Stradivari or Guarneri is now
beyond hoping for, whilst a Bergonzi is too rare to be obtainable
at desire; so a Guadagnini, the very best next instrument from
the up-to-date point of view, becomes the dream of youth.

" 'A tonal basis should be the ground as assessment of the
value of violins,' one is so often told by the half-informed, and
I am able to say that it is the fundamental of modern prices,
strange as the statement may seem. Seventeenth and eighteenth
century patrons of instrumental music appear to have made
little demand for power of tone in violins and violoncellos, and
the concerted expression of opinion of members of the orchestra
of the Grand Duke of Tuscany, describing the tone of the new
Stradivari 'cello as 'agreeable,' allows us to discern a sedate and
comfortable appreciation of instrumental tone, so different from
the standpoint of today.

"What is now positively needed in violin tone is power with
quality, in order that the concert artist of ability shall do himself justice in the largest of public halls, and those old violin
makers whose instruments have shown the greatest increases
of prices during the last thirty years, are those whose product
possess the required tonal combination. The lists of Italian
makers given by Fétis in 1856, brought together (without much
discrimination) a considerable number of names which have
since been re-assessed on very varying planes of value, and the
criterion has been the tonal qualification which I have detailed.

"The fine J. B. Guadagnini [the specimen of 1782 herein referred to] is a remarkable example of the master's best tonal
period, and in this connection, I can convey some technical information of great interest. In Messrs. Hill's life of Stradivari,

we read that the true Cremonese varnish is met with, for the last time, at Turin, on the works of J. B. Guadagnini, the maker no doubt operating under the auspices of Count Cozio. In the memory of the chief expert of the house of . . . . . the present instrument is comparable with another violin, similar in period, type and excellence, which the establishment once owned. The label of this latter specimen was inscribed by Guadagnini with a laudatory inscription to Count Cozio, for whom the violin was made, and the glowing terms of the inscription left no doubt as to the depth of Guadagnini's obligation to the nobleman.

"My own theory is that Count Cozio di Salabue obtained from Paolo Stradivari the recipe for the true Cremonese varnish, with possibly other particulars of Antonio's methods of working, and Guadagnini, after receiving these, felt himself sufficiently elevated to describe himself as 'alumnus Stradivari,' a distinction which he had previously never claimed, so far as I know. As a result of the application of the secret varnish, and perhaps with constructional improvements aiding, the tone of the Turin J. B. Guadagninis is better than that of those of other periods, as the harder varnish with which the rest, particularly the Parmeson ones, are covered, gives a sharp tincture to the tone.*

"In the document accompanying the fine violin now being described, we find the following phrase:—'Fine red varnish, of soft appearance.' Only a limited number of Guadagninis are precisely of the much-desired red colours, and the soft, rich gleaming Cremonese varnish of the instrument, gives an extraordinary beauty of appearance, and imparts to the tone a noble quality which is unsurpassed in my experience. The tone is very powerful and 'thick,' having that weight and reserve

---

* Mr. Dykes made a rash statement in thus rating Turin produced instruments above all others tonally!

which the concert artist adores, as it means that whatever he may demand of his violin in volume of tone, will be forthcoming.

"A second phrase of the record can be quoted to advantage, as it provides a text for other remarks of interest. The passage is:—'A finely preserved example!' This fresh and pristine specimen is, with the exception of the obligatory adjustments for modern playing, as left by the maker, and a view of the interior, through the end-pin hole, shows us the same clear and undisturbed surfaces which characterise some of the historic violins of the world.

"I have had the good fortune to be intimately acquainted, at one time and another, with some of the greatest masterpieces of the world of violins, and I have a feeling that with the finely preserved specimens, we draw far nearer to the illustrious makers than we can possibly do in the presence of defective, altered examples.

"We see more of their actual touch in workmanship, just how they finished the corners and edges, whilst from the extant and body of varnish we gain an idea of how the instruments may have looked when new, and lastly, when the violins have had sufficient use to develop their tone, we hear all the makers wished that we should hear when they first planned the instruments. A word of explanation is necessary here. We have seen that the general desire of the time was for fine tone of inconsiderable power, and the majority of the lesser old Italian makers catered for that requirement.

"The masters whom we now know to be great, possessed the superior mentality to foresee what future music would demand in the matter of violin tone, and consequently those intelligent men, whose instruments now fully satisfy us tonally, from Stradivari, Guarneri, and Bergonzi, down to Balestrieri, Guadagnini, and Storioni, consistently produced works which were in advance of their time. Giovanni Battista Guadagnini, better known by the Latinised form of his name, sometimes appears to me to occupy a somewhat similar position in the history of Italian violin making, to that which the consummate artist, Tiepolo, has in Venetian painting, the latter having been considered as the last of the ancient school, and the first of the modern.

"Guadagnini was working in the first half of the eighteenth century, and a specimen of his early Piacenzan violins which my father possessed, was an extremely brilliant one, yet in the majority of the maker's instruments, with their flat modelling, their broad massive corners, their general simplification of design, together with their abundance of wood and varnish, we have a complete modernity of style and feeling, and an entire severance from the antique types, which many of his lesser contemporaries, in various Italian cities, continued to affect.

"The subject of our illustration is a violin of compact form, with the body length of 13-15/16 inches, which is a frequent one with J. B. Guadagnini, and has a jointed back of the superior broad-figured maple, which was the matured choice of the Cremonese giants, it being probably the 'fine foreign wood,' mentioned by Lancetti. As a result of the remarkable preservation of this violin, the black edging of the scroll is still very abundant, and a further direction in which the master has followed Stradivari, is seen in the hollowing of the lower wings of the sound-holes, which work has been executed with taste and care.

"It is not likely that the violin hunter will encounter an unidentified Guadagnini, as these violins are too striking in appearance and in tone to remain submerged, but there are several special features of Guadagnini's work which the connoisseur should remember, as they are decidedly interesting. The lower terminal holes of many of J. B. Guadagnini's sound-holes are not round, but have a decidedly longer perpendicular axis, a treatment which gives the holes a very characteristic appearance. Regarding this point, it is necessary to say that it is less prevalent in the master's last or Turin period, this being possibly a further result of Count Cozio's 'Stradivarianization' of his *protégé*.

"Other characteristic 'landmarks' are the deeply pierced holes which are frequently found around the edges of the two bosses of the scroll, these being actually formed by the marking point during the initial outlining of the scroll design, but Giovanni Battista appears to have purposely deepened the impressions of the point, to give another personal mark to his work.

"What a pleasure it is to dwell with these noble pieces! The violin is by me as I write, and I have to say, after many years experience of fine violins, that I cannot easily conceive any truer gratification, to a person with a love of beautiful things, than that which is found in the contemplation and playing of fine Italian instruments."

* * *

The sentiments expressed by Mr. Dykes must awaken similar feeling in all who read his words, and the various points he brings out as characteristic marks to be found in J. B. Guadagnini's works are so clearly presented that it were idle to attempt to do better! Obviously, all Guadagninis are not varnished red, yet, as in the case of Stradivari's instruments, that seems the color most desired. The words of Charles Reade, in this respect, have weighty bearing here. The conscientious modern maker, who varnishes his creations with a plain color, let us say red or orange-red, must too often listen to critics who suggest shading, aging—or simulation of age and wear—not just the plain red violin! But that is the way Stradivari finished his, those wonderful pictures of glorious ripened hue now so desired; and so, also, did Guadagnini in the case of specimens such as the one which has been our subject here. What Reade said was this:—"We cannot do what Stradivarius could not do —give to a new violin the peculiar beauty, that comes with the heterogeneous varnishes of Cremona from age and honest wear. . . ."

*   *   *

In the November, 1927 edition of *The Strad,* Dykes wrote on "Cremona Violins and Varnish" and, suggested by the statement that in the varnish lay "the secret of the supreme excellence of the old Cremonese violins," proceeded to say:

"Actually this is only part of the complete answer . . . as the perfection of the instruments of the master makers of Cremona lies in the use of exceptional material, which appears to be now unprocurable in an ordinary way, together with a system of tentative construction radically different to the direct methods of the present day, the prepared violins being lastly covered with the incomparable varnish, the tone mellowing effects of which I was able to prove last month, in connection with Guadagnini."

Mr. Dykes wisely qualifies his reference to the difficulty of obtaining exceptional materials in adding "in an ordinary way," yet he is not far wide of the actual facts. Many of our native violin makers are finding good success in the use of American-grown wood and some contend that it is not inferior to that of foreign growth.

A Violin by
J. B. GUADAGNINI
Turin, 1783
ex Kleynenberg

The article by Mr. Dykes forwards an unusual and novel parallel:

"As regards the materials used in the Cremonese masterpieces, I would call attention to wise remarks contained in W. B. Coventry's 'Notes on the Construction of the Violin,'* in which the writer suggests a close and, to my mind, a perfectly just analogy between violin woods and the leaves of Havana tobacco plants, showing how products possessing perfect qualities are obtained from limited localities only, and that sometimes a distance of only a few hundred yards, in the case of the Havana tobacco areas, may mean a marked difference in quality.† A further point touches upon the inherent virtue believed by some to exist in the original, or at any rate the early growths from a soil. Charles Reade evidently held this view—'these veteran trees are all gone'—was his comment on a wonderful back at South Kensington, in 1872. An American student of violin matters observed a remarkable difference, for the purpose of violin making, between the first and the second growths of wood, his country, particularly perhaps in days gone by, presenting a good field for this observation."

TABULATION

1783* *ex* Kleynenberg. A violin of strong character, showing the maker, at seventy-two, still in full possession of his faculties of constructive ability. This specimen, as also others of the period, bear witness to the fact that no physical disability or mental impairment deterred him from full exercise of his skill. The violin has the original label, is in excellent state of preservation, and retains a full coverage of the original red-brown varnish. It was in the possession of Carl Becker when it was purchased by Peter Kley-

---

* The late Mr. Coventry was an American, a resident of Indiana.

† On this basis of reasoning, some millions of American addicts to the smoking habit would say "Agreed!"

A Violin by
J. B. GUADAGNINI
Turin, 1785
ex Wilhelmj

nenberg in 1924. In 1928 it was acquired by William Lewis & Son. Subsequently it was owned by Carlos Molina, well known orchestra leader, Ben Senescu, prominent Chicago violinist, through the intermediary of Kenneth Warren, by Dr. William H. Kane, of Oswego, Oregon, and lastly by Miss Marion McKinstry, of Los Angeles. *(Illustrated)*

1783* *ex* Hans Letz. A fine concert violin which was once owned by the famous violinist Hans Letz. Through the Wurlitzer Collection it was acquired by V. Bakaleinikoff. A finely preserved example with one piece back and reddish varnish.

1783 *ex* Brisson. From Albert Caressa, this violin came to Wurlitzer and was recorded in catalogues of 1917-18. Notations stated it to have been in the collection of Mme. Adolph Brisson, née Sarcey, publisher of *Les Annales*, Paris.

1783* A typical example of the period. Formerly in the collection of John Friedrich & Bro., Inc. Listed in a catalogue published in 1920 and described as having pretty small figure in the two piece back and sides, the varnish orange in color. Subsequent owners were Harold M. Turner and, presently, Harry A. Duffy.

1783 Listed in a catalogue of the Lyon & Healy Collection of 1913 as a specimen of the master's work which "outranks anything we have ever handled." Described as having a one piece back of curly maple of choicest selection, sides matching, original in all parts and in a fine state of preservation.

1785 *ex* Wilhelmj. One of the last works attributed to J. B. Guadagnini and so authenticated by Hart and Hill; the certificate issued by the last named includes mention that Giuseppe, son of J. B. Guadagnini, was at that time working with him, since adjudged an erroneous conclusion in favor of Gaetano. The Hart certificate, issued in 1905, bears a penciled note, "Good-bye, Yours, Wilhelmj," probably written when the great virtuoso parted with the instrument. It was long in private possession subsequently; at one time the violin was owned by Robert Bower. Messrs. L. P. Balmforth &

A VIOLIN BY
J. B. GUADAGNINI
TURIN, 178–
ex Steiner-Schweitzer

A VIOLIN BY
J. B. GUADAGNINI
TURIN, 178–
Uzes

A VIOLA BY

J. B. GUADAGNINI

TURIN, 1775

ex Trombetta

Son, of Leeds, acquired it in 1947. It is in almost mint, untouched condition and bears a varnish of warm red-brown color. Now owned by H. Tate. *(Illustrated)*

178– *ex* Steiner-Schweitzer. A violin of the late period in which the hand of his son Gaetano is apparent was acquired in 1933 by Rex Underwood, from Emil Herrmann, stated to have been in the collection of the eminent Swiss Dr. Steiner-Schweitzer. The violin has a top of fine grained wood, the back in two pieces is of softly figured slab cut maple, a characteristic head and varnish of red-brown color. Owned by Erich Lachmann. *(Illustrated)*

178- A late work sold by the late A. Koodlach of Los Angeles to François H. Uzes in 1923. It bears a false label of Milan dated 1753. While a student abroad in 1926, Mr. Uzes had its authenticity passed on by Maucotel & Deschamp and Albert Caressa of Paris; Mario Frosali issued a certificate at Los Angeles in 1948 stating the violin to be a part work of J. B. Guadagnini finished by his son Gaetano. The varnish is of a yellowish-brown color. *(Illustrated)*

VIOLAS

1773* From the Wurlitzer Collection, this viola, described as a choice example of the maker's work, was purchased by Dr. W. L. Mann in 1937. The instrument is in a fine state of preservation and has a plentiful coverage of the original orange-yellow varnish. The back is in two pieces of small figured maple, the curls extending upwards from the joint, unique in being marked with a distinct sap line in each side, visible in the lower bouts. The instrument is of medium proportions, the body length 15-3/4 inches.

1774* *ex* Wanamaker. From Albert Caressa, this viola passed to the Wanamaker Collection, and, subsequently, to Wurlitzer. The body length is 15-13/16 inches. The back is in one piece of maple showing a strong small figure. Fine orange-brown varnish plentifully covers the instrument. In the possession of John T. Roberts.

1775* *ex* Trombetta. An outstanding work, in high state of preservation. Albert Caressa is authority for the record that this viola

A VIOLA BY
J. B. GUADAGNINI
TURIN, 1781
ex Villa

at one time belonged to the violist of the Alard Quartet, by name
Trombetta, acquired July 5th, 1927 for the Wanamaker Collection, the viola was purchased by Milton Blackstone of the Hart
House String Quartet from Wurlitzer in 1934. The viola has varnish of deep reddish-brown color. The proportions are: body
length 15-7/8 inches; across the bouts, upper 7-1/4, middle
5-3/16, lower 9-5/32 inches. In the Lewis collection at the time
of this recording. (Illustrated)

1778   ex Chavy. For many years the solo instrument of M. Chavy,
"Alto-solo de la Société des Concerts et du Theâtre National de
l'opéra" in Paris. In perfect condition; small curled maple in two
piece back, and sides, almost fully covered with original dark
red-brown varnish. Body length 15-3/4 inches. Collection of Emil
Herrmann.

1779   A viola formerly in the Wurlitzer Collection and listed in the 1917
catalogue.

1781* ex Villa. The viola of 1781 pictured has an interesting historic
background. As related by the late Alfred Hill in a letter to Alfred
Hobday of Bayswater, England, dated January 14, 1930, he first
became aware of its existence in the early 1890s. It was then in a
collection of instruments owned by Signor Maurizio Villa of Turin.
Villa published a booklet about his collection in 1888 under the
title "Imici Violini" in which this Guadagnini viola was illustrated.
Wishing to sell the collection later, he entrusted the viola to Signor
Simonetti, a fine violinist and chamber music player, who brought
it to this country and about 1896 offered it to Emil Ferir, eminent
violist, with whom he frequently played in ensemble. Ferir eventually became the owner in 1931 and retained possession until September, 1947, when it was purchased by William D. Peiffer. (Illustrated)

1784* ex Dr. Leyds. A fine example, this viola was in the possession of
Dr. W. J. Leyds of The Hague, in June, 1923, at which time he
obtained a certificate attesting its authenticity, including the label,
from W. E. Hill & Son. Through the intermediary of Albert

A Viola by
J. B. GUADAGNINI
Turin, 1784
ex Leyds

Caressa, the Wanamaker interests acquired possession which subsequently passed to Wurlitzer. The viola is in a prime state of preservation; it has a body length of 15-13/16 inches and breadths at the bouts 7-3/8 upper, 5-1/4 middle and 9-3/16 inches lower. (*Illustrated*)

1785   *ex* Ara. One of the maker's works left uncompleted at his death to which Gaetano affixed one of his father's labels, dating it 1785. The viola was long played upon in the Flonzaley Quartet by its then owner, Ugo Ara, passing eventually to Wurlitzer and then to the late Herbert Straus. Now owned in California.

VIOLONCELLOS

1772   *ex* Popper. Owned by Mr. A. F. Metz, this violoncello was for many years the solo instrument of the famous virtuoso, David Popper. It passed to Mrs. Hede Wiener, of Beaconsfield, England, through the intermediary of August Herrmann. Acquired subsequently by Emil Herrmann, the instrument was brought to this country and purchased by Mr. Metz. The back is in two pieces, the varnish of dark orange-reddish color.

1779   *ex* Gutmann. The name of Baron Gutmann is recorded in connection with a number of fine instruments which at one time or another were in his possession. This cello was acquired from him by Emil Herrmann, who subsequently sold it to a Dr. Becker of Prague.

1780*   *ex* Davidoff. A magnificent instrument, once owned by the famous Russian cellist, Charles Davidoff (Davidov). It was part of a quartet of fine instruments for some years in the possession of the late Joseph Haft, after whose death it was acquired by the eminent artist, Kurt Reher, in 1947.

1783   A characteristic work recently in the collection of Rembert Wuriltzer. Handsome broad figured maple two piece back, with sides of similar wood. The varnish is of a reddish-brown color. The

A Violoncello by

J. B. GUADAGNINI

Turin, 1783

ex Huxham

dimensions of the cello: length of body 28-5/16 inches; across the bouts, upper 13-1/4, middle 9-5/8, lower 16-3/4 inches.

1783* *ex* Huxham. Although the work of a man well up in years, this instrument allows no doubt of his undiminished powers as a workman. All details are carried out in highly excellent manner, the material is of choice quality, and the varnish, of a dark red-brown color, remains in ample coverage. The body length is 28 inches, across the bouts, 13-1/8 upper, 9-5/8 middle, and 16-5/8 inches lower breadths. It was in the collection of Charles Tunsch of Berlin at the time Maucotel & Deschamp issued their certificate of authenticity in 1923; Erich Lachmann brought it to this country and it passed to Wurlitzer possession, to be purchased by Sidney H. Huxham. He retained possession until 1944 when it passed to William Lewis & Son. Frederick E. Perfect became its owner in 1949. *(Illustrated)*

PART VIII

J. B. GUADAGNINI'S LABELS

It is the hope of the writer that this treatise, the first of its kind devoted particularly to the life and works of J. B. Guadagnini, will enthuse others to pursue the subject further. Although serious thought has been directed towards the end that a true biography of the new famous *liutaro* might emerge, what has been heretofore available for the layman to consult consists largely of reiteration. Certainly, had the same sincere, intensive research, which, for over a century was devoted to the great Cremonese masters, with collaboration of church and civilian officials at the points where the makers lived, been similarly directed to the Guadagninii, a better record concerning them might exist. That which has been entered herein is the result of a considerable experience with authentic works of the makers under consideration without opportunity for research otherwise in the far removed localities of their activities. The results achieved, therefore, must not be regarded basically other than circumstantial, yet assured by the evidence of actual works of their hands and with dating on labels providing mute witness.

It will be said, and rightly, that a true story cannot be evolved through mediums depending on labels found in old violins. Fortunately, the majority of J. B. Guadagnini's works still retain the original tickets; unlike the fate which deprived the works of Lorenzo, his father, of their labels, thus destroying that means affording recognition due him as the producer, the strong individuality that marks those of J. B. Guadagnini from the early years of his career, hold them immune to misrepresentation as works of other makers. This has largely delivered them from vandalism such as has been practiced in other cases, although there have been instances where his instruments were supplied with false labels purporting Cremonese origin.

Certain works on our subject that stand in high repute from a literary viewpoint, present many irregularities in pictured labels. The work of Jules Gallay names the period of J. B. Guadagini as "Plaisance, 1755-85," but illustrates a label of the Turin type with date 1765, or six years before the maker's arrival at that city; and another, of the Milan type, with date 1775, thus post-dated by a score of years! Lütgendorff pictures a Parma type of label with date 1741 (the period was 1759-1771); another of the Milan type, date 1760, when the maker was working at Parma.

Dealers of the past and present, as well as private owners, studying their instruments and finding the dates out of accord with periods indicated by such printed examples, cannot be severely censured because they thought to correct seeming inconsistencies by altering the figures on labels. Thus we find Guadagnini violins bearing their original labels, but showing the evidence of such tampering, sometimes carefully, at others crudely done.

The various forms of labels used by J. B. Guadagnini were type-set: the first in use at Piacenza were imprinted with only his given and family name, in the Latin form of Joannes Guadagnini. Two forms are known:

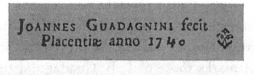

In the second type the floral ornament is replaced by a circular device in which appears, intaglio, the maker's monogram GBG (representing the Italian form Giovanni Battista Guadagnini) surmounted by a cross, with the letter "P" beneath the monogram to designate Placentina (Piacenza) as the locality of his origin. Of further significance, the label shows the maker's relationship as son of Lorenzo in including the words "filius Laurentii." At this period Lorenzo asserted his separate individuality by referring to himself as "Pater" on his labels.

The third type, used by J. B. Guadagnini at Milan, omits mention of the father, but retains the "P" with the monogram and in the text unmistakably establishing his origin as of Placentina:

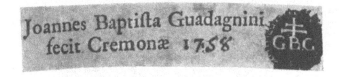

At Cremona, Guadagnini ceases mention of Placentina in the text of his labels but continues to use his monogram device including the letter P, thus still designating his natal city.

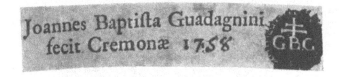

At Parma we find the letter "P," signifying Piacenza as it did also on the earlier tickets (rather than Parma), remaining under the monogram. Whether another form was used prior to the introduction of the "serviens" and "C. S. R." signs of service at the ducal court, I cannot say.

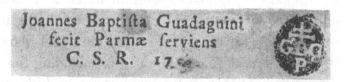

Nor is there an explanation other than what has been previously discussed to account for the further introduction of "Cremonensis," which appears on the next Parma type; as has been remarked, it was probably employed in order to further the maker's prestige:

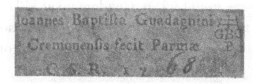

Using the same form of wording, but apparently struck with an idea that the usual oblong form of label could be improved upon, we find the type set in a manner which permitted the ticket to be cut in graduated steps. The form originated in Guadagnini's last years at Parma; used in the year 1771 the label provides convincing evidence that the maker was still working in the city at that time. Significant also, the letter "P" remains as part of the monogram.

A similar form was first used at Turin; reference to Cremona continues, but the initial "P" under the monogram is replaced with "T." Having asserted Cremonese connection, the maker found it expedient to renounce allegiance to Piacenza, therefore, the substitution of the "T" for "P," obviously to proclaim Turin as the city of his then residence:

There is good reason to believe that Count Cozio regarded it as essential to establish Cremonese origin for J. B. Guadagnini in order that he should be so recorded by Lancetti among the "worthies" of that city. We have Cozio's letter to Lancetti offering the news that he had obtained, *from Turin*, information that the Guadagnini family was Cremonese, written subsequently to his original report that any connection with Cremona, whether by birth or habitat, had no sustaining evidence. Had there been such, it would have come to his knowledge during the years of his close connection with the maker, and further investigation would not have been called for. However, his (presumed) suggestions that Guadagnini assert claims brought results in labels of which the following setting shows the form:

Jo: Bap: Guadagnini Cremonen:fecit
Taurini directione D.I.A. Cotii   GBG
Typis Antonii Stradiuari 177   T

A label of this type is found in the violin recorded as the *ex*
Salabue of which the label bears false dating 1770, obviously
through the tampering of an uninformed owner at some previous time. If it is one of the violins made by Guadagnini for
Cozio, which its wording indicates, as the Count was not in possession of Stradivari's residue until early in 1776, it suggests
a work of that year, removal of the upper turn of the number 6
resulting in the cipher. On that form of label it should be noted
that Guadagnini does not speak of himself as a disciple of Stradivari, contenting himself to state the work as of the *type* of the
Cremonese master. We do see reference to Stradivari incorporated in a form frequently met with in the late works, a type
reproduced in many books on our subject and widely reprinted:

The idea of alluding to himself as of the Stradivarian school
obviously impressed the aging Guadagnini to such a degree
that, probably subsequent to the epoch of the Cozio relationship, some of his labels from about 1780 onwards, emphasizes
the Cremonese master's name in prominent type:

Examples of this form are found in the violin of 1782 now
owned by Miss Launspach, and the cello of 1780 known as the
"Davidoff."

This last form was also occasionally used after the maker's death by his son, Gaetano, probably inserted in partially finished works of his father which he completed.

Labels contained in old violins can only be photographed under certain conditions; removal for the purpose is apt to damage or destroy these fragile bits of old paper and only when opening of an instrument is necessary may their insides be exposed to the camera.

(I am indebted to my colleagues Emil Herrmann, Erich Lachmann and Rembert Wurlitzer for collaboration in supplying photographs of Guadagnini labels.)

TABLE OF MEASUREMENTS OF J. B. GUADAGNINI INSTRUMENTS IN INCHES

	Length of Body	Widths Across Bouts		
		Upper	Middle	Lower
Piacenza: 1740, Lewis Collection violin,	13 15/16	6 1/2	4 11/32	8
1742, the *ex* Bazzini violin,	13 27/32	6 9/16	4 1/2	8 1/16
1750, the *ex* Moulton violin,	13 15/16	6 15/32	4 3/8	7 15/16
1743, the Graudan violoncello,	28 3/16	14	9 9/16	17
Milan: 175–, the *ex* Vieuxtemps violin,	13 7/8	6 1/2	4 1/2	7 15/16
1750, the *ex* Birkby violin,	13 7/8	6 1/2	4 7/16	8
1757, the *ex* Herten violin,	13 29/32	6 9/16	4 3/8	8 1/16
1754, the *ex* Gerardy violoncello,	28 3/16	13 3/16	9 9/16	16 1/2
Cremona: 1758, the *ex* Knapp,	14	6 3/8	4 3/8	7 7/8
Parma: 1766, the *ex* Krasner violin,	13 15/16	6 9/16	4 7/16	8
1769, the *ex* Kingman violin,	13 15/16	6 1/2	4 1/2	8
1770, the *ex* Millant violin,	13 15/16	6 9/16	4 1/2	8
Turin: 1773, the *ex* Van Atta violin,	13 15/16	6 5/8	4 11/16	8 1/16
1774, the *ex* Kochanski violin,	13 15/16	6 9/16	4 7/16	7 15/16
1778, the *ex* Hart,	13 15/16	6 1/2	4 1/2	7 9/16
1779, the *ex* Serdet violin,	13 15/16	6 5/8	4 1/2	8 1/16
1780, the *ex* Tarisio violin,	13 13/16	6 17/32	4 19/32	7 63/64
1773, the Dr. Mann viola,	15 3/4	7 3/8	5 1/4	9 1/8
1775, the *ex* Trombetta viola,	15 7/8	7 1/4	5 3/4	9 5/8
1784, the *ex* Leyds viola,	15 13/16	7 3/8	5 1/4	9 3/16
1783, the Huxham violoncello,	28	13 1/8	9 5/8	16 5/8

J. B. Guadagnini was not careful to set the notches in the sound holes of his violins at the usual 7-5/8 inch "stop".

SUMMARY OF THE WORKS OF J. B. GUADAGNINI AS HEREIN ENTERED

	Violins	Violas	Cellos		Violins	Violas	Cellos
WORKS AT PIACENZA				**WORKS AT PARMA**			
1740	5	..	..	1759	2	..	2
1741	3	..	..	1760	5	..	2
1742	2	..	..	1761	3	..	..
1743	1	..	3	1763	1	..	..
1744	5	..	1	1765	3	..	..
1745	6	..	..	1766	3	..	..
1746	3	..	1	1767	6	..	..
1747	3	..	..	1768	2	..	..
1748	1	..	1	1769	4	..	..
1749	1	..	1	1770	9	..	..
174?	1	..	..	1771	1	..	..
	31	0	7		39	..	4
				WORKS AT TURIN			
WORKS AT MILAN				177?	8	..	..
				1772	6	..	1
1749	2	..	..	1773	7	1	..
1750	13	..	..	1774	8	1	..
1751	8	..	..	1775	12	1	..
1752	4	..	..	1776	7	..	..
175?	1	..	..	1777	1	..	..
1753	12	..	..	1778	2	1	..
1754	2	..	1	1779	5	1	1
1755	11	..	1	1780	6	..	1
1756	2	..	..	1781	3	1	..
1757	7	1	..	1782	4	..	..
1758	1	..	2	1783	5	..	2
175?	1	..	..	1784	..	1	..
	64	1	4	1785	1	1	..
				178?	2	..	..
WORKS AT CREMONA					77	8	5
1758	7	0	1				
				TOTALS	218	9	21
	7	0	1		Violins	Violas	Cellos

PART IX

THE DYNASTY GUADAGNINI

With the passing of J. B. Guadagnini in 1786, the strongly individualistic touch which marks his productions and makes them readily distinguishable disappeared from the works of his successors in the family. His son Giuseppe built some excellent violins, used good varnish, but failed to rival the works of his father. Gaetano also made good violins, and is recognized as having been a faithful helper to his father. None of the succeeding Guadagnini generations were prolific in their output of violins; they are known to have been engaged in repairing and also as having produced many fine guitars and other types of instruments. Violins actually made by them do not show a definitely recognizable type in their style or methods of construction. Although authentic examples must exist in fair number, they are far exceeded in quantity by falsely labeled works which in some detail or other show features resembling the style of Guadagnini. This class of instruments has contributed to the general confusion which surrounds the works of the great maker's descendants, and make it difficult to separate the false from the real.

It is also to be considered that some of the later Guadagninii sold instruments not the work of their own hands, which they supplied with labels bearing their names, providing a class of "genuine" Guadagnini works in the making of which they had little or no part. Although we find catalogue listings of violins attributed to the various later members of the family, the subject of the careers of these makers is one which has been largely avoided. It is one which this writer, to his personal regret, must

VIOLIN MAKERS OF THE GUADAGNINI FAMILY

Laurentius Guadagnini (Lorenzo)

Neither place nor date of birth definitely established. Presumably born at Piacenza about 1695, died there, the year undetermined, about 1745.

Giovanni Battista (Joannes Baptista)

Believed born at Piacenza (some say Cremona), 1711. Certified works date from 1740. Died September 19, 1786, at Turin. Worked at Piacenza, Milan, Cremona, Parma, and Turin.

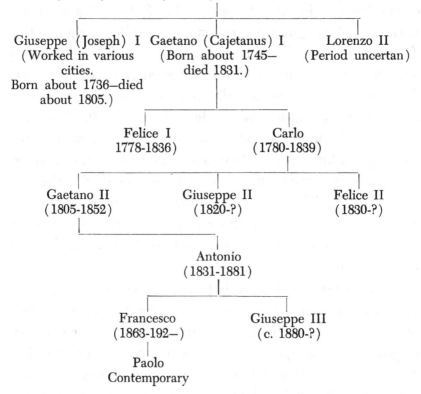

Giuseppe (Joseph) I   Gaetano (Cajetanus) I   Lorenzo II
(Worked in various   (Born about 1745–   (Period uncertan)
     cities.   died 1831.)
Born about 1736–died
    about 1805.)

Felice I   Carlo
1778-1836)   (1780-1839)

Gaetano II   Giuseppe II   Felice II
(1805-1852)   (1820-?)   (1830-?)

Antonio
(1831-1881)

Francesco   Giuseppe III
(1863-192–)   (c. 1880-?)

Paolo
Contemporary

also leave as an inconclusive and sketchy closing chapter to this review.

Factual evidence lacking concerning the origin of the Guadagnini family it is the opinion of this writer that the violin-making line may be attributed to Piacenza, a thesis to which early writers not influenced by Yusupov subscribed. Their findings were based on very real evidence provided on the actual labels employed by Lorenzo and Giovanni Battista which gave the facts. Both declared their origin in the text of their labels; Giovanni Battista so continued to do until his advent at Parma where, although he no longer employed the word Placentinus on his labels, he did the letter *P* in connection with his monogram. The migrations of this maker were correctly recorded by Count Cozio, who also names his two violin making sons as Giuseppe and Gaetano.

Thus we have what appears to be incontrovertibly a true rooting of a family tree of which branches have continued to pursue the art into the years of our generation. This genealogical table is offered as presenting the best opinion of this time.

As one who applied himself assiduously to the accumulation of data, Baron von Lütgendorff sometimes overextended his notices to actual as well as rumored violin makers and as fitting to this review, his remarks concerning the descendants of Lorenzo Guadagnini will be analyzed. Certainly, had it been possible for him to pursue his investigations in the various cities that were their habitat, von Lütgendorff would have provided not only more information concerning the founder and his descendants, but would also have been spared the errors his remarkable work perpetuates.

Writing about the Guadagninii, Lütgendorff produced some characters in his compilation who apparently never existed. Of these so recorded mythical figures one appears under the name of Giovanni Antonio Guadagnini. That name, at least as long as Lütgendorff's work survives, is now permanently inscribed in violin chronology—born of an unsound hypothesis advanced by an earlier French writer. This will be discussed later and is mentioned here to explain why "Giovanni Antonio Guadagnini" does not appear in the geneological table here submitted.

Another, concerning whose violin making activities there seems no real evidence, is recorded as Lorenzo II, son of Giovanni Battista. Lütgendorff provides an extended notice, leading his readers to infer that he, Lorenzo II, was the author of a number of violins which now pass as the work of his illustrious antecedent, Lorenzo, founder of the line!

The story of the family, as presented in Lütgendorff's survey, which is part of the portion pertaining to Turin, reads as follows:

"He (J. B. Guadagnini) was a worthy apostle of Stradivari and passed his art to his son Gaetano I, so that he too could build excellent violins, although the fashion of the day compelled him more and more to manufacture Guitars, which his son Carlo did by choice, while Lorenzo II appears to have built violins exclusively and probably died young. Violins by him are rarely seen, which may be attributed to the fact that they are accredited mostly to his grandfather whose works they resemble. Carlo Guadagnini raised three sons, Gaetano, Giuseppe, and Felice, as violin makers who certainly did not reach the eminence of their antecedents, yet still were quite capable. Gaetano II however was a true disciple of the family and so his talented son and pupil Antonio again became a better violin maker than he; of Antonio's sons the still living Francesco is unquestionably the best contemporary maker. He states himself to possess the original Cremona varnish and so still prepares it from the same recipe left by Giambattista at his death. Less important is his brother Giuseppe III. It is said that other members of the family, not mentioned here, also lived in Turin as violin makers."

It is a truism that great genius rarely remains, or is reborn in later generations of the same family. Lorenzo Guadagnini has been appraised as a very excellent master; the very few existing authentic works of his hands do not admit of a broad appraisal of his capabilities. On the other hand, the output of his son Giovanni Battista attests his industry as well as his ability.

As proof of the old axiom, neither his own sons nor their progeny approached a like eminence; their achievements fail emulation of the example set by their gifted ancestor, either in quality or quantity.

With reference to the name Giovanni Antonio Guadagnini, mentionel by Lütgendorff, the entry may be traced to the writings of Laurent Grillet (1851-1901), French violoncellist, composer and writer, who was the first to record the name of Giovanni Antonio as a maker of violins by reason of a label dated Turin 1750, said to have been found in a violin. While this offered Lütgendorff a pretext for entering the name in his account, Grillet's mention of the label surely provided uncertain ground on which to venture comments, and should not have been enlarged upon to the extent of further details. This Lütgendorff did, however, describing the violin mentioned by Grillet (thus an inference that he had actually examined it!) as being entirely a counterpart of one by Lorenzo Guadagnini and, further, that "also this Guadagnini calls himself a pupil of Stradivari and was probably a brother of Lorenzo, and the first of the family to go to Turin. We find this relationship reiterated on page 88 of Lütgendorff's survey of Turin, but on page 52, in speaking of Parma and J. D. Guadagnini's removal to Turin, we read: "Whether his removal was due to *his older brother,* as we may well believe, cannot be stated with certainty, *as nothing is known about this Giovanni Antonio.*"

The label mentioned was pictured in the Lütgendorff book and is palpably fictitious, but now, where there was once a single violin so falsely named, many others have been consigned to an equally dubious status by the insertion of reproductions of the label.

Next calling for notice is "Felice I," nephew of Giovanni Battista (Nepos Joannes Baptista, etc.). No mention of this Felice I is found in Lütgendorff's survey, but we do find that the designation "Felice I" is there transferred to Felice, the son of Carlo! The biographical notes (in all editions) inform us that the violins of Felice I are often confused with those of Felice II—a situation very like that which formerly centered about J. B. Guadagnini I and II, now resolved into one, but in the instance of the makers named Felice, not entirely cleared of doubt.

❁   ❁   ❁

Returning to the sons of J. B. Guadagnini known to have followed his vocation: Giuseppe (Joseph), produced a number of instruments; Gaetano (Cajetanus), who continued the operation of his father's shop after his decease, assumed importance in the history of the family through having been the progenitor of the later line of instrument makers of the family name; and, lastly, there was Lorenzo II, regarding whom Count Cozio made no mention at all in his notes, and of whom there is little to record as a maker of violins.

GIUSEPPE (JOSEPH) GUADAGNINI I
Son of Giovanni Battista
Born about 1736—died about 1805

Giuseppe evidently inherited, besides such talent for instrument making that he possessed, a lust for wandering from his father. He is said to have worked in many northern Italian cities—at Milan, Turin, Como, Parma, and Pavia. Of this, proof seems to exist in actual works.

An excerpt from Lütgendorff's survey regarding Giuseppe at Parma reads:

". . . the son Giuseppe Guadagnini, called Soldato, not quite the equal of his father, tarried for a time at Parma. Perhaps he hoped that the good reputation left there by his father might bring to him good success, which he had in vain sought elsewhere."* Lütgendorff's notice in the biographical section tells us that "He called himself Cremonese but if he was born or worked there is unknown. He built after the patterns of Stradivari and Guarneri; flat broad model, good work, less successful acoustically. 1760 he was in Parma; 1763 he lived at Como, in Contrada di Porta; 1790 in Pavia. Towards the end he came to very reduced circumstances. . . ."

Giuseppe is presumed to have been the author of a goodly number of instruments of which, however, there is small trace today. He apparently remained with his father and brother at least until the beginning of the Parma epoch, as evidenced by several examples possible to record here. His death occurred at Pavia about 1805.

---

* Reference is made to a plate illustrating a violin by Joseph Guadagnini ("Tafel 76") dated Parma 1770, from the Hamma collection, which turned out to be a work of J. B. Ceruti and through Erich Lachmann later passed to a player in Budapest.

A VIOLIN BY
GIUSEPPE GUADAGNINI
CIRCA 1781

A violin ascribed to Giuseppe is illustrated. It bears a presumably genuine label of his father, thus from Turin, dated 1781, but probably a work of later years. It is known that his brother Gaetano used such labels in instruments completed by him remaining unfinished by his father, and is said also to have inserted them in some of his own, but I can neither affirm nor deny that Giuseppe also may have obtained and used them for his own purposes. In the case of the violin pictured, it was acquired in the 1920s by the late Alexander J. Stuart from the collection of Wittmann of Vienna and in this country passed through Otto K. Baumann to Emil Herrmann.

Instruments attributed to Giuseppe Guadagnini:

VIOLINS

1762, label Parma, 1762. Formerly in the Friedrich collection and illustrated in a catalogue published April, 1921.

1780, label Como. From the Parisian dealers Caressa & Français.

1781, label Turin type of his father, believed a genuine ticket. *(Illustrated)*

1782, label Turin. Coming from Hill to Wurlitzer, this violin was sold to Max Silverman.

1788, label Pavia. Described in a catalogue of the October, 1926 Friedrich collection.

1801, label Pavia. Acquired from the Stübinger Collection, Vienna, by Erich Lachmann and brought to this country by him. Passing to Wurlitzer, it was purchased by the late Dr. Charles A. Haff in 1932.

VIOLAS

1780, label Como. From the collection of Emil Herrmann, acquired by Albert F. Metz.

1780, label Milan. Acquired for the Wanamaker Collection from Caressa & Français. Pictured in the 1931 catalogue of the Wurlitzer Collection. Now owned in San Francisco.

1793, label Parma. Also part of the Wanamaker Collection this viola came from Silvestre & Maucotel and was listed in the Wurlitzer 1931 catalogue.

In addition to the instruments tabulated as American possessions, an article appearing in *The Strad*, edition of December, 1943, was devoted to a violin by Joseph Guadagnini then owned by Albert Arnold of London. It was accompanied by plates and was described as a work produced at Pavia. The label is stated to be the original, with the last figure partially obliterated but apparently having been of the late 1790s. Comparison of the plates showing the Joseph Guadagnini here pictured, with those in *The Strad* article show an unmistakable affinity of workmanship. The article also mentions Joseph's brother, Gaetano, regarding whom we have next to remark.

GAETANO GUADAGNINI, I
Son of Giovanni Battista
Born Piacenza about 1745—died Turin 1831

The article above mentioned as having appeared in *The Strad* was evidently from the pen of a writer well informed on his subject. Quoting further, it continues ". . . Gaetano, who worked in Turin, produced instruments of equal merit, but, is chiefly known as a skilled repairer."

The later makers of the Guadagnini family are more or less generally spoken of as repairers and makers of guitars; this should not be accepted, however, to mean that they did not, on occasion, produce good violins. Others of the great Italian

A VIOLIN BY
GAETANO GUADAGNINI
CIRCA 1796

violin makers occasionally occupied themselves with other types of instruments, Stradivari, as an example, having also made guitars, of which several are now existing. To meet the demand of his time, Gaetano no doubt was compelled to produce the wanted types, which, with repairing, provided employment and sustenance. We know of several excellent violins produced by him.

VIOLINS ATTRIBUTED TO GAETANO GUADAGNINI I

c.178– A fine example bearing label of J. B. Guadagnini is in the possession of Rodion Mendelevitch of Los Angeles.

c. 1796 Illustrated in the catalogue of the August, 1923 Friedrich Collection. The violin was in the possession of Harry J. Kimball of Hollywood in 1946. Through Erich Lachmann, ownership passed to Miss Carol Launspach.

c. 1798 Listed in the 1931 catalogue of the Wurlitzer Collection.

1799 Wurlitzer Collection. Listed in the catalogue of 1925 and described as being of a flat model, the work bearing resemblance to that of his father and mentioning that "one frequently finds the labels of his father in the violins of Gaetano."

1821 From the violin maker George Ullmann of Zurich, Erich Lachmann purchased this violin in 1927, selling it the following year to Albert Müller in New York. An exceptional work of the maker, in the style of Guarneri del Gesù.

*   *   *

It is in order to discuss Lorenzo II, who has been recorded as another violin-making son of Giovanni Battista. He is so spoken of by von Lütgendorff and was no doubt so regarded by the worthy writer. However, his manner of recording illustrates a failing, reprehensible in the fabrication of details now found contradicted by fact, and further showing how far fantasy may carry one to enlarge on a fiction. Lütgendorff wrote, as concerning Lorenzo II:—

"Son and presumably also a pupil of Giambattista II. As Lorenzo I on some of his labels terms himself 'Pater,' Lorenzo II had been up till now regarded as his son. Through a lately discovered label in a wonderful violin owned by Max Sternau in Weimar, it is now possible to state that Lorenzo II was a grandson of Lorenzo I. As his work resembles that of his grandfather closely many of his violins surely have been attributed to him and the dates 'corrected' to accord, which explains their rarity. He used very light golden-yellowish varnish and is notable for elegantly carved scrolls. His label: Lorenzo Guadagnini figlio di Giovanni Battista, fecit in Turino (sic) an. 1790."

For the sake of future recorders, it is to be hoped that the "rarity" spoken of will so remain, not to be augmented by numbers of instruments supplied with fictitious labels reproduced from the sample pictured by Lütgendorff.

It so happens that the true story of the identical violin which duped the author of the aforementioned paragraph can be told. Our esteemed colleague, Mr. Erich Lachmann (whose long experience has placed him in possession of a vast fund of data concerning violins as well as owners thereof) was well acquainted with the late Baron von Lütgendorff, the violin under notice, and also Max Sternau, in whose possession it reposed at the time it came before von L. and prompted the notice by him. Lachmann's marginal notes on the page on which Lütgendorff's mention of the violin occurs signify (in English) "Humbug," "Fake!" "An old Füssen fiddle."

Without regret or obituary we may take leave of this presumably mythical violin making son of Giovanni Battista Gua-

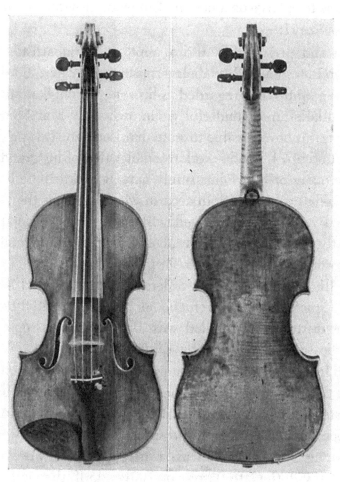

A Violin by
CARLO GUADAGNINI
Turin, 1798

dagnini. If in reality he did fashion any violins, this writer has
no knowledge of any.

＊   ＊   ＊

The continuation of the line of violin makers of the name
seems definitely to repose with Gaetano I, for he was the father
of two sons, Felice and Carlo.

FELICE GUADAGNINI I
Son of Gaetano I
Turin 1778–1836.

It is not given to me to provide information regarding this
maker. Such data pertaining to Felice Guadagnini as is available to me, will be reserved for another Felice, Son of Carlo.

CARLO GUADAGNINI
Son of Gaetano I
Turin 1780–1839

We find in Miss Stainer's "Dictionary of Violin Makers" that
Carlo (a bracketed question mark follows the name) Guadagnini received mention as "son of Gaetano, grandson of
Giambattista Guadagnini. A maker of guitars at Turin about
1780. He also repaired instruments. His three sons, Gaetano,
Giuseppe, and Felice, were all makers, but chiefly worked at
repairing old instruments." Lütgendorff was equally sparing of
words in mentioning Carlo, and to the same effect.

That this maker produced violins, perhaps small in number,
is indicated by our illustration. This depicts a very excellent
work, dated at Turin 1798, such an one which suggests a workman of good training and superior ability. The violin was

A Violin by
GAETANO GUADAGNINI (II)
Turin, 1831

brought to this country by Lino Rossi, a well known violinist; he acquired it in 1939 in Milan from the dealer G. Ornato, who certified to its authenticity. It passed later to the Lewis Collection in Chicago. The violin is built on fine lines, the material is excellent and the rich varnish is of a red-brown color. The Hamma book illustrates a fine specimen, a later work of the master, dated 1829. Max Möller offers comment in his book that Carlo was a better maker than his father, and that several good instruments from his hands are known to his house.

GAETANO GUADAGNINI II
Son of Carlo
Turin 1805-1852

Gaetano (Cajetanus) Guadagnini II was the first born son of Carlo. Aside from the fact that his name is signed to a number of violins, we must regard Gaetano II as important because he was the chosen instrumentality to continue the family line in the violin making craft, through his son Antonio. Antonio is said to have been a better violin maker than his father. Although Gaetano II does not receive much credit from the various chroniclers, it must be said to his credit that some fine works bear his label. Max Möller states in his book that Gaetano never left the city of his birth—Turin. In this, it is evident that he must have had reference to Gaetano II, son of Carlo, as Gaetano I was born at Piacenza. The violins of Gaetano II agree quite well, however, within the description given by Möller, as of a more effeminate type, lacking the strong features generally associated with the work of earlier members of the family. Gaetano II seems to have been correctly associated with the making of guitars, but the violin of 1831, illustrated here, indicates that some very attractive and meritorious works emanated from his shop. The violin is also pictured in Hamma's book. Another, of similar characteristics, was in the Lachmann collection at the time of this recording.

A very characteristic work bearing original label dated 1830 was in the possession of Onofrio Manzella a few years ago, and later in the collection of Vincent Cardillo.

A violin, authenticated by Hill and bearing the original label dated 1835 was acquired from Philip Hammig of Berlin by Royal K. Johnson while studying in Germany. It passed later to Louis Krasner and from him to Wurlitzer.

A violin of 1851 by Gaetano II is described in a catalogue of the August, 1924 Friedrich Collection as a fine work, patterned after the model of Stradivari.

GIUSEPPE (JOSEPH) GUADAGNINI II
Son of Carlo
Born about 1820—death ?

Giuseppe, the second son of Carlo, is said to have worked at Turin and at Rome. Not having had any experience with works by this maker, and being without data concerning his career, no further remarks can be offered in his tribute.

FELICE GUADAGNINI II
Son of Carlo
Born about 1830—death ?

Carlo Guadagnini's third son, Felice, receives favorable mention by Lütgendorff; he wrote that: "He outranks his father . . . his violins have sonorous tone and are well built, also the boldly designed head is beyond criticism. Only the varnish—often of red-brown or yellow-brown—leaves something to be desired.

His better works already command good prices." Although suggested acquaintance with a number of specimens in the quoted notice, such experience has not been ours for which reason further comment is not permissible.

A violin attributed to Felice Guadagnini was brought from France early in this century by the dealer I. Stern, and was acquired from him about 1915 by the late John Hudson Bennett. From his possession it passed to John Friedrich & Bro. It is now owned by John Harding. The instrument is built on a broad flat pattern, has a two piece back of curly maple and rich red-brown varnish. The label bears the date 1837, the period, however, more correctly of later years.   *

ANTONIO GUADAGNINI
Son of Gaetano II
1831–1881

Just as Gaetano I continued the Guadagnini line through his son Carlo, the latter's son Gaetano II trained his son, Antonio, as a violin maker, and through him the family tradition was carried on to another generation, and to our times. Lütgendorff wrote about Antonio:—"Son of Gaetano II and grandson of Carlo Guadagnini. A capable and excellent copyist of the old masters; repairer and regular purveyor to the 'Musiklyzeen' in Turin and Pesaro; an extraordinarily industrious violin-maker." Antonio was a good maker, his work being of a type similar to that of Stefano Scarampella, Luigi Fabris, Raffaele Fiorini, etc.

THE LATE GENERATION

Antonio Guadagnini's two sons, Giuseppe III and Francesco, were taught by him to follow the art of violin making. Of Giuseppe III we can learn but the bare facts of his being, and having worked during the years shortly previous to and after the turn of the present century.

FRANCESCO GUADAGNINI
Turin 1863–192–

Lütgendorff presents the following data concerning Francesco:—

"Francesco Guadagnini. Turin, 1889. 1910. Son and pupil of Antonio Guadagnini. At this time the only descendant of the famous family in Turin. A learned and able master, who worked on the models of his great-great-great-grandfather, Giambattista. Regarding his varnish, he states that he still uses the same as that employed by his ancestor and that it fails only in not possessing the qualities which age alone contribute. It is true that his varnish (of lustrous red color) shows many characteristics of the old Italian varnish. Up to this time* he has been working without assistants; he has three sons of whom the oldest is now but seventeen years of age. . . . He states the establishment of his House to have been 1690, which does not quite accord with fact. . . ."

Francesco Guadagnini was not overrated by Lütgendorff. His work is regarded as among that of the best of the moderns, carefully executed, his materials well chosen, and his varnish of excellent quality. He was a steady producer and a fair number of his instruments are known. He was still working at Turin as late as 1924 when Mr. Rembert Wurlitzer visited his shop and acquired one of his violins. Several types of labels are found, usually embellished with armorial bearings.

Francesco was awarded gold medals for his instruments at

---

* Lütgendorff, 1922 edition.

Turin in 1884, Antwerp in 1885, Vienna in 1892, and at Turin in 1911.

Several violins by the maker have passed through my hands; a cello made in 1897 was brought directly to Los Angeles. It was in the possession of Helmuth Ellersieck in July, 1949. The maker's name is branded in several places; it is a Stradivari copy with varnish of a deep red-brown color.

Of the sons of Francesco, Paolo was working as late as 1937. No data concerning this contemporary maker being at hand, there remains nothing more to add to this review.

*   *   *

And so, leaving much untold, I regretfully bring this chapter to a close, and with it this story of the Guadagnini Family of violin makers.

I venture the hope—I would prefer to say prediction—that as a result of this work an interest may be awakened, particularly closer to the habitat of the descendants of Lorenzo and Giovanni Battista Guadagnini, which will bring forth a better knowledge of all who followed in the tradition of their forebears.

Faithfully,

ERNEST N. DORING

GENERAL INDEX

Oft-recurring names of dealers omitted; names of owners in italics.

BIBLIOGRAPHY

OF SOME OF THE PUBLISHED WORKS TO
WHICH REFERENCE OCCURS IN THE TEXT

✿   ✿   ✿

RENZO BACCHETTA: *Stradivari, vita e opera del celebre liutaro*, Cremona, 1937; *Cozio di Salabue, Carteggio*, Milan, 1949.

CARLO BONETTI, AGOSTINO CAVALCABO, UGO GUALAZZINI: *Antonio Stradivari, notizie e documenti*, Cremona, 1937.

GEORGE DUBOURG: *The Violin* (etc.), editions 1836; 1837; 1850; 1852; 1878.

FRANZ FARGA: *Geigen und Geiger*, Zurich, 1940.

FRANÇOIS JOSEPH FÉTIS: *Notice of Anthony Stradivarius* (etc.); original French edition published by J. B. Vuillaume, Paris, 1856; English Translation by John Bishop, London, 1864.

JAMES M. FLEMING: *Old Violins and Their Makers*, London, 1883.

JULES GALLAY: *Les Luthiers Italiens* (etc.), Paris, 1869: *Les Instruments des Écoles Italiennes*, Paris, 1872.

LAURENT GRILLET: *Les ancêtres du violon et du violoncelle* (etc.), Paris, 1901.

GROVE'S *Dictionary of Music and Musicians;* London, 1879; various subsequent editions.

EMIL AND FRIDOLIN HAMMA: *Meisterwerke Italienischer Geigenbaukunst.* Stuttgart, 1930.

GEORGE HART: *The Violin, its Famous Makers and Their Imitators,* London, 1875; other editions 1880; 1884; and later.

HUGH R. HAWEIS: various writings, *Music and Morals; My Musical Life; Old Violins.* Many editions.

ED. HERON-ALLEN: *Violin Making as it was and is,* London, 1884. Many reprints.

WILLIAM E. HILL & SONS: *Antonio Stradivari* (etc.) 1902; second edition, 1909.

GEORGES HOFFMAN: *Stradivarius l'enchanteur,* Paris, 1938; second edition, Geneva, 1945. *Edition in German,* Zurich, 1947, titled *Der bezaubernde Stradivarius.*

PROF. WILLIBALD LEO VON LÜTGENDORFF: *Die Geigen- und Lautenmacher* (etc.), Frankfurt, 1904; three subsequent editions.

ALFONSO MANDELLI: *Nuove Indagini su Antonio Stradivari,* Milan, 1903.

FRITZ MEYER: *Berühmte Geigen und ihre Schicksale*, Cologne, 1918-1920.

MAX MÖLLER (AND SON): *Italiaansche Vioolbouw*, Amsterdam, 1938.

JOSEPH PEARCE: *Violins and Violin Makers*, London, 1866.

HORACE PETHERICK: *Antonius Stradivarius*, London, 1900 (as among others).

HENRI POIDRAS: *Critical and Documentary Dictionary of Violin Makers* (translated from the 1924 French). Rouen, 1928. Volume II, 1930.

FEDERICO SACCHI: *Count Cozio di Salabue*, edited by Towry Piper, London, 1898.

SANDYS & FORSTER: *History of the Violin* (etc.); London, 1864. Many reprints.

CECILIA STAINER: *A Dictionary of Violin Makers*, Oxford, 1896. (Several reprintings.)

The Strad: A journal published monthly at London since May, 1890.

STRADIVARI BICENTENARY EXPOSITION: *L'Esposizione di Liuteria Antica*, Cremona, 1938.

RENÉ VANNES: *Essai d'un Dictionnaire Universel des Luthiers*, Paris, 1932.

ANTOINE VIDAL: *Les Instruments à Archet* (etc.); Paris, 1876; *La Lutherie et le luthiers* (1889).

PRINCE NICOLAI YUSUPOV: *Luthomonographie, Historique et Raisonnée*, Frankfort-on-Main, 1856.

LIST OF SUBSCRIBERS

Ansett, Mr. and Mrs. R. L., Ind.
Applebaum, Samuel, New Jersey
Archambault, Ed., Canada
Arneson, Mrs. E. A., Washington

Backus, Merton L., Ill.
Balfoort, Dirk, Holland
Balmforth & Co., L. P., England
Bardin, Lester F., Calif.
Beaty, Florence and Clifton, Calif.
Becker, Carl, Ill.
Beggs, A. Grant, N. Y.
Benson, Harry, Ill.
Benson, S. C., Calif.
Berger, Dr. Isador, Ill.
Bethany College Library, Kan.
Beyer, George W., Ill.
Bigley, Nicholas D., Ill.
Blandin, E. M., France
Bohnak, Joseph J., Mass.
Bolander, John A., Jr., Calif.
Bollacker, Charles H., Ill.
Bowden, Sidney, N. Y.
Brooks, Louis E., Mich.
Brown, Faris M., Calif.
Brown, James, Ohio
Buscemi, Paul, N. Y.

Callier, Frank J., Calif.
Cameron, Alexander, Ill.
Cañas, Dr. Martinez, Cuba
Cane, Dr. William H., Ore.
Carlo, Alphonse, Fla.
Carlson, John E., Ill.
Carroll, Martha, Tenn.
Catlin, Dr. David, N. Y.
Caton, Harold, Calif.
Cerf, Raymond, Kan.
Chaffee, J. G., N. J.

Chapek, Joseph E., Ill.
Chassman, Joachim, Calif.
Chausow, Oscar, Ill.
Cherry, Milton, N. Y.
Clark, Dudley LaZelle, Wash. D. C.
Clifton, W. S., N. C.
Clouter, Thomas E., Wash.
Cohen, Herbert L., Conn.
Cohen, Jacob, Ill.
Commander, Doris, Tex.
Csehy, Wilmos, Ohio

Dali, Eduardo, Argentina
Davis, Chester F., W. Va.
Davis, Dr. Neal, Ind.
Deveny, John, Calif.
Dickson, Harry Ellis, Mass.
Diedrich, Fred J., Ill.
Dietz, Raymond, Tex.
Dietz, Robert, Ohio
Di Tullio, Joseph, Calif.
Dreger, Alvin Brice, Ala.
Driggs, W. H., Calif.

Ellersieck, Helmuth, Calif.
Engstrom, George E., Ill.
Everhart, Eugene, Mich.

Fawick, Thomas L., Ohio
Field, Richard E., Mass.
Field, S. H., Penn.
Fitzmaurice, Robert M., Ariz.
Français, Emile, France
Franko, Joseph, N. J.
Freeman, Jay C., N. Y.
Frier, Dr. Ernest A., N. Y.

Gallagher, A. Norman, Md.
Gerber, Lewis Franklin, Jr., Md.
Gordon, Dr. W. C., Calif.

Graham, Prof. John Wallace, Ore.
Graudan, Nicolai, N. Y.

Hamma & Company, Germany
Happ, Eugene, Ind.
Henstridge, William H., England
Herrmann, Emil, N. Y.
Hesse, Helen, Ill.
Hiebel, Leonard B., Ohio
Hill, William E., & Sons, England.
Hirashima, K. B., Hawaii
Hoing, Clifford A., England
Homeyer & Co., Charles W., Mass.
Houghton, Ellis, England
Hug & Company, Switzerland
Humphrey, George, Mass.

Ibison, Charles E., Ill.
Indiana University Library, Ind.

Jacklin, Walter A., Canada
Jeffery, F. Campbell, N. Y.
Jellison, Jack E., Ohio
Jepson, Oscar W., Wis.
Johnson, Hugh, Ill.
Johnson, Thruston, Mo.
Jones, Dana H., Calif.
Jones, Horace A., Colo.
Jones, L. DaCosta, Ind.
Junkunc, Laddie W., Ill.

Kalter, Robert, Ill.
Karr, Mrs. Elma Eaton, Mo.
Kaufman, Louis, Calif.
Kennedy, Leon, Conn.
King, Harold, Mo.
Kirschner, Herbert, Ill.
Knitzer, Joseph, Ohio
Kolbe, Alexander H., N. Y.
Kolbinson, Stephen, Canada
Krogdahl, Sven J., Ill.
Kucera, Hubert, Iowa

Lachmann, Erich, Calif.
La Fosse, Leon, Ill.
Lanini, Alfred, Calif.
Larsson, Leo D., Calif.
Lavender & Co., J. H., England
Leggett, W. H., Mich.
Le Leux, Lionel, Ala.
Lindsey, W. Paul, Penn.
Locke, J. H., England
Logan, John, Jr., Ill.
Lohberg, Ernest, Ill.
Ludington, Nelson A., Mass.
Lustgarten, Samuel and Alfred, Ill.

Mangold, Rudolph, Ill.
Mannik, Marius, Calif.
Marchetti, Theodore, Ohio
Marlin, Jack, N. Y.
Mason, C. L., Ga.
Mazzi, Francesco, Calif.
McGowin, Floyd, Ala.
McKinstry, Marion, Calif.
Meadows, Lyle J., Ia.
Metz, Albert F., N. J.
Meyers, William, Mich.
Moglie, Albert F., Washington, D.C.
Möller, Max, Holland
Moyer, Guy H., Penn.
Muenzer, Hans, Ill.

Nathan, Morris, N. Y.
Neff, Owen W., Kan.
Nordenholz, G. P., N. Y.
Note, John, Penn.

Olson, Reuben, A., Ill.
Olson, Richard A., Ill.
Orner, George, Fla.
Osterman, Albert M., Calif.
Ostrander, Carl T., Calif.

Palmieri, Armando, Penn.
Parsons, Giehl Irving, Calif.

Peiffer, William D., Canada
Perfect, Fred L., Ind.
Petersen, C. S., Ill.
Petersen, T. C., Calif.
Petschek, Charles, N. Y.
Pickhardt, Dr. R. J., Ind.
Porter, W. F., Canada
Posner, Nathan E., Calif.
Pratt Free Library, Md.
Puljer, Peter, Penn.

Reid, Joseph V., Canada
Remenyi, Laszlo, Hungary
Rice, W. H., N. Y.
Roberds, Joseph, Calif.
Roberts, Stella, Ill.
Rook, A. Gordon, Calif.
Rose, Kenneth, Tenn.
Rosen, Jerome D., Mo.
Rosenfeld, Jay C., Mass.
Ross, Dr. Edgar S., Penn.
Ross, Harry, Ill.
Rossi, Giovanni, Washington, D. C.
Roth, Heinrich, Ohio
Ruben, Dr. S. A., Penn.

Saam, Frank, Mich.
Sager, Leander J., Ill.
Salz, Ansley K., Calif.
Schmidt, Albert, Calif.
Schmidt Brothers Company, Ohio
Schmoll, Rudolph F., Ore.
Schwab, Henry, Calif.
Scott, Dr. Thornton, Ky.
Shepard, George E., Mass.
Simon, Edwin G., Calif.
Sirois, Everett D., Mass.
Smith, Charles D., S. C.
Sorantin, Dr. Eric, Tex.
Sorenson, Ferdinand, Ore.
Sorkin, Leonard, Ill.

Spring, Albert, Washington
State Teachers College, Ia.
Stein, Charles F., Md.
Stoffel, William Peter, Wis.
Supala, Vladimir Jan, Conn.
Sutherland, Dr. James K., Mich.
Sutcliff Co., Gerald F., N. Y.
Szigeti, Deszo, N. Y.

Talley, Helen Dvorak, Ill.
Taylor, Vernon L., Ill.
Thomas, Paul J., Washington, D. C.
Thompson, Harold W., Canada
Thor, Peter E., Ill.
Towle, Thomas S., Penn.
Traner, J. W., Calif.
Traub, Dr. D. S., Ky.
Truetschler, Fred, Ill.

Uzes, François H., Calif.

Vail, Bert C., Mich.
Vidoudez, Pierre, Switzerland

Walecki, Herman, Calif.
Walters, Gibson, Calif.
Warren, Kenneth, Ill.
Weld, Theodore Vance, Penn.
Werchman, John, Ill.
Wertz, Allen, Calif.
Whatley, J. H., Tex.
Whistler, Harvey S., Calif.
Widmayer, Frederick H., Penn.
Wiegand, Fred L., Ga.
Wild, Ernest, Mont.
Willis Music Company, Ohio
Wilson, E. Clem, Calif.
Woodworth, Dr. William P., Mich.
Wunderlich, Curt, Mich.
Wurlitzer, Rembert, N. Y.

Zafos, Harold, Calif.